Curious Tales of Old West Yorkshire

Marie Campbell

Published by Sigma Leisure – an imprint of
Sigma Press, 1 South Oak Lane, Wilmslow, Cheshire SK9 6AR, England.

British Library Cataloguing in Publication Data
A CIP record for this book is available from the British Library.

ISBN: 1-85058-703-5

Typesetting and Design by: Sigma Press, Wilmslow, Cheshire.

Cover Design: MFP Design & Print

Cover photograph: Haworth graveyard *(David S. Brett)*

Printed by: MFP Design & Print

Foreword: by Mollie Sugden

It is many years since I lived in West Yorkshire so it was with great pleasure and interest that I read the draft of this book which revived so many memories.

To the best of my knowledge my father's family has lived in Keighley for many generations, in fact there were Sugdens involved in the battles to repel the Scots when they invaded England. My formative years were spent in Keighley. I dimly remember the pinfold, and going down from the bottom of Oakworth Road through the derelict house to a little stone bridge over what my brother called 'The Dark River Stink!' Then up again to near where the Upper Chapel used to be. Now it is all filled in and become what I remember as 'The New Road'. There were wonderful characters – Freddie Gramophone, who used to busk near the old post office with a wind-up gramophone with a horn, fitted on a push cart, and Sally Matchbox, selling matches in the street from a tray she held. Then there was Old Three Laps, so nicknamed because he was so mean he asked the tailor to add three laps of material to clothing that didn't fit

rather than spend good brass on new. As for his son Bill, he retired to bed until the day he died after being jilted at the altar by Mary Smith of Newsholme Dene. Rumour had it that when he died the wall of his cottage was knocked down to get him out because he had grown so fat. Looking back it seems to have been a more gentle, safer, slow-moving era. Yet on reading this book one wonders just how gentle, safe and slow-moving it was in reality. Certainly it is most fascinating reading and I am honoured to have been asked to write this short foreword.

Mollie Sugden.

Preface

They say that West Yorkshire's towns and cities had little or no history before the Industrial Revolution pressed itself hard upon them, but this is not so. Imagine real flesh-and-blood knights defending England at the sides of our kings and lords; but these are now nothing more than shadowy figures flitting silently through the centuries. Their manors in Yorkshire still exist today, although some have mysteriously vanished without trace. Oh! What stories they could tell us if they still lived. And what of the battles hard-fought on the moors about us? Remember to take care when you next stroll out on the wild, heather-spattered moors for Emily Brontë is surely not alone in her wanderings. She has many friends in the soldiers who were buried where they fell here in bloody battle – Royalists and Parliamentarians alike. Think, too, of the weary traveller, unhappily lost forever, dying alone and never found. His bones picked clean by wild animals and birds glad of the unexpected tasty morsel. These numbers now belong to a more ghostly army. Perhaps if you should care to stop and listen awhile you may, if you are lucky, hear a ghostly chorus sighing, 'Lost! Lost! Lost!' Their voices swelling the sound of the wind moaning and swirling over the bleak and desolate moors long after night has fallen.

And now to the darker side of Yorkshire's towns and cities, where visitors are not always welcome – for the souls of the long dead, who believe they still live, are loath to leave this earthly plane. They continue to share their old places with those who have not yet lived their lives out and who cannot comprehend the restless dead souls' plight. Consider also the Bradford and Craven witches and wizards, and others who cast their magic spells and dispensed their curious prescriptions about the towns and villages. Superstitious folk looked to them for protection against the Black Art, widespread in Yorkshire and Lancashire. Let us not forget the power of the stones – the magic contained within these and other charms was diligently used to protect the innocent from those they feared wished to harm them. Remember too the fate of those who refused to give up the Old Faith in dangerous times and who, for their crime, when death finally came, were cast out by the Church at Skipton into filthy ditches, there to be eaten by pigs.

Think too of ancient customs practised by our forefathers for centuries but now long forgotten: of souls mourned by the Passing Bell rung in the dead of night, of cottage lights extinguished while the winter night was still yet young for fear of execution. What of the old parish church at Keighley, once containing stained-glass windows depicting Old Father Time flying high in the air while a skeleton looked bleakly on? Consider the old pews once used by local high-ranking dignitaries, and their tombs, containing nothing more than dusty old bones. Remember Miles Gale, the Rector who believed in witchcraft, and all the relicts destroyed by unthinking past generations. No, the old ways should not be forgotten. They are a legacy left in our keeping so let us not forget the darker side of our heritage.

Acknowledgements

Many thanks to all who have assisted in the preparation of this book, their efforts are deserving of recognition: Mollie Sugden, Sandy Pimm, Vera Jalil, Alan Butterfield, A.S., M. Morley, Mr and Mrs Rose, Doris Emsley, K.B., Tommy Wilkinson, Edith Wild, Keith, Tim Stanley, Revd Paul Slater, St Michael & All Angels Church, Haworth, Elaine Hitchcock, Murdock, Brian Moorhouse, Denny Lincoln, Ruth Taylor, John Kershaw and Mark Jennings. Sincere thanks to the staff at Keighley Reference Library for all their help and for extensive use of archive material, and to the library staff at Skipton, Bradford, Colne, Thornton, Leeds, Halifax and Hull. I am also grateful to the staff at Cliffe Castle Museum, Keighley; Mr Malcolm Hoddy, Editor of the *Keighley News;* the *Telegraph & Argus; The Yorkshire Post* and Haworth Tourist Information Centre. Keighley Registry Office, the Home Office and the Public Record Office have also given invaluable assistance. Thanks also to the Craven Museum staff – Siobhan Kirrane and Mrs Kath Kershaw; and the Society of Friends. I should like to thank Mr Steven C. Wood of Haworth for his time and patience in proofreading the draft of this book. And to long-suffering Jake Newiss of Oakworth – many thanks, Jake!

Photographs and illustrations have been reproduced by kind permission of the following individuals and local newspapers: Mark Jennings, Sandy Pimm, Dr Ian Dewhirst M.B.E., Jake Newiss, J. H. Rhodes, Mollie Sugden, Mrs Betty Humphries, *The Keighley News*, The Craven Museum, Skipton, Keighley Reference Library, and The Religious Society of Friends, Bradford. Thanks also to Concord Photo Service, Keighley Business Centre, South Street, Keighley.

The cover photograph of Haworth graveyard is by photojournalist Dr David S. Brett. Most other photographs are taken by the author.

'Until daybreak when the shadows shall flee away.'

Marie Campbell

LOCATION MAP

•Burnsall

Bolton Abbey

•Skipton

Beamsley

Carleton Addingham • •Ilkley

Elslack Kildwick Rombalds Moor

Barnoldswick Silsden

Lothersdale Steeton East Morton

Cowling • KEIGHLEY •

Colne • Laneshaw Bridge Laycock Bingley •

•Trawden Oakworth • Harden

Nelson Haworth • Wilsden •

Bowlesworth △Hill Oxenhope Denholme

•BURNLEY Walshaw Dean Reservoir Thornton •

Heptonstall Moor •Walshaw Clayton •

•Pecket Well

Heptonstall • Hebden Bridge

N

•Todmorden HALIFAX

Cragg Vale Elland •

•Ripponden

M65

M62

5 miles

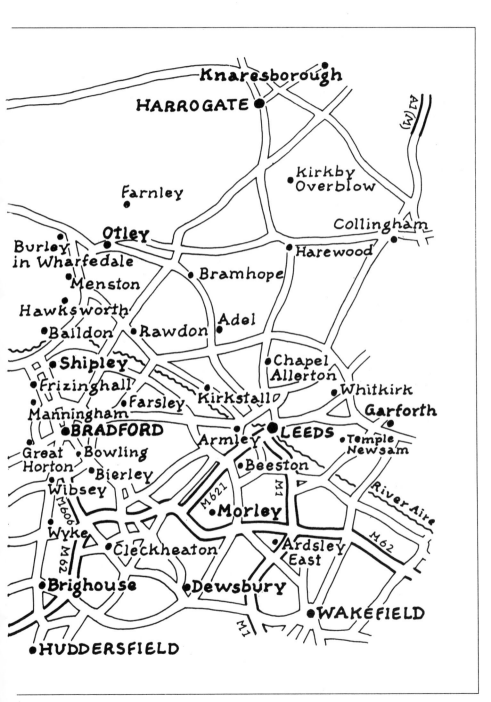

Contents

Chapter 1

Two Wise Men in the Village of Haworth

'In memory of a Haworth stargazer and a famous reverend gent.' *M.C.*

'The tribe of these impostors (Wisemen and Astrologers),
notwithstanding the spread of general intelligence, and the progress
of civilisation, is still numerous, and continues to thrive on the
credulity of the lower class inhabitants. So lucrative has the
profession of fortune-telling in this neighbourhood been, that many
of the adepts in it have died worth considerable sums of money.'
A Bradford observation made in 1842.

Patrick Brontë v Jack Kay

'More celebrated in the Black Art than any man throughout the length and breath of Yorkshire and Lancashire', Jack Kay was born on 11 October 1766 and named after his father, John Kay. Jack's career as a celebrated occultist (who, unlike the majority of his counterparts, *never* made a fortune from his art) was already well established in the 1820s when Patrick Brontë and his family arrived in the village of Haworth. The old ones, such as Jack Kay and Tabby, the Brontës' servant, who had been born in the 1700s, still clung to ancient local beliefs of fairies, boggards, dogs of death and mischievous elves. Tabby would relate to the Brontë children the time when her own mother came hurrying home 'on the edge of dark, freyed out of her wits' after seeing 'a fairish in the hollow'. Perhaps it was Tabby's accounts of hobgoblins and fairies which encouraged Charlotte Brontë to write in her novel *Shirley* the words, 'I may well fear what looks like a great dark goblin meeting me in the moonlight.'

Jack Kay lived only a stone's throw from Haworth parsonage with his wife Rebecca. Revd J. Whalley tells us that, 'one of the by-streets diverging from the outer gates of St Ann's leads to the residence...of Jack Kay.' *(St Ann's was James Whalley's name for St Michael's, Haworth. Whalley was called to a higher place on 24 August 1882 and was interred at Haworth's old churchyard. He began his working career as a grocer's apprentice in Halifax before training for the ministry.)*

The census confirms that in 1841 John Kay (now a widower) rented number 6 Acton Street, Town-end from John Sutcliffe. He lived here with his woolcomber son, Thomas. Other occupants of the house were his grandchildren Mary and Rebecca – both aged fifteen and working in a worsted factory. Sarah, a year younger, was employed as a servant girl, while the eldest, Edwin aged twenty, earned his living from woolcombing.

Kay was venerated by many as of one of the most distinguished of professed prognosticators. He was a practitioner of the old word and widely known to be well versed in its mysteries. As a self-taught astrologer and weatherman he believed the heavenly planets mapped out a person's destiny at the time of birth.

A Soothsayer's Reputation

Jack Kay's reputation in the Black Art was recorded in a diary kept by Thomas Wood, a Bingley man born in 1822. These pages reveal an interesting account of a mysterious tale of a dying hexed victim. It is the story of a young girl fading away, affected by a sudden unexplained illness. Thomas describes how local women whispering together in hushed tones croaked, 'She's just done poor thing, she's wasting away like a sweating candle. She used to be as young a lass as ever sun shone on till she were "wished". It's no use that doctor's stuff, it'll do no good while that's lifted (the hex). Better go to Jack Kay's and he'll make t'aud witch squeak at's done it.' Thomas adds that wise men and women were sought out to exorcise the evil spirit by charms.

The following detailed account of one of Jack Kay's sittings comes from the pages

of *The Wild Moor*. This was written by a native of Oxenhope, the Revd James Whalley of Cross-stone, Todmorden and was, he said, founded on fact. Wealthy clients he claimed, 'came from towns and villages far beyond 'the wild moor' to present themselves before him (Kay). Mr — who had just arrived in his private carriage, after a long and cold journey over "the wild moor", was shown to the easy chair in the snug little room beside a warm, bright fire, and in which room was suspended a striking and life-like picture, in oil, of the famous soothsayer, or, as he was locally designated, "the wise man".' The artist is thought to have been John Bradley (1787-1844), who gave painting lessons to the Brontë children.

'In the meanwhile, the astrologer arranged his "study", chairs, crystals, &c., and, finally, "the books" were opened. Then rapping attention gently at the snug

This life-like oil painting of Jack Kay adorned the wall of the soothsayer's small but cosy parlour where he dispensed his own brand of celestial arts.

little room door, he said in a half musical, bewitching, and enchanting voice, "I'm now ready, sir, step this way, please, will you!" The gentleman, trembling like an aspen leaf from head to foot, and quivering and shaking as if now possessed with a demon, fell into a swoon. Regaining his consciousness, the "wise man" muttered, "Don't be alarmed, sir; you are, I believe, born under a lucky planet. Will you be good enough to tell me your residence, name, age, and *present* position in life!" He answered the question on the way to the "study". Having ascertained the year, the month, the day, and the very hour and minute of the gentleman's birth, he put on his silver spectacles, and discovered the solution of the gentleman's "problem". He pretended to read from the old "black art" book the future destiny and fortune of the comparatively young victim...closing the book he held up the "glass", and professed that he could discern certain of his aged relatives passing off the stage of life, and leaving behind thousands of broad acre land.' Jack Kay cast the querist's fortune using the signs on his zodiac chart and various astrological and mathematical tables and scrying (looking) into a crystal ball, turning it widdershins. 'Concluding this portion of the prediction, he moved most gracefully to the gentleman, and respectfully solicited him to take the glass into his *own* hands, and behold with his own eyes. He did so.

'"Now," continued the astrologer, "don't you perceive something *white* in the midst of something like *yellow* liquid!" "O yes," replied the gentleman, "what is it, Mr Predictor!" "It represents sir, that you will shortly realise a very handsome fortune ... The white in yellow liquid signifies hosts of Bank of England notes intermingling with yellow gold, and *all* for *you*. But mark, sir you have enemies. Beware! beware! beware! Read Psalm —, and call down the vengeance of heaven upon his soul!" At this startling and unexpected news, the gentleman was aghast! But his consternation was immediately suppressed by the soothsayer, who continued – "Sir, you interrupted me in my revelation; I was going to add, I will render you perfectly safe in the midst of your most deadly foes. I will put you in possession of a magical charm, it will be worth more to you than your future estates. If you continue to wear this bright 'spell', it will never fail to ward off the sword of your enemy, prevent the raging fires from destroying your halls, servants, cattle, sheep, and your carriage from overturning in crossing 'the wild moor' (for the purpose of consulting me in case of imminent danger, or sudden emergency), and it will protect you from ten thousand other dangers to which mortals are all subject in a world like ours, which is liable to the fate of so many unlucky planets! I have now, sir, withdrawn the dark veil of futurity, and you have had bright glimpses of your future fortune, success, and happiness.

'The carriage and horses which have this day safely brought you over 'the wild moor', will soon – very soon- be yours. You are, I have unmistakably discerned, destined to live in peace, abound in wealth, and shine in splendour." The gentleman was now almost lost in wonder and joy, and appeared as if he were on the presence of Mercury, the god of eloquence. Then came the closing scene...As the "wise man" received his "fee" from the gentleman, a bright ray of sunshine beamed through the little window in the corner of the "study". "There," said he, "that is also an additional indication of the sunshine which will greet your pathway through your future career." A gentle smile then came over the harsh and severe features of his countenance, and his eye sparkled with delight, as he beheld in his hand *the white* which was most certainly "destined" to 'intermingle with the *yellow liquid,* which he had already accumulated. The famous astrologer thrice pronouncing the word farewell, the gentleman withdrew for the return over "the wild moor!'"

It appears the church at Haworth may have condoned the use of astrology long before Kay's time. The parish register on 20 August 1652 records, 'A storm of Wind and Hail did much damage to standing corn...It was the effects of a Conjunction of Saturn and Mars; these Planets being then supposed to be conjoined in the sign of Leo at the Storm of the Hail.'

Revd Brontë and the Occult

On one occasion two refined ladies arrived in Haworth searching for Jack Kay. Nearing Main Street they stopped their carriage to make enquires of a village girl as to the abode of Haworth's wisest man. Realising the visitors were in search of Jack Kay, the mischievous servant girl directed the ladies to the back door of the parsonage. Expecting to meet the astrologer, they found themselves confronted instead by Patrick Brontë. When he learned the true nature of their errand Brontë led them directly into his drawing room. He delivered a stern lecture exhorting both ladies to guard themselves against all forms of evil but particularly contact with soothsayers. He then ordered one of the misdirected females to open the bible that always lay on his study table and to read aloud verses 31 and 32 of Leviticus 19: 'Regard not them that seek familiar spirits, neither seek after wizards, or be defiled by them: I am the Lord thy God.'

Revd. P. Brontë in the winter of his age.

With the stern words of the old parson ringing in their ears and reflecting upon the contents of Leviticus 19 they hurriedly exited Haworth. Whalley said of Revd Brontë, 'The venerable vicar was celebrated for his learning, and he observed that persons who were under the influence of familiar spirits were under the influence of demons. The 31st verse of Leviticus advises that one should avoid all real dealers with familiar spirits, or necromantic or magical superstitions, and also all pretenders to the knowledge of futurity, fortune-tellers, and astrologers.'

Soothsayer and Brontës?

Branwell Brontë may have consulted Jack Kay on a number of occasions unbeknown to his father. If Branwell's friend Grundy is to be believed, the pair also consulted a ninety-five-year-old Haworth crone as to their future fame and fortune. A yellow silk square reputed to have belonged to Branwell Brontë and decorated with detailed tarot or occult symbols survived him. It was last seen in private hands a few years ago. Where is this relic now? It is possible that Jack Kay and his art influenced Emily Brontë in her novel *Wuthering Heights* where Mrs Heathcliffe calls Joseph a scandalous old hypocrite as he removes a long dark book from a shelf. She warns him how she herself has learned the black art of witchcraft and even threatens to model the household in clay and 'fix' the first person to cross her.

Strange Visitor

An eccentric old man arrived at the Brontë residence on 22 June 1830, begging to see the parson. Tabby informed him her master was ill and confined to his bed. The elderly yeoman insisted he had come with a message from the Lord, saying, 'He desires me to say the bridegroom is coming, and that we must prepare to meet him, that the cords are about to be loosed, and the golden bowl broken; the pitcher broken at the fountain.' Young Charlotte, who was in the kitchen at the time, took this to be an omen of impending doom. Afterwards it transpired that the old man had lost his mind and he spent his remaining days locked in a lunatic asylum.

Mechanics' Institute

On 12 June 1829 Jack Kay became a member of the Keighley Mechanics' Institute and was the following year elected Vice President. Both Patrick Brontë and John Bradley, a painter, were active members of the Institution, together with other notables of the day. Bradley was a founder member of the organisation. In 1835 Jack Kay seconded a proposal: 'That 2 shillings (10p) a night be paid for the use of Gas by the Temperance Movement Society for each public meeting when gas was used.' The Temperance Movement bitterly complained to the committee that they were being much overcharged! On 13 January 1837 Kay delivered a lecture at the hall to students of astronomy on the Perihelion of the earthly universe 'that point in the orbit of a planet or comet, etc., at which it is nearest to the sun.' At the close of Institute business, members might retire to a local tavern to mull over the night's events. This may account for Joseph Constantine's portrayal of Patrick Brontë before he became a teetotaller.

'When a boy I frequently saw the Revd Patrick Brontë on his way home from Keighley, and many times I have watched him unitl he was lost from view. Knowing who he was my boyish curiousity was excited to see him making a great effort to walk without staggering... His fondness for liquor may account for allowing his son Branwell to idle away his time at public houses and contact habits which carried him to an early grave...'

Death of Owd Jack

Haworth's burial register confirms that Jack Kay died on 24 January 1847 aged eighty years. His death certificate shows Thomas Kay was present at the time of his demise. The actual cause of death was registered as unknown. Revd Patrick Brontë officiated at the soothsayer's funeral. On 28 January the *Bradford & Wakefield Observer and Halifax, Huddersfield and Keighley Reporter* addressed the astrologers passing thus,

On Sunday Last, In The 81st Year Of His Age, And Much Respected MR JOHN KAY, Long And Widely Known As 'The Wise Man Of Haworth'

A more fitting obituary appeared in the death columns of the *Leeds Intelligencer* on 30 January 1847:

John Kay, The Celebrated Astrologer

'This personage had been well known in the West Riding generally, and some parts of Lancashire, for a great number of years, persons in the highest rank, as well as those of a lower station, in splendid equipages, having visited him for various information respecting matters past and future. He was a man held in respect by his neighbours, and formerly was frequent in his attendance at the church at morning service, but in later years the singularity of his avocation caused him to seek the utmost privacy. The last week he had an unusual press of business, and breathed his last on Sunday morning, after half-an-hour's sickness, in the same house he had occupied in Haworth town-end for upwards of forty years, at a very advanced age, probably not less than eighty five years. His proper name was John Kay, but from the earliest period of life he was known as Jack Kay. An ancestor of his was so distinguished for a rhyming propensity, that at the baptism of his father, a clergyman was greatly perplexed, yet amused during the ceremony – Correspondent.'

Thomas Kay registered the death on 2 February 1847, giving his father's occupation as 'soothsayer'. Soon after the old skyologer's death, Arthur Nicholls officiated at the

Death certificate dated 1847 confirming Kay's occupation as that of soothsayer (Keighley Register Office)

wedding of Thomas Kay and Hannah Firth (née Crabtree). On this occasion, for some unknown reason, Thomas altered his father's occupation from that of soothsayer to butcher. Jack Kay left no last will and testament nor did he leave a fortune. The site of his burial place in Haworth churchyard remains an unsolved mystery. In 1879 a number of tombstone slabs were removed from the side of the old church in the execution of the Revd T. Wade's grand new rebuilding programme. This may explain the missing Kay family's tombstone as the new church site took in land, which had been previously used for burials.

No Death Toll

The Bradfordian published these lines on 1 September 1861,

Obituary Notice

'On Friday, June the 7th, the good old man of Haworth breathed his last in the grey old parsonage, amid the scenes of his long labours. For six years he has been alone in the world, wife and children all departed; the last lingering remnant of a race whose name will in the future be described in the annals of British Literature.'

Reporters from the *Bradford Review* who were present at Patrick's simple funeral ceremony published these lines:

Funeral Of The Late Revd P. Brontë

'The funeral of the late P. Brontë took place yesterday at noon in Haworth Church. Great numbers of people had collected in the churchyard, and a few minutes before noon the corpse was brought out through the eastern gate of the garden leading into the churchyard. The Revd Dr Burnet, vicar of Bradford, read the funeral service, and led the way into the church, and the following clergymen were the bearers of the coffin: The Revd Dr Cartman, of Skipton, Revd Mr Snowden, of Hebden Bridge: and the incumbents of Cullingworth, Oakworth, Morton, Oxenhope and St John's, Ingrow...There were several gentlemen who followed the corpse whom we did not know. All the shops in Haworth were closed, and the people filled every pew, and the aisles of the church, and many shed tears during the impressive reading of the service for the burial of the dead, by the vicar. The body of Mr Brontë was laid within the altar rails, by the side of that of his daughter Charlotte. He is the last that can be interred inside of Haworth church. On the coffin was this description: Patrick Brontë, died June 7th, 1861, aged 84 years.'

Kay Home Demolished

During August 1970 a petition of over 2000 signatures, including those of Councillor Smith Midgley and Alderman Snowden, was presented to the Council to stop the demolition of Acton and North Street cottages, Townend. Sadly, it was not then known that number 6 Acton Street was of special interest, otherwise the cottages might have been saved and sightseeing tours organised of the famous Brontë soothsayer's temple. The organiser of the petition, Mr James Gill (78) of number 47 North Street, Haworth, told the *Keighley News*, 'When people come to Haworth they come not only to see the museum, but to see Haworth as it was in the days of the Brontës. If anything else is pulled down, there will be nothing of old Haworth left.' Unfortunately, the petition failed and the humble abode of owd Jack Kay for over forty years was reduced to a pile of rubble to make way for a tourist car park opposite the Edinburgh Wool Shop.

Dark Undertones?

An anonymous correspondent sent this curious note about the Brontë family to the *Keighley News* in 1874. 'There are those amongst us who could have told Mrs Gaskell of many a little incident happening in the family circle which combined to undermine the health of those ladies more than all the black tombstones and poisonous gasses which she could conjure up.' What could he or she have been hinting at?

Haworth Railway

According to his history *'Haworth Railway's Oppnin' Serrimony'*, Bill o' Hoylus End, in delivering his speech to the natives of Haworth, spoke of Jack Kay and his brand of wizardry in glowing terms. 'And although ye been behind wi' yer Railway, ye been up i' different arts an' sciences. Wet nashun my friends can boast of a majishun like yer oud Jack Kay. He wur a credit to you all, an' yo wur sadly indetted to him; he proffesied twenty year sin 'at this event wud come to pass an' if he'd been livin' this day, it's a hundred to one but th' Railway would hev been made to sum weere else ner Keighla, for ha feel convinced et Keighla is not worthy of amalamashun wi' a rispectable city like Haworth. The village...was founded by folk from Eastern countries because they tuk fearful after em in Haworth i'th line o' sooth-sayers, magishuns, an' istralegers...and that the West End an th' South End wur de-stroyed, but it's a mack a settled on by th' wiseuns it wur witchcraft...'

Since the great Jack Kay was dead and buried, the inhabitants of the village sought out the services of another local skyologer who duly went off weather-gazing and planet-ruling. On his return he prophesied that a flood would soon descend upon the Worth Valley in raging torrents and the omens were against the coming of the railway. In Bill o' Hoylus's words the skywatcher told them:

> Stars wur shoiting in an' aat,
> An' gravel rathces wur abaat,
> An' th' folk, he sed they little knew
> Wat mischief it began to brew.
> An' news he spred abaat the taan
> Wat lots o' rain wud tumble daan;
> ...Sum tried to stop its course wi stones,
> An' sum dropt on their marrow bones,
> An' hoped that if the world wur draand,
> The railway wud be saafe and saand.

As soon as the waters began to rise as the soothsayer had predicted the men of the vil-lage went in search of him. After searching for some time they found the old man peer-ing into a tunnel. 'Sum sed he wur lookin' at th' mooin, others sed he wur lookin' into futurity, hasumever, they axed him to cum daan an' look at th' railway, an' tell em whether th' flood wur baan to tak it away or not, but the saucy oud haand refused at first, for he sed at he wur flaid at sum on em wod'nt be able to stand th' shock if he tell'd em th' warst, so the ould lad sed,

If my advice yo want, poor things,
An cannot do withaat it,
Go arm yor seln to th' teeth, he sed,
An' doan't be long abaat it;
Both rakes an' powls an' props an' ropes
Yo cannot get too sooin,
An' take the Cowinheaders' plan
When they discovered th' mooin.
Doant gape abaat, but when arm'd
Tak each a different rowt,
An' let yor cry be ivery man,
Th' poor railway's up the spout.'

Note

The author of this book would be very pleased to pass on any further information about Jack Kay to his descendant, Mrs Rose.

Chapter 2

Witches, Wizards and Prophets of Fore-Speak

'A consulter with spirits is one who converses with Satan or uses means devised by him to obtain knowledge of things secret or future.' *Deut. 13.12.*

George Mason

George Mason of Calverley Carr near Bradford – a dark and dubious character – practised the art of astrology. He died in April 1807 and left behind him a tidy fortune of several hundred pounds acquired by his 'extensive impostures' practised upon the ignorant and gullible.

Planet-Ruling Hannahs

The Ling-bob witch, Mrs Hannah Green, was a successful rival of George Mason and had more than £1000 when she died on 12 May 1810. This was amassed during forty years of fortune-telling and associated arts. All classes of society consulted her, including a number of wealthy Bradfordians. Requests were often made of her to rid houses of 'any stray vision of evil intent, which might chance to locate itself on their premises'. The wealthy folk of Otley and Leeds regularly drove up to her home at Novia House between Yeadon and Charlton Moor, believing her skill surpassed all others at finding lost or stolen items. It was not unusual to find an orderly queue outside her cottage of those awaiting their next instalment of the future. A curious legend surrounded the Ling-bob witch. It was said that Hannah Green could only be disposed of by shooting her with a silver bullet when she appeared in the image of a hare.

The witch's obituary appeared in the *Leeds Mercury* on 17 May 1806.

'Hannah Green, alias "The Ling-bob witch", departed this life on Thursday night last, in her hovel at Yeadon, where thousands of inquisitive maidens have for years resorted to enjoy by anticipation their destiny.'

Hannah, however, was alive and well. She fumed when hearing of her supposed death for her 'demise' had lost her lucrative clients. The witch was convinced the culprit was none other than her old adversary George Mason, in a bid to take her custom. Hannah wrote a curt note to the editor of the newspaper on 21 May:

This is to inform Mr Baines that if he does not contradict my death in next Saturday's paper he must stand to the consequences of the law. Hannar Green.

Mr Baines, seeing the witch was quite determined, wrote this piece in the following Saturday's edition of the newspaper:

```
Whether we were imposed upon last week by the person who brought us
the article announcing the death at Ling-bob, or whether any
attempt is now made to mislead us, we have not skill enough in the
occult sciences to divine; but the above letter certainly does not
appear to be the production of a witch.
```

When old Hannah died her daughter Hannah Spence, who kept a dame's school at Ben Delph (Albert Square), took over the lucrative fortune-telling business. It was recorded that in 1820 'in the township of Yeadon there resides a professor of divination, Hannah Spence by name, the daughter of and successor of Hannah Green, the renowned sybil, popularly called 'The Ling Bob Witch'.

As Hannah Spence's powers were inferior to her mother's she charged only one penny a sitting. Those who consulted her were nicknamed 'penny fooils' and so it was that the area in which she lived became known as Penny Fooil Hill.

Rough Robin

A hermit named Rough Robin lived on Rombalds Moor near Keighley until 1806. He was supposedly able to predict all manner of things, ranging from a maiden's future husband to foreseeing major world events and hidden mysteries of the past. He was said to give the precise date of when his predictions would come to pass. Besides local people, others from afar would make special pilgrimages to consult him. The Kendal and Penrith carrier's wagon was ambushed and robbed in 1790. The owner consulted the famed sage as to the identity of the thief. Robin predicted that 'if the thief did not restore the property before a certain day, it should be the worse for him.' The carrier departed believing Robin would conjure up the devil to raise the wind against the guilty person if his goods were not returned before Thursday, 25 February. The appointed day arrived and a hurricane duly raged, damaging much in its path. Those who lived in the vicinity of its wake knew of the prediction and battened down their cottages, thus escaping the awful wrath of Satan. Of course, the robber was never discovered and nor did the carrier ever see his stolen goods again.

In 1806 Robin removed to Leeds where his following gathered pace. The editor of the *Leeds Mercury* took exception to the soothsayer setting his stall out in his town. On the 7 August he wrote, 'If he did not beat a quick march out of the town he would be before Monday night tipped with a magic wand called a constable's staff, and lodged at an enchanted castle, where he may confer with his familiars without degree of interruption, – except from the turnkey.' Robin heeded this prediction and left Leeds immediately.

Wise Man

Abraham Lockwood was as popular a figure in his day as Rough Robin, and earned a good living from fortune-telling until the 1830s. However, his opponents claimed he was nothing more than a false oracle.

John Hepworth

'There were a number of fortune-tellers in Bradford at the early part of the present century, who were all actively engaged in the exercise of their art. The credulity of the inhabitants was so intense that it did not require an adept to succeed. In every industrial part of the town there was at least one amateur fortune-teller, or witch, to minister to the wants of the populace of the district. Many of them earned more by their humbug than their ordinary callings.' Mr Fieldhouse 1889.

Old Bradfordians, although in many ways a practical race, were nonetheless given to superstition and a belief in witchcraft, fortune-telling, planet-ruling, boggards and ghosts. Many thought nothing of parting with hard-earned cash to consult a wise man

Wycoller 'tree spirit'

or woman. This was the case with Robert Sutcliff, a poor and infirm handloom weaver who believed his home at Blackshaw near Halifax was visited regularly by an evil spirit summoned up by unkindly neighbours. In an effort to banish the evil spirits from his abode he sent word to John Hepworth a wondrous and well-established fortune-teller in Bradford to call at his home. Hepworth was able 'to perform the most marvellous miracles, to have foretold, with perfect truth, marriages and deaths, and to have evicted evil spirits from bewitched premises...' As soon as the Bradford Oracle arrived, on the 14 May 1803, Sutcliff begged him lay the malicious spirit that he believed was dogging him. During the course of the consultation Hepworth concocted a mixture of human blood and hair which he corked up in large iron bottle. He then threw it into the open fire whilst reciting a magic spell. This was designed to break the witch's evil charm. If the bottle should burst the witch would die or beg forgiveness and admit to the curse. In this case neither happened for within thirty minutes the witch bottle exploded, killing Sutcliff outright and badly damaging the property 'to the utter of astonishment of the impious exorciser'. It is not known whether John Hepworth was prosecuted for killing the superstitious weaver. Other less dramatic ways of ridding oneself of evil spirits employed by this infamous character included a concoction of herbs, mistletoe, motherwort and wood betony mixed together with sugar, raisins and honey. John Hepworth was only one of many charlatans operating in and about Bradford, all ready and willing to relieve the gullible of their hard-earned cash.

Witch Hole

Skipton was once widely famous for its wise men and witches. References can be found from as early as the 17th century to Witch Hole, a name still borne by a field here. An entry in the parish register for 1715 states, 'Kildwick – One Thomas Stott, Hugonnem Blakey & Chr'ferum Smith, for pr'tending to tell of stolne goods & telling of ffortunes.' All three were excommunicated from Skipton Church as transgressors.

Native of Halifax

Skipton's most famous wise man was Timo-thy Crowther who was born at 11am Thursday, 20 December 1694, near Halifax. His family moved to Skipton when he was a young boy. Crowther married a local girl named Ann who bore him eight children. In his early years his interests turned to astronomy and astrology. He collected and concocted numerous spells, incantations and weather signs, which he wrote down in his charm book. He cast nativities (birth charts), counteracted evil spells concocted by demonic witches, exorcised evil spirits and had stolen items returned to their rightful owners.

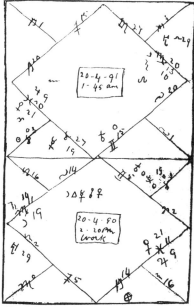

Hand-drawn nativity chart discovered in the back of an 1887 occult book

Spell Reveals a Dead Man

The famous Evangelist John Wesley (whose own parents had suffered the attention of poltergeists) heard of a strange story concerning Crowther from a boy named Jonas Rushford or Rushworth of Bramley on 24 July 1761. Jonas said that two years previously a man in his village had mysteriously been missing for three weeks so two neighbours had sought out the magician Timothy Crowther. He ordered them to bring a young boy under the age of thirteen to him. Jonas was chosen and journeyed to Skipton. The boy was put on a bed and told to take hold of a looking glass while the magician read from a curious book *(Molle's Living Librarie?)*. He was then covered from top to toe with a bed sheet and asked what he could see in the mirror. Jonas replied that he could see his mother holding some wool in her hands. He looked a second time for the missing person. A picture gradually formed which revealed a drunken man riding along the old Windhill Road towards Idle, near Bradford. He saw him stop at a beerhouse along the way and drink two pints of ale, which he paid for with a golden guinea. The landlord enquired if the man had far to go. On hearing his reply two men tipped each other the wink and rode to Windle Common near Windhill Wood Top to await the drunkard. As he passed by the thugs pulled him from his horse and rifled his pockets. Gagging the unfortunate victim with his own handkerchief, they threw him down a deep coal shaft. Jonas returned to Bramley and took his neighbours to the place he had seen in the magic mirror. A volunteer climbed down into the pit and found the murdered man's remains. Wesley pondered on the tale before writing in his journal, 'Is it improbable only or flatly impossible, when all the circumstances are considered, that this should be pure fiction?'

> 'Float murmurs of mysterious crime
> And tales of secret shame.'
> Anon, Windhill.

Crafty Crowther

Timothy Crowther was for many years the parish clerk at Skipton Church. His handwriting can be examined in the records of the day. In 1756 Crowther requested that the five bells in the tower of Skipton Church, stolen during the Civil War and returned in 1655, be replaced. The Church Board refused, stating it was out of the question. He asked instead for new bell clappers and the Board willingly granted this request, believing it to be a cheap compromise. Crafty Crowther ordered clappers of the largest size, which on contact reduced the bells to a pile of broken pieces. A new peal of six bells cast by Lester and Pack was installed at the church in 1759 – leaving Crowther triumphant! His only remaining son, Samuel, eventually took over the work of his father as parish clerk. Some of Timothy Crowther's hand-written manuscripts mysteriously resurfaced, one hundred and fifty years after his death, on a bookseller's stall in Leeds, and were purchased by the author and historian Mr W. Harbutt Dawson.

Magic Cult Continues

The practise of the occult in Skipton did not die with Timothy Crowther. Some twenty years after his death Bramley Overseers' accounts for the year 1783/4 set out payments for,

> 'Dec. 8th – Expenses on bargaining with conjurer from Skipton to cure Matthew Hudson's daughter, 1s. (5p).
>
> Feb. 1st – Astrological doctor for Hudson's daughter, 12s.6d (62½p).'

Subsequent entries reveal that Mr Hudson's child took fits. A widespread belief at this time was that to suffer a fit meant evil spirits possessed the person concerned. Magician's services were often called upon in cases of this nature. The same accounts also show that a Bible was purchased for the sum of 2s (10p) in 1709 for the moral welfare of one Abraham Burn.

Molle's Living Librarie, 1612

'Some magicians (being curious to find out by the help of a looking-glass, or glass viall full of water, a thiefe that lies hidden) make choyce of young maidens, or boyes unpolluted, to discern therein those images or sights, which a person defiled, cannot see...In our time conjurers use christall, called the divination chrystallemantia, or onychomantia, in the which, after they have rubbed one of the nayles of their fingers, or a piece of chrystall, they utter I know not what words, and they call a boy that is pure and no way polluted to see therein that which they require.'

Will Span

Nicknamed 'Will Span', this tall, gaunt-looking individual from Keighley was well known in his day for 'his supposed power of seeing wraiths or the spectral appearances of persons about to die!' Lanky Span was the last bull-baiting champion of Exley Head, an event which used to take place in the week of the old Parish Feast of St Peter until the custom was abandoned in 1794.

Bertha and the Unbeliever

Old wife Bertha practised the black arts from a squalid, remote, single-roomed habitation. One fine day in the 1700s Thomas Parkinson visited the wise woman out of nothing more than idle curiosity. He rattled the door of the hovel and was invited in. Looking about him he saw three stools, an old deal table and a few kitchen utensils, amongst which nestled a blackened cauldron. On the wall were three pictures of wise men: Merlin the wizard, Nostradamus and Michael Scott. Parkinson bid Bertha perform some incantations to prove her powers. The old woman, on seeing her visitor was a disbeliever, said, 'Then you doubt my power, think me an impostor, and consider my incantations mere jugglery. But sit down by my humble hearth, and in less than half an hour you shall see such an instance of my power as I have never hitherto allowed a mortal to witness.' Parkinson did as he was bid, nervously watching the old crone as he sat down close by the peat fire.

Hone's Table Book takes up the tale, 'She then with chalk drew a circle on the floor, and in the midst of it placed a chafing dish filled with burning embers. On this she fixed the cauldron, which she had half filled with water. She then commanded me to take my station at the further end of the circle, which I did accordingly. Bertha then opened the sack, and taking from it various ingredients, threw them into the 'charmed pot.' Amongst other articles I noticed a skeleton head, bones of different sizes, and dried carcasses of some small animals. While thus employed, she continued muttering some words in an unknown language; all I remember hearing was the word *konig*. At length the water boiled, and the witch, presenting me with a glass, told me to look through it at the cauldron. I did so, and beheld a figure enveloped in the steam. At the first glance I knew not what to make of it; but I soon recognised the face of N——, a friend and intimate acquaintance. He was dressed in his usual mode, but seemed unwell and pale. I was astonished, and trembled. The figure having disappeared, Bertha removed the cauldron and extinguished the fire.'

Bertha looked triumphantly at Thomas, 'Do you doubt my power? I have brought before you the form of a person who is some miles from this place: was there any deception in the appearance? I am no impostor, though you have hitherto regarded me as such.' Parkinson edged his way towards the safety of the outside world. The old witch stopped him by saying, 'I will show you something more wonderful than the appearance of this evening. Tomorrow, at midnight, go and stand upon Arncliffe Bridge, and look at the water on the left side of it. Nothing will harm you: fear not.' Bertha insisted he must go and go alone so as not to break the charm. The following night curiosity drove him to do Bertha's bidding.

The evening was calm and in Parkinson's words a, 'full-orbed moon was sailing peacefully through a clear blue, cloudless sky, and its beams, like streaks of silvery lustre, were dancing on the waters...and the moonlight falling on the hills, formed them into a variety of fantastic shapes. Here one might behold the semblance of a ruined abbey, with towers and spires and Anglo-Saxon and Gothic arches... the stillness which reigned around, broken only by the murmuring of the stream, the cottages scattered here and there along its banks...composed a scene of calm and perfect beauty... I waited...nothing appeared.'

Signalling the hour of midnight, the village clock struck twelve long, hollow strokes. Parkinson cast a glance into the stream, from whence he fancied he heard a low, moaning sound. The sound continued for a moment or two then ceased. The deadly silence caused a sudden fear to sweep over our adventurer, who turned and ran as if his very life depended on his immediate flight from the scene. He later related, 'On turning the corner of the lane that led to my father's house, a huge dog apparently of the Newfoundland breed, crossed my path, and looked wistfully on me.' Believing the poor animal to be lost he encouraged it to follow him home. Upon arrival he turned to look for his large companion but the dog had vanished.

The following day Parkinson returned to the witch's hovel. Bertha asked if anything had happened the previous night. Shrugging his shoulders he said nothing other than that he had spoken to a stray dog. To which Bertha replied, 'That dog never belonged to mortal; no human being is his master. The dog you saw was Bargest!' Parkinson had heard tell of the ghostly Bargest and knew death followed at his heels. He asked who would die, but the witch would tell him no more. Three hours later Parkinson was shocked to learn that his friend N——, whose image he had seen in the cauldron, was dead. He had committed suicide by drowning himself below the spot where Parkinson had stood on the bridge the previous evening.

Becca Brigg

This once-noted fortune-teller lived in a cottage at Jack Field, not far from Thwaites, between Keighley and Bingley. Only one reference to her is known to exist for her name had almost slipped away into the wreaths of time.

Old Wizard and his Dog

Tommy Fanny was born in Keighley about 1690. He walked from the town of his birth to Rugby, where he found work as a professor's assistant. Under the professor's guidance Tommy became a scholar well versed in the art of magic and animal doctoring. When the professor died Tommy inherited his savings and antiquarian occult books. In 1721 he wed a farmer's daughter, Susie Whitebait. With her encouragement, he set himself up as a magician. Quickly gaining a reputation throughout a wide area, he became well known 'of the period for possessing a through knowledge of love philtres, potions and the like. Old farmers and their wives, young couples, lovesick girls, and amorous swains, even little children would go for advice to the famous soothsayer.' In 1763 he wrote a book about unrequited love. After his wife's death he bought himself a dog and gave it the curious name of Silverarm. Local inhabitants thought the dog had been conjured up using demonic forces. Rumours were rife that Silverarm was a reincarnation of the recently deceased Susie. Dog and master became inseparable. Remarkably, both expired on the same day: 17 May 1769. Churchgoers argued amongst themselves as to whether or not the infamous magician should be allowed to rest in holy ground. The more credulous amongst the number were convinced that the magician and Silverarm should be buried together within the church confines since the animal had really been Mrs Susie Fanny, previously reincarnated by her husband.

Kilnsey Nan

Nancy Winter was up hours before dawn to walk twenty miles or so from her 17th-century home, a corner of the old manor house, Kilnsey, to collect herbs to prepare and sell as magic potions. These were renowned for their healing virtues. She also concocted her own brand of incantations and special charms, using herbs to foretell events and protect the inquirer from 'thunder and the wiles of evil spirits'. In the 1820s she sold her special preparations from a small shop in Bag's Alley, Skipton, on market day, and always carried on her breast a familiar in the guise of a guinea pig. The old crone forecast a person's future for a small sum of money. Craven folk made special pilgrimages to ask her advice and have their fortunes read in the cards, by crystal gazing or by the use of a divining rod. At the turn of the century, a correspondent used the *Craven Herald's 'Antiquarian Notes and Queries* to advertise for information about Kilnsey Nan. Sadly, none appears to have been forthcoming. Very little else is known about her occult career. Not far from Nan's abode, Dan Cooper once saw fairies out prancing in his rented field. On his next visit he found a circle of mushrooms in the exact spot where he had seen the little people perform their dance ritual. His aunt, on hearing the story, said, 'My dear, you saw the fairies and the mushrooms were a gift to you because you were good and did not disturb the dance.'

Joe Brown

On 25 October 1810, charlatan Joe Brown was executed at York for poisoning a Leeds woman. Brown had been a respected church watcher until he trod the path of demons. After committing several acts of fraud he was forcefully evicted from the church. He later took up with a man of low character and together they devised a plan to earn easy money. Donning disguises, Brown acted the part of deaf-and-dumb fortune-teller while his partner-in-crime interpreted Brown's actions to their gullible clientele and pocketed the cash. Brown and his accomplice were eventually caught and brought to justice. At the hearing Joe Brown cleared his already overburdened conscience by confessing to the cruel murder of a Leeds and Selby carrier.

Roving Astrologer

D.H. Dawson included this story in his *Gleanings of Craven*. 'In common with my fellow-creatures I enjoy any sight possessing peculiar novelty. I therefore walked to see this Lancashire Aesculapius, for he is not a native of the District of Craven, expecting to find a man, if possible, thinner than myself, and with a more care-worn expression of countenance, the natural result of lamp-work or, being an astrologer, lamp black is perhaps a more proper term. Judge my surprise upon being shown a tall fat man, in a blue sparrow-tailed coat, the picture of health and ignorance: – and this elephant of wisdom with a carpet trunk visits all over Craven – dispenses his quacks – his charms – and his knaveries, to the injury of good sense and the ignorant poor, upon which he commits his speculative peculation's: I wonder whether he has ever yet visited a magistrate; I think not, I would publish this shameless person's name, but he cannot read; yet I think without the aid of any sorcery he will be able to discover this true portraiture, and I trust that he will return to his first web, where he earned, if not so much money, at least it weighed not upon his conscience.'

David Lund

David and his brother, Thomas Lund, owned an engineering business at Albert Foundry, Keighley, but owing to the economic climate the business failed. Turning his attention to the occult David Lund established and circulated a paper entitled *The Astrologer,* and thus earned his living selling copies at three pence an issue. However, in June 1887 news of Lund's new business venture came to the ears of Superintendent Ireland. Together with police sergeant Tom Kendall Mellor, Ireland entrapped the soothsayer by writing to him using the alias of 'John Feather' and requesting 5s. (25p) of prophetic forecasts by return post. This was to be called for at Ingrow Post Office (attached to the Great Northern Inn before being burnt down a few years later) on Halifax Road. Lund obliged by sending 'Feather' an astrological birth chart and a list of things he should avoid or expect from life. Ironically, Lund calculated that, 'Mercury being the strongest planet in the figure of the earth...the business for you (Feather) is a literary occupation...or you would do well in the legal profession. You would have success in the law. Also, the Sun being conjoined with Mercury and Venus will make you a good businessman and cause you to be ambitious...you will do well in a partnership.' How right the fortune-teller was! Poor Lund was prosecuted under the Vagrancy Act.

During the court case the soothsayer was compared to the Lancashire witches. John Briggs, the magistrate, imposed a fine of £3 plus costs. In the month of May 1890 Lund was again charged and brought before the court on two separate counts – purporting to be a fortune-teller and pretending to tell fortunes and deceive Her Majesty's subjects. The prosecution called two witnesses. The first was Lily Wrigley, a common weaver who told the court how she and a friend Annie Stott had consulted the defendant one Friday. They had walked to his home close to High Shann Farm. He lived alone in a single-storied building known as Fern Cottage, at the top of Highfield Lane, Keighley. 'The lane was country-like, wi' ruts big enif to bury a cart in and a fair old hike on foot I can tell you,' Lily said with feeling. On reaching the cottage door the two women knocked and Lund opened it. Lily asked, 'Are you the person that tells fortunes?' David Lund replied, 'I suppose I am.' After going inside they noted that he carefully barred the door behind them. The price for chart casting was fixed at 1s.6d (7 ½p). However, Lily had only about 1s (5p), which the soothsayer accepted as full payment. He asked how old she was, which day of the month she was born and if she was a resident of Keighley. After chalking some magical symbols on a slate and reading pages from a book he told her that she should have been married last year to a small, dark man. However, she would be given another chance. At this juncture the normally sombre courtroom burst into fits of laughter. Not to be outdone in her hour of glory, Lily ignored the outburst and went on to describe how Lund advised her of the best way of actually catching a husband (more laughter in court).

David Lund then cast an astrological chart for Annie Stott for less than a shilling, which was all her purse contained. She asked his advice relating to a personal problem, saying she wished to heal a rift between herself and her parents that had forced her to leave home. Lund advised her to return to her family where she would be safe from harm. The prosecution asked him why he charged for his services. The defendant replied that if a person consulted him and wished to ask him a question he had the right to answer it. As a student of mathematics and political economy he did not always charge for this service, usually only charging for time spent drawing astrological maps and doing complicated calculations. The court's attention was drawn to the theosophist's handbill, which clearly stated 'I charge only for the time and calculations' and was accompanied by a list of prices:

ASTROLOGY

1st Any particular question, such as business money, property, legacies, removals, partnerships, courtship, marriage, sickness, &c· **1s. 6d.**

2nd Birthday figure, showing all the important events in the current year of your life · · **2s 6d.**

3rd When to buy or sell stocks and shares, Consols, bonds, warrants, &c · · · · · · · · **2s 6d.**

4th Nativity of birth, giving a general forecast of all the affairs of life, such as the best businesses to follow, who to marry, diseases predisposed to, best direction to live, riches, children, journeys, friends, and enemies· **5s. 0d.**

5th Nativity of birth, giving all the above particulars, as in No. 4, together with a description of the most prominent events will occur, all through life · · · · · · · · · · · · · · · · · **10s 0d.**

For natives of birth please state age, time of birth, sex, and birthplace.

All questions may be answered by letter.

D. LUND, Herbalist, Fern Cottage, Keighley.

Lund was found guilty on both counts and sentenced to spend one month at Armley Jail, Leeds. Before he was taken down he told the court that there was a person practising the science of astrology in nearly every town in the country. People in Bradford, Halifax and Hull openly advertised the practice without fear of punishment from the law; therefore it was unfair to continue to persecute him as an occultist. 'Why,' Lund asked, 'were men allowed to practise astrology in other towns without interference, whilst he was being persecuted?' This was certainly a justifiable question. William Seed (Wise Willie) of Low Moor, Bradford, for example, was, like Lund himself, a self-taught mathematician, astrologer and almanac maker and openly plied his trade. Even the *Keighley News* accepted and printed fortune-telling adverts as early as December 1880.

Lund was the first ever theosophist to be held at Armley Jail. The depravations of prison life suffered by the ordinary man were not so great for Lund. On his arrival the prison authorities found him well prepared. He neither smoked nor drank and was used to living the life of a hermit. He was also a strict vegetarian. After his release he returned to Fern Cottage and continued to carry on the practice of predicting future events. Receiving another summons, the soothsayer called at the police station to ask the Superintendent what he thought the result of a further court case was likely to be. 'What?' he was asked. 'You pretend to be an astrologer and can't foresee that?' 'Nay,' retorted Lund, 'I dare not look.'

The 1891 census lists Lund (mis-spelt Lunn) as a widower, aged 52, born in Keighley. He boldly describes his occupation as a teacher of astrology and mathematics. He spent the last week of his life in bed. His death earned him a place in the *Keighley Yearbook.* 'Mr David Lund astrologer, herbalist, and theosophist, closed his eventful life on January 20th 1903 at the age of 63. Originally a mechanic, he became an astrologer of more than local fame. He was twice fined, and once imprisoned for fortune-telling. During his lifetime he accumulated quite a tidy fortune particularly after his imprisonment when he flew in the face of the authorities and continued to practise the occult and gathered a large clientele most of whom were female.' David Lund owned a large and valuable library, 'consisting chiefly of works on astrology in which subjects he seems to have been regarded as one of the chief authorities.' He was also an active member of the Keighley Foreign Affairs Committee, which was 'founded at the end of the Crimean War to save England from the hands of Lord Palmerston.' (Palmerston was thought to be in league with Russia.)

Only hours before his death Lund had Keighley solicitor William Dewhirst draw up his will. '...a legacy of twenty pounds to my niece Elizabeth Crabtree of Brow Haworth... and Lydia Lund Mitchell of Royal Hotel, Settle... ten pounds to Mary Holmes of Spencer Street, Keighley...' Fern Cottage and its contents were left to his niece Mary Robertshaw Lund of 7 Dean Lane Head, Allerton, Bradford. 'To have the use and enjoyment thereof during her lifetime...after her death the proceeds arising from the sale and realisation of my said dwelling house garden and herediments...shall be sold and the proceeds given to the Keighley and District Hospital to be applied and used by them for the purposes of support and maintenance...'

The said hospital, which was described as a human slaughterhouse by Guardian Jefferies in 1884, was to receive several hundred pounds almost immediately, and could expect to receive a further three hundred pounds after the sale of Fern Cottage. Although persecuted for practising occultism within the parish of Keighley, David Lund was obviously a very forgiving man. His remains were laid to rest at Utley Cemetery.

Urgent Notice!

Attics, cellars, drawers and cupboards should be diligently searched for copies of *The Astrologer,* written by David Lund and originally costing only 3d per issue.

Prosecuted

At Keighley Police Court on 3 September 1897, Henry Hargreaves, moulder, of Victoria Road, Keighley, was charged under the Vagrancy Act of pretending to tell fortunes. He pleaded guilty to the charge although he objected to the wording of it. Mrs Sophie Roe of Hainworth had described a consultation with Hargreaves to her husband, whereupon he had marched her directly to Keighley police station. Superintendent Greyson suggested they concoct a plan to catch the fraudulent trickster out. Mrs Ellis, the wife of a Bingley policeman, agreed to accompany Mrs Roe to Victoria Road. They were to ask Hargreaves to foretell their futures after feeding him fictitious information.

On their arrival Hargreaves took the two women to an upstairs bedroom and asked them the exact time and date they were born. After consulting a book and staring into an oblong glass he wrote something down on a bit of paper. He told Mrs Ellis she suffered from heart trouble in the previous year but if she took care of herself she would live to be middle-aged. He asked if she had any questions for him. Ellis wanted to know where her husband went at night. Hargreaves looked into the glass and declared her husband was with another female. He saw him drinking on the top floor of a large, newly built property with a fair and a dark woman. She then enquired about her fictitious family, whom she said she had not seen for some time. Hargreaves told her that her father was very ill and had almost died two weeks past. Death would visit him within the next two weeks. A legacy would be left to her which she would receive the following October. He warned her not to go to the law as it would mean trouble for her. Knowing her father to have been dead for nine years she said nothing. She asked what he charged for his service and he asked for a silver shilling (5p).

A regular visitor to Hargreaves' home, Sophie Roe handed over her shilling. He told her she must leave for New York the following month (November) because her husband would turn her out of their home. After leaving Hargreaves' house the women hurried to meet with Inspector Dempster who had been hiding around the corner. They returned to the house, where Dempster charged Hargreaves with pretending to tell fortunes. The fortune-teller flatly denied the charges then tried to bribe Mrs Roe. Returning her shilling he said he was 'not to a pound or two if she said nothing!' Mrs Roe told the court she had believed in his powers but did not anymore. When she last visited the fortune-teller alone he had taken her into the bedroom and had made an immoral proposal to her. She showed the court a small bag Hargreaves had given her to wear in her corset for luck. Hargreaves claimed the women had not been duped as they did not heed his predictions. He said he could predict the future by means of studying the art of astrology. Giving evidence for the prosecution, a well-respected gentleman told the court his wife had consulted the fortune-teller and as a direct consequence of the charlatan's advice she had left him. Hargreaves, married with two children, promised to abandon his art and pleaded for leniency. The magistrate fined the occultist £3 plus costs, warning him that should he continue telling fortunes he would receive the maxim penalty of a £20 fine.

Roger the Wise Man

This account of a visit to a wise man who lived in a cave at Knavely Knoll is taken from the *Craven Minstrel's Legend of Peter King* by James Henry Dixon. 'He wor a queer lookin shop, an' furnished efter a mack on it's own. A roarin fire o' Turf blozed on the floor, for there wor nother grate nor dogs. Smoke 'scraped thrro' a holie it roof, which what wit reek, lamp blacks an' bacca smoke, wor as black as t' back o' my hat! Liggin afore t' fire wor a girt Tom Cat, a verra suspicious lookin animal. He wor purrin loud as onny bumfiddle, an' weshing his cheeks wiv his paws...There wor an old jack-door perched top of a long settle; he wor blinned an ee-shoo nan liked him! Roger then axed a lot ov questions day shoo wor born-time-o'day-age ov her fether an' muther at time, an' so on; this shoo gave him quite correct. Then he gat a bit ov paper an' a pencil, an' lookin into owd Paddywatch to ascertain what planets wer in disjuntion at t' hour o' her birth he preceded to draw her telescope.'

Wise Man or Impostor?

Meanwhile at Addingham 'a simple weaver of cotton has become a weaver of the intricate web of life, and with the practice of herbal medicine, he foretells events casts nativity's – and puts futurity into a nutshell. It was not long ago when a simple man consulted this eminent person as to the health of his grand daughter. The doctor shook his head, and pronounced judgement that the girl was bewitched, – he then took a fowl, and roasting its heart, visited four corners of an adjacent field, muttering some unintelligible jargon, and then bade the witch to come forth; but as it seemed not to obey his mandate, he took his fee and departed. The poor girl was removed to a house to be near this learned person, who said it was a very hard case, and after four months' charming and fees, he was forced to give it up.' This account in Dawson's *Gleanings in Craven* continued, 'it was indeed, a very hard case for it was the grandfather who was bewitched – out of his money.'

George Hey

The Kirkstall prognosticator George Hey saw himself as a Christian, and as such advertised on 3 January 1801 that he had been 'commissioned by heaven to announce, that on Whit-Sunday, in the year of 1806, the world would be destroyed by torrents of fire'. He hoped the announcement would stop the masses from committing wrongdoing against God. To this end he placed a further advert that he himself concocted in October 1802.

To the World at Large

'Repent that ye may be saved! and live and dwell on the earth for ever in peace with God; for I foretell the length of every man's and woman's life that liveth upon the earth, unless they live forever and never die; for on WHITSON MONDAY, in the year 1806, it will rain down fire and brimstone until all shall be consumed that know not God; but all that live in His fear and strive to do His will shall live on the earth for ever. Think not much of me for telling this, for as Noah was the end of the Old World, and beginning of this, so I do declare the ending of this world, and the beginning of that which shall follow, and of that there will be no end.
GEORGE HEY Kirkstall Forge, near Leeds, Yorkshire, May 2nd, 1801'

Hey was emulated by a man known as the Sheffield Tailor, who predicted the end of the world would commence in 1805 and not 1806 as George Hey stated. In any event, both wise men were wrong. The Sheffield Tailor was first to fall by the wayside when his prediction failed to materialise. Hey's disciples waited with baited breath for the marked day. It began very hot and humid and large crowds thronged the streets of Leeds – both in anticipation and trepidation. The restless multitude cautiously shifted from place to place until the orange orb sank over the westward hills accompanied by a blood-red sky. They all held their breath and waited for the end to come. Emotions ran high as the sun at last slipped from view and all remained well in the world. A chronicler of the day wrote, 'such a night in England ne'er had been, and ne'er again would be.' Residents of Leeds heaved a great sigh of relief as the following morn dawned bright and clear.

Billy Cryer

Billy Cryer of Tow Top, Carleton gained local popularity as a weather prophet and watchmaker. Unfortunately, little is recorded of his abilities. It is believed that the self-taught rustic owned a wheel-cutting engine, which enabled him to make the parts for the clock at St Mary's Church, Carleton in 1833. After a grand procession round the village with Billy Cryer holding the mechanical clock parts for all to see and wonder at, he marched into the church to assemble the clock. The church clock kept excellent time and was declared a mechanical wonder. Billy was hailed as a genius! After instructing the Revd Busfield to lock the door to the bell tower, Billy told him that the timepiece would strike for the first time on Saturday at twelve noon. To everyone's amazement it did precisely that!

Billy was also interested in sundials. Mrs Gatty's *Book of Sun-Dials* contains a strange letter written by Billy, which allows us a further glimpse of his character. He had been asked to design a sundial for a Kirkby Malham village tavern. This was fixed not in the full light of day, as one would expect, but by moon and starlight.

```
Carleton, July 1843
Dear Sir,
Ever since I have imbrased every applicable oppotuntity possible
for a complition and yet after all defeated! the model will take
two or three days yet to finish it, you need not be afraid of any
preposterous executions (because it might fright Her Majesties
Horses* as her Royal Highness and her Consort Prince will ride over
every day) . . . if I am well shall not deny another hour till it
is finished, but every process requires its own time, say two days
to finish the Model, one day in casting, when I take it to Keighley
(on my way to Wilsden to see my sister whom I've anxiously
expected), then to its paint and Gild, . . .
Your humble Servant,
Wm. Cryer
```
*Note the inn's signboard

Billy's obituary, strangely dated 1u.10.30, appeared in the *Pioneer*, as follows:

Billy Cryer Of Carleton
Noted Clock Maker – Once Acclaimed Village Hero

'Mr Cryer evaded marriage for a good many years (or marriage evaded him) until he finally gave up waiting for the hand of the cook at Stonegappe. He went and married instead, in his own words '...a little elderly body with clogs on.'

A small, dark-coloured oleograph of the smiling Cryer, dated around 1806, can be seen at the Craven Museum at Skipton Town Hall.

Fathers of the Rosy Cross

'Seeking to know what is forbidden, spirit under the ray of Thoth, will be in a few years blown to the wind.' James Gillingham

The Lamp of Thoth

In the early 1880s, a group of men covertly met behind the anonymous exterior of number 14 Parkwood Street, a small, newly erected house. (According to the census an out-of-work engineer by the name of William Dugdale and his family resided here in 1881.) The small but select group led by Daniel Murgatroyd practised magic rituals and discussed the secrets of the universe and mystical wisdom – hence the group's name of Thoth. The sect had in some way come into possession of a copy of Lord Henry Clifford of Skipton's medieval spell book. Calling themselves Fathers of the Rosy Cross, they explored the clandestine rites of Yorkshire's medieval Dragon Lands.

Parkwood Street, Keighley, where the secret sect calling themselves The Lamp of Thoth met in 1880 to practise the mysteries of the universe.

Who was Zanoni?

Liberal MP Sir Isaac Holden and a small number of other influential men appear to have been linked to this covert group. In the early part of 1880 the sect produced a magazine, which revealed to the subscriber 'mysteries of the great unknown'. The editor signed himself only as Zanoni.

Golden Dawn and Theosophists Intervene

Both Madam Blavatsky, a founder member of the theosophical sect, and McGregor Mathers of the Golden Dawn had devotees in the nearby towns of Bradford and Todmorden. When the rival sect was uncovered Blavatsky and Mathers joined forces to put an end to its activities. They charged the Fathers with plagiarism and copying the philosophies of the Theosophists and Golden Dawn. Furthermore they accused them of employing dark forces in the hope of discovering knowledge of the forbidden kind purely for self-gain. They condemned the sect for practising black magic, raising elementals and sacrificing young goats.

Mystic Map

Little is known about the Fathers' activities other than from excerpts in various occultist manuscripts retrieved from a Bradford tip (now in private ownership). A title page shows a hand-drawn map entitled *The Lands of the Dragon*. The drawing depicts a burning hill between a swastika and a dragon – the centre point was probably once the meeting place of a medieval magic coven. The ancient monks of Bolton Priory practising with Gothic alchemist Clifford no doubt employed similar illustrations. The towns of Skipton, Keighley, Bingley, Ilkley and Bolton Priory feature as focal points within a hexagon and form the triangle of the Dragon, whose lands are supposed to have great magical powers.

Property Torn Down

The meeting place at 14 Parkwood Street was torn down almost before its stone and mortar had time to set, due to the Midland Railway Company's widening scheme of 1881. The vacant lot now serves as a car park for the Globe Inn. There may be a surviving copy of the magazine produced by Zanoni in the 1880s lurking in a dusty corner or carefully stored in a private collection. Keighley historians are on a quest to discover it.

Terror at Parkwood Street

Long after the Fathers had left Parkwood Street, a family living there fell victim to a series of terrifying events. On moving into the rented house, three children shared an attic with a painting of an old woman seated in a rocking chair. The watercolour had been inherited from the previous tenant. Scratching noises heard late into the night terrified the children so much that the police were called for. They found that a small dividing door connecting to a neighbour's attic had been forced open. The neighbour was unable to give an account of the noise or scratch marks found on the door. The children were convinced their ordeal was in some way connected to the painting of the old woman and refused to sleep in the attic. The whole family huddled together down-stairs until they found a new home.

Henry Harrison, Charlatan

Henry Harrison from Leeds was a fortune-teller by trade and figured in the Dove murder case. An account of the occurrence comes from the pages of *Mayhall's Annals Vol. 1.* 'On March 1st 1856 Harriet Dove, daughter of Mr Jenkins of Bramhope, aged 28, the wife of William Dove, Cardigan Place, Kirkstall Road, Leeds, died in great agony, under circumstances which left no doubt but that she had been poisoned. A *post mortem* examination by Mr Morley, and Mr Nunneley, surgeons showed clearly that she had died from the effects of strychnine. Mr Dove, the husband, was taken into custody on suspicion of having administered the poison. After four days' inquest...the jury returned the following verdict: – "We find that Harriet Dove has died from the effects of strychnine, wilfully administered by her husband William Dove..." Dove was taken to York Castle to await trial set for a few months later on 16th July.'

The post mortem showed that the prisoner Dove had often treated his wife cruelly and wished her dead. To this end he consulted Henry Harrison, a Leeds wizard, asking the best way to do away with his wife. Harrison advised him to poison her. Dove acquired strychnine twice or three times from a Mr Morley's surgery, telling him he wanted to poison stray cats. Instead he administered the drug to his wife Harriet. As she lay dying in great agony he pretended to cry and was inconsolable at her funeral.

Mr Bliss, for the defence, pleaded insanity. A number of witnesses came forward in support, relating to the court instances of strange acts committed by the prisoner. Since his earliest childhood days these acts included. 'Chasing his sisters with a red hot poker, – setting fire to the curtains of his bed-room – his tormenting of cats and kittens – his buying a pistol at twelve years of age to shoot his father, and his schoolmaster – his attempt to poison his master's horses, &c., &c.' Nevertheless, Dove was found guilty of wilful murder, although the jury recommended mercy on grounds of defective in-

AN ANXIOUS INQUIRY.

Mrs. Pickles : Oh, Mr. Postmaster, I've called to inquire about a letter with money in it which the fortune-telling lady said last week was certain to arrive for me.

Victorian cartoon poking fun at fortune-tellers *(The Yorkshireman)*

tellect. The judge, in pronouncing the death sentence, cautioned him not to expect that his life would be spared, although he would forward the recommendation of the jury to the proper quarter. The prisoner's solicitor and his friends tried to obtain a commutation of the sentence but the Home Secretary refused to comment. Dove was executed in front of York Castle at noon on Saturday, 9 August 1856.

In his confession he blamed Harrison the fortune-teller for his wife's death, but Henry Harrison carried on his evil practices after the trial. On 30 September he was sentenced to serve nine months' imprisonment in the House of Correction for having obtained money by false pretences from Elizabeth Croft and for violating her person. On 8 November he was committed to York Assizes for bigamy. He received his final sentence on 9 December 1856 – four years' penal servitude.

Smuggling Gypsies

In the reign of Queen Mary a massive fine of £40 was levied against any person caught smuggling into the country gypsies and all those who professed to tell fortunes or other like craft.

Curate Crabtree

Melinus Rusticus Almanack, printed in 1685, was the brainchild of Henry Crabtree, the third curate of Todmorden (1660-1691). Crabtree saw himself as a prognosticator of fortune, astrologist and healer of the sick. He was probably the only cleric to produce an almanack of this kind. His pages advised the reader to 'rise early, walk in the fields by running streams of water, and feast the lungs with fresh air. Sage and Sweet Butter is an excellent breakfast…' In the month of August our cleric advises, 'Beware of purging, vomiting, and blood letting, especially when the air is hot, for then the Dog-Star will bite both by his manifest and occult quality.'

Mr Jollie, in his pamphlet entitled *The Surey Demoniack, or an account of Satan's dreadful and strange actings in and about the body of Richard Dugdale, of Surey, near Whalley, in Lancashire, 1697,* wrote, 'Then they sought oute a reputed wise man for help, viz., Dr Crabtree. Dugdale said he was amazed at several things which befel him whilst under his charge, as particularly at his precise fore-telling various sorts of matters, he at last confessing (as some have told us) that there was no help for him except from the ministers.'

In reply to the publication, Zachary Taylor wrote in Crabtree's defence, 'This is a devilish insinuation of some bodies to abuse a minister of the Church of England, for such this Dr Crabtree (as he calls him) was. He was, as far as I can learn, no great scholar, a blunt but honest man, and served at a poor place for about twelve pounds a year, which he augmented by venturing to give physic to the country people. But this would not do Mr Carrington's (one of the Exorcist's) turn; you must be made to believe that he was a conjurer, (and Mr C., in one of his letters, expressly tells him so, though his correction in the Narrative mollifies it into a reputed Wiseman)…Poor Mr Crabtree's dead, and dead men cannot bite nor box neither, else Mr C. might have heard of it on both sides of his ears. But what were those unlawful means poor Crabtree used? Nothing in the world, saith Richard, his patient, but *Phisicking* and

Blooding... Crabtree's reputation, however, for 'physicking and blooding,' appears to have been more wide-spread than for divinity or astrology.'

This outlandish curate established a register in 1662 of all baptisms and burials that took place in his church. There are some strange entries! 'John Bairstow, of Hollowspin seeing both his daughter and his wife departed in peace, presently began to offer sacrifice unto Bacchus for joy. But he continued so long adoring of him that Apollo, the God of Wisdom and Physick, was enraged at him, and struck him with a Pestilential fever, which thing John felt it violently raging in him he confessed his sin and humbly implored Apollo to cure him...And he purged not only the morbific matter and malignant humour but also cleansed his body of ij Jugs of old Ale and his throat of ij muttons stakes yt' (stuck in it). But just as Bairstow began to feel better he weakened and fell back to the drink. He 'swallowed an ocean of old Ale.' When it had all gone he returned home alone to Hollowspin, an isolated, barren place high on a mountain top, where his heart 'burst for very grief, and he died in a rage for want of ale, and came to Todmorden to be buryed – May 1, 1667'.

Sadly, nobody bothered to enter Crabtree's burial in 1696 in the registers and we are left with only the words of Zachary Taylor to serve as the curate's epitaph.

Chapter 3

Spiritualism and West Yorkshire

'Camouflage it as you will, Spiritualism with its kindred superstitions, such as necromancy and occultism, is a recrudescence of the old, old practices cultivated in the days of long ago.' Revd J.A.V. Magee also warned the nation to '...keep away from the seance-room as you would an opium den. The Devil has a mysterious power still over persons, places and things...there are hidden forces of evil waiting in this unseen world, which is so near us, for their prey, and waiting to find a lodgement in the human soul.' – *Father B. Vaughan*

Foundation of Modern Spiritism

In 1848 the Fox sisters claimed to contact departed spirits. Soon messages from the dead heralded the beginnings of the modern Spiritualist Movement. Seances were organised but attracted mainly those of a curious or morbid disposition. Alcoholism eventually claimed the lives of both sisters. They died in abject poverty in 1891 but their powerful message outlived them. Sceptics believed spiritism opened the door to demonic possession and lunacy. In 1877 a Victorian doctor, Forbes, claimed that 10,000 people possessed by demons were confined in lunatic asylums. He was of the opinion that many had committed suicide due to meddling with occult forces:

'Where e'er we look, to right or left,
'Tis mine' or 'thine' by cunning theft,
We claim the whole thus God's bereft -
But does he faint!
The world at large is in distress,
Through want of knowledge more or less,
More than the tongue can well express.
Or artist paint.

Stray Thoughts Joseph Scaife, Keighley

From Temperance to Spiritualism

Businessman David Weatherhead bought a hall sandwiched between Green Street and Sun Street for the sum of £300. Its maintenance was funded from the rents brought in from the cottage dwellings below. In this way Weatherhead was able to finance the first Temperance and Working Man's Hall, which opened its doors to welcome artisans willing to turn their backs on the evils of drink and once more take up the tools of their trade.

Keighley Spiritualists' Temple Jubilee souvenir commemorating founder members David Richmond
and David Weatherhead

Owenite contacts Weatherhead

Hounded out of his native Darlington by hecklers, David Richmond's wanderings
came to an end when he reached Keighley. In America he had become a disciple of
Robert Owen of Harmony, Indiana and his mission was to convert England to spiritualism. Richmond invited Weatherhead to join him in his crusade. The first venue from
which the message of spiritualism reached the ears of Keighley townsfolk was the
Working Man's Hall (a move strenuously opposed by the Temperance Movement).
Casting aside Methodism and the Temperance Movement, a small number, including
Weatherhead, took up the new religion and its motto: 'Fear God, honour the King,
love the brotherhood, honour all men.'

Table Rapping

The novel art of table rapping, practised regularly at the hall, opened up lines of communication between the dead and the living. From 1853 those possessed of one penny
could purchase pamphlets communicated by the dead. The following extraordinary ti-
tles were available from the Market Place, Keighley: *Divine Illumination Communicated from Spirit Spheres, The Voice of Good Spirits or The Road to Heaven, Spirit
Rapping, Communications from the Spiritual World, What is the use of Spirit Manifestations?* On 16 August 1853, the door of a secret address in Bingley opened to admit a select, invited few. Those attending the private party were treated to a
posthumous treatise delivered by Robbie Burns, which provided the content of *Table*

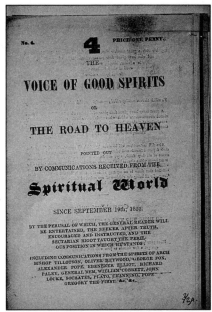

Spiritualistic penny pamphlets sold in Keighley market place

Moving Extraordinary! (Harrison & Son, Bingley printers, published this but the date of the meeting was mistakenly printed as 1854). No time was lost in presenting this to the public as a penny sheet. Joining its sister pamphlets hawked in the marketplace the broadsheet carried the following warning, 'It is through sin and wickedness that we are permitted to visit you, and lead you to repentance.'

An Extraordinary Warning

Amidst outpourings of poetry during a seance at Sun Street a Keighley medium who was about to embark on a voyage to the Americas was warned to abandon her plans, otherwise she would drown. The medium took heed and cancelled her trip. News arrived that, 'after the ship had left Liverpool it landed again in Ireland, had gotten half way to America, being driven back again...through a terrible tempest, which, for three days, kept every one in momentary expectation of going to the bottom, and the captain, in despair, jumped into the sea, and was drowned.'

Spiritualist Messages

The Society for Investigating the Phenomena of Spirit Intercourse was founded in Keighley and the dead were soon busy contacting believers in Bradford and its environs. Robert Jenkinson, who died in 1663 aged eighty-one, passed the following wise words to a Keighley medium on 19 February 1856. 'If men would only in all things be guided by good sprits, crime and poverty, oppression and vice, would at once come to an end. Books, ignorantly styled infallible: Religious corporations, called venerable, And Priesthood's, imagined sacred; Will ever keep the mass of people in ignorance and slavery, And prevent them from establishing their manhood.'

James Hardcastle, who died in 1707, was next to come through the ether. Telling the medium that in life he had lived eight miles from Bradford, he continued, 'Rejoice! That mankind will soon be able to destroy the power of Priesthood's: seldom wise; – never honest; – often ignorant; – always selfish. Knowledge, is daily increasing; so ignorance – which has been to them a power In the same degree, diminishing. Therefore, seek to improve knowledge, and you will help promote the truth; for ignorance is the friend of falsehood and deceit.' *Spiritualists Penny Pamphlet no. 4.*

Temperance Society Condemnation

In November 1853 the remaining stalwarts of the Temperance Society became the authors of the *Keighley Visitor*. In the pages of the first issue they took the opportunity to publish their own thoughts on spiritualism.

Table Moving Extraordinary

'Strange and incredible as this announcement may appear to a large number of our less credulous readers, there are not wanting those who place implicit confidence in "Table Moving" as being the means by which we are now enabled to hold intercourse with the spirits of the departed. For our own part, with the belief in such intercourse we have no sympathy; and when we express ourselves in its entire rejection, we are only reducing to paper the opinion entertained by far the greater number of those who have at all thought upon the subject. While however, we may feel disposed to question the truthfulness of the *conclusion* to which these men have so prematurely, and in our opinion, so illogically arrived. We do not for a moment doubt their sincerity; on the contrary, our acquaintance with the parties, – the apparent earnestness with which they prosecute their experiments the desire they manifest to convince and win over those who oppose them – and above all their own pledged word are in our opinion evidence sufficient to place their sincerity beyond question. It is quite possible to be sincere and yet at the same time mistaken. Sincerity by no means argues correctness. The men who advocate the "pancake" theory of the earth are undoubtedly sincere; but then a more enlightened philosophy, and a better educated judgement, condemns their suppositions as absurd and erroneous. The contents of the pamphlet under consideration, which lay claim to a spiritual origin, include a sermon and a few verses of poetry. Like men who boast the possession of wisdom because of the greatness of their ancestors, the little fame they have acquired is more owing to the popularity enjoyed by their *alleged* authors, than to any intrinsic merit of their own. In addition to these, the tract contains a very nicely written introduction, in which certain opinions, more or less of the speculative nature, which have been advanced by Professor Farraday and others as attempted explanations of "table moving," are briefly examined and as briefly dismissed...signed simply Guielmus.'

Spiritualism Defended

From the second issue of *The Visitor* comes the following extract presented by THE THIRTEEN WHO PREFER FACTS TO BARE ASSERTIONS in the defence of Spiritualism. 'Although we did not positively say that the phenomenon was the effect of spiritual agency we know perfectly well that, our remarks inclining that way, would subject us to the ridicule of all parties...who would treat us as a kind of simple people, carried away with something near akin to witchcraft and fortune-telling; yet since, neither the writer of the article, nor any other, has advanced any thing to alter our opinion.'

The editor of *The Visitor* retorted, 'It is quite easy to see from this, the writer here alludes to a long digression respecting the scepticism of the age, and what he takes to be the ignorance of the professing world as to the true nature of the spirit, and origin of man. We have admitted it for two reasons: 1st, because it bears no relation whatever to the article of which this is pretended refutation; and, 2nd, because its insertion would involve us in religious controversy, and that, as he well knows forms no part of our mission. Then "fair play is a jewel;" we esteem it the most valuable in our casket.'

The Keighley Thirteen

Jonas Bottomley, Joseph Scaife, Thomas Bentley, Hiram Haggas, Crispin Barret, William Bland, Samuel Smith, Joseph Moorhouse, Thomas Pickles, William Scott, John Garnett, John Hardacre the Medium and John Smith the Querist made up The Thirteen. These men held the first seance in Keighley. Using the alphabet method, they believed they had successfully made contact with those who had passed over. In reply to the *Keighley Visitor* they imparted the following lines, 'You will see from this, that it depends neither on the intensity of the wish, the length of time the hand is on the table, nor the accidental action of the muscles; but that the operation is performed by *some invisible* agency acting *independently* of all those causes, and moving in a manner frequently contrary to the wishes and expectations of the parties.' The article concludes, 'we are compelled to come to the conclusion, that the *table moves the hand,* and not the *hand the table.*'

Spirit Propaganda

The first spiritualist journal made its debut during 1855. Published in Keighley and financed by Weatherhead, the *Yorkshire Spiritual Telegraph* appeared on a monthly basis for two years. In 1873 Weatherhead paid for the erection of the Lyceum on East Parade to promote the dissemination of spiritual knowledge. The following is from the 1894 *Keighley Year Book.* 'The present Lyceum in East Parade, was erected more than 21 years ago by David Weatherhead. There is a good Sunday school connected with the society, held in the morning and afternoon. An offshoot of the above society began work in the Albion Hall about nine years ago, and subsequently removed to the Co-op Assembly Rooms. These rooms proved inadequate, and in November last removed to a building at the top of Dalton Lane, formally used as a Wesleyan Church.' David Weatherhead, the champion of British spiritism, died on 3 September 1875.

Mother Church

The Spiritualist Society purchased a defunct chapel from Keighley Wesleyans for £500 on 9 March 1895. £50 had been received in donations for painting and decorating. The Society relocated from the Lyceum to the Wesleyan Chapel on Heber Street after the Wesleyans moved to Malsis Road. The building was re-named the Heber Street Temple of Spirtisim. A board attached to the front of the building proclaims the temple to be The Mother Church of British Spiritualism. Its opening was celebrated with a ham tea extravaganza. On the 20 July 1895 the *Keighley News* reported that the first meeting was well attended. At the opening ceremony Mrs Britton 'spoke with dramatic fervour'. She spoke of the adversity that the religion had had to endure and of the joy with which they had expected to be received. 'Instead of which the message was cursed in every pulpit, was sneered at in every paper. The unfortunate ones, in whose presence of the signs of the powers were manifested, (mediums) were robbed and cruelly used. Their houses were stormed, and their goods destroyed. But the power went on and the rappers rapped on, and the eyes of the multitude were opened...after 47 years of power in this grand old Yorkshire town with one of the first veterans of the movement (David Weatherhead).' Mr Campion of Leeds congratulated the brethren upon their success in uniting together and acquiring such a beautiful temple and proceeded to speak of the blessings he claimed to have experienced from embracing spiritualism. He told of how fifteen months earlier he had become so ill that he had to be fed by spoon and bottle, but through spirits and through the angels he was still alive, 'a miracle of the 19th century'. Four years into the zealous mission, the temple in Heber Street proudly welcomed over one hundred believers at each weekly meeting. Sir Arthur Conan Doyle in his *History of Spiritualism* notes that Keighley 'brought spiritual phenomena under the notice of the people of Yorkshire'.

Seance at Keighley

In 1855 Turkey Street, situated in one of Keighley's poorer quarters, attracted many curious townsfolk. On entering a tenement they were shown to an upstairs bedroom and greeted by a fourteen-year-old girl spiritualist seated at a table that had been carefully prepared in the centre of the room. Observing the alphabet laid out on the tabletop they waited for the glass to move as the girl invoked the spirit of any dear departed soul who cared to communicate. The visitations from Heaven spelled out cures for headaches and other ills and were accompanied by knocking and rapping. As the seances progressed the rapping grew louder. The noise was said to resemble that of a joiner driving nails into a floor with a hammer. Those assembled then joined in hymn singing, adding to the din from the rappings of the dead. The noise could be heard throughout Turkey Street and beyond but neighbours' complaints fell on deaf ears. The young medium's talents continued to flourish. Tales of unearthly visitations to Turkey Street abounded. Still in its infancy the *Yorkshire Spiritual Telegraph* despatched a reporter to Turkey Street. The paper was eager to publish news of these marvellous manifestations. On his arrival the investigator found all made ready for a seance and five believers in attendance. After asking the gathering to spread their hands out on the tabletop, the medium at once began to invoke spirits in her usual fashion. Rappings interspersed with loud bangs soon filled the darkened room. The table rose into the air and remained suspended for several seconds. Back on the floor it wobbled wildly whilst a misty vapour slowly swirled out from beneath, forming itself into a luminous apparition. After publication of the Turkey Street phenomenon sceptics proclaimed the events to be a hoax and the medium fraudulent. Without exception all that had attended the seances defended the girl, declaring her talent to be genuine.

Life after Death?

Phenomena could not always be satisfactorily explained away. A reporter for the *Keighley News* wrote of a spiritualist meeting held in 1914 prior to the First World War — 'To combat materialism by proof of man's survival of the changes called death.' The reporter said, 'Eminent men found themselves at a loss to explain the phenomena they had witnessed by any natural means.'

James Gillingham, a declared disbeliever, attended many seances in his quest for the truth. This is his own account of a seance from his book *Errors of Spiritualism*. 'It was a summer evening on 23rd May 1873, at the private residence of a friend. It was in full daylight. The table at which we sat was by a bow window, over which muslin curtains were drawn to exclude the sunbeams. In the centre of the table was a vase filled with spring flowers, among which were some large branches of lilac. Suddenly the curtains moved. A hand emerged out of the daylight and drew them aside, first one then the other. Presently a hand...appeared passing over the table. Slowly it moved before our wondering eyes to the vase of flowers. With finger and thumb it took one of the pieces of lilac and made repeated attempts to break the flower from the branch...At length it succeeded. Then it carried the plucked flowers across the table...not six inches away from me. I requested that it would touch my hand. It moved to me, patting it thrice, during all which actions the others and I examined it curiously and closely could distinctly see the blue veins and the pink nails. Its touch was warm and soft. The daylight fell full upon it, and it was as distinct, definite, and apparently as solid as any hand upon the table. I could discern no arm. The hand was plainly visible as far as the wrist, but there it seemed to end, not with a definite outline, but melting away, as it were, into a hazy cloud or shadow it returned across the whole width of the table – a space of eight feet – as slowly as it had come, vanished, and we saw it no more.'

Outrageous Epitaph

When death visited Denholme doctor Mark Illingworth his remains were laid to rest in the graveyard at Southgate Baptist Chapel, Denholme. But the trustees of the chapel found the old doctor's epitaph so outrageous that they took it upon themselves to place the offending tombstone face down, thus hiding the words set out below from the sight of all those who passed by. This action caused the old doctor's son, Jonas, to snatch the corpse from the graveyard and bury it elsewhere.

'Are the mysteries of the past and future of human life, then so plain and so clear to the Christians of Denholme? Who has drawn aside the curtain of the Past? What were you and I before we came into this world? What was our soul before it inherited this bodily frame? Did it exist at all before it entered the tabernacle of flesh? Are these questions anywhere answered? And if not, cannot a believer in God say truly that no living man has drawn aside the curtain of the Past of human existence? And the Future! Has that curtain been drawn aside? If so; surely our knowledge of the after-life is distinct and clear; surely the all-pervading light of the Eternal – that Eternal which lies beyond that of the grave, – would have revealed with absolute distinctiveness, and beyond the possibility of doubt, the future of all human life! Will the body rise again at the last day and live forever, or will only the soul exist eternally? When death lays his icy hand on man, does the soul sleep in the tomb until the day of judgement, or does it at once go to the everlasting abode of bliss or misery; or does it inhibit some unknown spot until that period arrives when 'all flesh shall be judged?'

Brontë's Warning

On the subject of necromancy the Revd Patrick Brontë referred all those he deemed to be in its grip to *Leviticus 19*: 'do not practise magic, or witchcraft...Do not turn to mediums or wizards; do not seek them out, be defiled by them...There shall not be found among you anyone who practises divination, a soothsayer, or an auger, or a sorcerer, or a charmer, or a medium, or a wizard, or a necromancer. For whoever does these things is an abomination to the Lord...When you say you consult mediums and the wizards who chirp and mutter, should not the people consult their God? Should they consult the dead on behalf of the living – surely for the word which they speak there is no dawn – they will look to the earth, but behold, distress and darkness, the gloom of anguish; and they will be thrust into thick darkness.' Furthermore, Brontë directed interested parties to the last pages of the *Old Testament Malachi 3 v 5*. 'I will draw near to you in judgement, and I will be a swift witness against sorcerers...'

Charlotte's Experiment

In a letter to Mr James Taylor, dated 15 January 1851, Charlotte wrote that she had met the writer Harriet Martineau and had visited her at her home in Ambleside. Martineau indulged in the fad of table rapping, which was fashionable at the time. Harriet

Professor Kershaw.

Halifax mesmerist Professor Kershaw earned his living by putting volunteers into trances on stage.

Martineau asked Charlotte if she shared her interests in mesmerism (hypnotism), which was first discovered in 1842. Charlotte wrote of it to Taylor, 'Scarcely, yet I heard miracles of its efficacy and could hardly discredit the whole of what was told to me. I even underwent a personal experiment; and though the result was not absolutely clear, it was inferred that in time I should prove an excellent subject.' Was Charlotte hoping to contact her dead brother and sisters or was she simply willing to try mesmerism in the hope of benefiting her fragile health? According to Professor Kershaw, a stage hypnotist, mesmerism had been hailed as a cure-all for those suffering from a wide variety of illnesses. He claimed it 'caused the lame to throw away crutches, the epileptic and paralytic to be restored to health'.

Charlotte's Friend's Fear

In the days when doctors understood little of comas, they sometimes confused them with death. Frantz Vester invented safety coffins – the earliest in 1862. Harriet Martineau was terrified of being buried alive, even though waiting mortuaries were set up for the express purpose of keeping a corpse for seven days before committal to the earth. Harriet paid her doctor £10 to cut off her head after death to avoid premature burial.

A Bevy of Bradford Spirits

In 1876 Bradford Saunterer asked a friend, 'What is your idea as to the influence of spirits?' His friend Barnacles replied, 'My idea is that if you take a sufficient quantity they'll make you beastly drunk.' The Saunterer, alias James Burnley, explained he actually meant spirits as in those of the dead. The enlightened Barnacles said he thought the whole idea complete bosh! Bradford had long since rid itself of spiritualists duping and degrading the town. However, he was shocked to discover that there were, in fact, several colonies thriving in the township as he spoke. The Saunterer begged his friend to accompany him to a spirit meeting that very evening in the vicinity of Bowling.

Secret Meeting Place

The pair arrived in the area and as Barnacles whistled a tune from the *Tramp Chorus of Rob Roy* under the light of a street lamp, Saunterer went in search of the spiritualists' secret meeting place. He had been informed that this was to be found somewhere within a huddle of mean looking, cottage-type houses. Unsuccessful in his attempt, he returned. The companions stepped back into the shadows and waited until they saw three women pass quietly into a nearby stable yard. Following behind they found themselves inside a tumbledown stable. These details are from the pen of Saunterer. 'We had to mount a pair of wooden stairs, where there was very little light. "Mind where you are going," whispered Barnacles in a tone of awe, "don't tumble over that spirit," as he pointed to a dark indistinguishable object laid to one side of the steps. I startled back, and if my hair did not stand on end it ought to have done, considering the shock that my nerves experienced. What could it be? As I strained my eyes to look at it I almost fancied I saw it move and I am quite sure I heard something groan…Had the spirits become aware that enemies were on the threshold of their temple…Barnacle struck a light. The threatening object turned out to be nothing more than a sack of potatoes!'

Spirit Talk

On gaining the top of the stairs they were confronted by a dozen spiritualists, mostly women, dressed in humble attire and seated on wooden benches. There was a raised platform to the centre front. A gruff Yorkshireman called Spade bid the friends, 'Come forred, gentleman; come up to t' fire; it's nobbut a cowdish sort of a neet.' After waiting around for almost an hour the stable owner (Spade) said, 'I'm flayed there's not bonn' to be onny speykers to-neet.' A man dressed in greasy attire arrived and whispered, 'Little Vault was with us.' Spade hurried round passing out hymn books and saying, 'Lewk for t' twenty-fift' hymn, long meter.' Meanwhile Little Vault took the platform, seating himself on an armchair and closing his eyes while the others sang. 'As the singing proceeded the presence of the spirits manifested on all sides. Even Spade could not give the hymn out without much jerking and twitching, and several young women seemed to have been suddenly attacked by palsy, they shivered and shook to such an extent. It made one feel as if I had gone into some hospital for patients suffering from St Vitus' dance, and I almost expected to find myself shaking and twitching before I had done.'

Spirit Possession

When 't' twenty-fif't hymn' had been concluded, 'Little Vault began to wriggle about and all eyes were directed towards him. He did not wriggle long, however, the Vault evidently believed in doing his spirits gently. He rose to his feet, laid his hands on the little desk before him, and with firmly closed eyes, allowed the spirit within him to hold forth. I was unable to ascertain whose particular spirit it was, but, whether it was "a spirit of health or goblin damned", it knew little about the ordinary rules of grammar or the common usage of English pronunciation. Even such a word as "spiritism" – which one would have expected a Spirit to deliver correctly... Instead he uttered "spiritimiss". Little Vault let out a stream of verbal garbage. "Spiritimiss is give to us to make our own ter-ruth; spiritimiss is to give us for salvation of our souls..." the flow carried on in this manner for a full twenty minutes until Vault, temporarily released from spiritual thraldom, sat down until we had another sing... Little Vault, who had not yet opened his eyes, was again possessed by a spirit.

'He rocked to and fro in his chair...jerked to his feet, and allowed spirit no 2 to address the assembly. It was soon evident that this spirit had belonged to a person who had come to an untimely end. From the look that Vault put on when he jumped to his feet, I should imagine that the hangman had been the spirits liberator in this case. It spoke slowly and solemnly, "I say unto ye," it said, "ye know not the day nor the hour... It is done in the twinlin' of a high. Ah! My friends, I was cut off in a moment. I never felt the shock; it was as sudden as a gun." "It's some'dy' at's gotton killed," whispered Spade to a man next to him. "It's happen that falla 'at gat killed t'other day," whispered some one else; and the congregation, with the exception of the crowing infants, seem deeply impressed. The spirit droned on "Ye might go from this room to your little dwellings, well and hearty, a many on you, and ye might be dead to-morrow. A many is dropping down dead in your streets every day...take warning by me; I was well and hearty in the morning afore dinnertime it was all over." Two more hymns were sung before Vault silently slipped away.

Spirit Faith Healing

'A young boy suffering from an incurable disease was hoping for a miracle cure. Conventional doctors had advised amputation of his arm. A woman faith healer began to rub the afflicted part of his body aided by the spirit of a dead foreign doctor. Spade chose that moment to spring to his feet his mind and body possessed by a spirit shouted "Mango – wish-scrath-mush-ditch-lobberty-sisty-mack-dlabbero-bosh!" And indeed that is exactly what it appeared to be.'

Spirit Photography

Barnacle and Saunterer next visited the studio of a spirit photographer. Saunterer's imagination had been fired after being loaned a strange photograph of carte-de-visite size. The image was of a woman medium on a chair flanked by a chubby angelic being floating in the air. A group of disembodied angels' heads, their wings sprouting from their necks, rested on a cloud of incense above the medium. The owner of this remarkable photograph said the picture had been taken in the ordinary way and it was not until the photograph was developed that the uninvited angelic beings emerged. The photographer was said to have been 'ommost freeten'd aht of his wits' when he saw what he had captured on camera, and never fully recovered himself afterwards. The artist, wrote Saunterer, 'who is a party by the name of Johnson, ought to come forward and corroborate. Although I do not claim to have any spirit acquaintance, I must say that I have seen several of the angels before, and, as they are by Sir Joshua Reynolds, they are not unpleasant to look upon.'

Visit to a Medium

'On the night following my visit to the stable-loft, I and Barnacles made another raid upon the spirit-land, and again we had to go Bowling-wards. How is it the spirits are so partial to Bowling? What has Horton done to be so neglected? What has Manningham done? It is passing strange, this favouritism. It is not likely that in other parts of the town, as well as Bowling, there will be found persons echoing the words of the poet, and crying – "Ah, Christ, that it were possible. For one short hour to see. The souls we loved, that they might tell us. What and where they be?" May not the desire for a touch of the vanished hand, and the sound of a voice that is still, be as strong amongst the dwellers of Manningham and Horton as amongst the denizens of Bowling? We went our way to a cottage house in Cotewall Road, Bowling Old Lane. Our informant the doctor-medium advised us we should see a card with 'Pills' printed on it in the window, so we had not much difficulty in finding the place. We were requested to go upstairs, and up we went. It was a small unfurnished chamber that we entered, and near the window a number of females were gathered round a little table, at the head of which sat a tall, gaunt albino, his long white hair thrown back from his forehead and his preternaturally pink eyes flashing strangely in the deepening twilight. The service – if service it can be called – had already commenced, he of the pink eyes being in the act of offering up a prayer. Barnacles and I seated ourselves at the foot of the table, a sort of magic circle being thus formed, and those who came into the room afterwards had to content themselves with a back form. After the prayer had been concluded, the albino, who was the officiating medium, threw himself back in his chair, shut his eyes, and placed his two hands upon the table. A spirit seemed to take possession of him immediately, for he began to strike his fists upon the table excitedly, and wriggled and bobbed his head as if he were trying to shake it off. "A screw loose there, I fancy," whispered Barnacles, as the man's head banged against the table. These antics went on for a minute or two, and then the medium darted out his hand and grasped the arm of a woman who sat on his right. He stroked it, he patted it, and moaned over it awhile, and then delivered himself something after this fashion: – "Eh lass! (*bobs his head*) eh, lass! I've been watchin' thee an' I couldn't do bud come." The spirit of the newly dead husband of the woman had come through the ether. The widow bent her head and began sobbing into her handkerchief. "Well" she said wiping her tears "I wanted tha to come." "Ah, bud," continued the Spirit "I didn't dew altogether reyt to tha when I wor upo' t' earth." "Wah, nut awius thah didn't," his widow replied. "Noa," said the Spirit, and the medium gave the widow's arm a violent jerk, "theer wor things they wor;

theaze fowk doesn't know what I mean, do they?" "No" muttered the widow, "they don't lad." The disembodied voice continued "Things were noan so weel wi me at first after I left t' eearth," the Spirit proceeded, "but I'm progressin' my burdon's getting' leeter ivvery day." "I'm glad to hear it, lad," said the widow. Then the Spirit began to moan and weep again, and hinted darkly at the bitter past, and ultimately, with an appeal for forgiveness and a warm shake of the hand, it passed away, and the widow dried her eyes and was comforted.'

Other spirits came and went during the course of the evening. A woman sitting by Barnacle received a message. 'The voice was a living voice to her' for it was her dead mother, 'a queer owd stick'. The Spirit spoke in a strong Halifax dialect, telling her middle-aged daughter she would soon join her in heaven and that she had met her friend Nancy again. The Spirit asked if the daughter had felt 'summat touch thee o' t' left shoolder o' last Setterday t' neet?' The daughter nodded her head. 'That wor me, lass, that wor me, ah watched thee buy them potatoes.'

'I'm in Heaven'

The voice of a little girl who had died six months earlier came through the medium, addressing her grief stricken father. 'It began in a thin, high-pitched tone. "Hee, daddy, daddy, I tum to peyt tull ye, daddy, I tuddant bide a bit longer. Hee! Hee! Hee! It is drand up here. Hee! Hee! Hee! It is bonny. I've dotten a pair o' wings on nah, daddy, an' I've lots o' playmates wi' wings on; reyt drand 'uns; reyt bonny uns, I've dot no pain i' my heead nah, daddy; I've got no pain in my little tummack nah, daddy. Dre's a lot on us in dis room nah. Dare's a little angel dere; dare's an udder here; an' anudder dare; an' dare, an' dare, an' dare!" At this juncture the medium began to wave his index finger right, left and right again. The little voice faded away into the distance with words tinged with lamentation. "Dood neet, daddy. Don't try, daddy, I'll tut adean daddy." One more spirit came then it was over. A hymn was sung after which "a ghostly visitor" came to tell those assembled to congregate at the same place the next Saturday when the albino medium would deliver a speech on "Which way to heaven." The medium's performance was finished for the night and the gas which had flickered at its lowest throughout the session was now turned up full.' Saunterer and Barnacle's footsteps turned towards home, where they would digest the night's bizarre entertainment. Bradford inhabitants were, it seems, very involved in spiritualism and the occult. Idle Spiritualists met at the Old White Hart on Highfield Road, which was erected by Richard Farrer in 1693.

Chicanery at Huddersfield

In 1876 at the West Riding Police Court, Huddersfield, the Revd Francis Ward Monck, a former minister turned spiritualistic medium, stood charged under the Vagrancy Act. It was alleged that, 'on the 23 October he used certain subtle means and devices to deceive and impose upon Her Majesty's subjects, to wit, George Hepplestone, general dealer, Huddersfield, and Henry B. Lodge, woollen merchant, Huddersfield.' As Dr Monck was a medium of some standing, spiritualists and other interested parties filled the courtroom.

The first witness was Mrs Ellen Hepplestone, the wife of George Hepplestone. The court heard that on the evening of Monday, the 23 October 1876 a seance had been held at the Hepplestones' home in Arthur Street. The witness's square dining table measured about 2 metres, had no drawers in it and was covered with a cloth in readiness. The 'doctor' complained that the cloth was not long enough and insisted it be exchanged for a larger one. Those assembled handed over £2 each to Monck and were instructed to sit with their feet under the chairs and their hands on the tabletop. Monck said a gentleman must sit with a lady but that he himself must sit alone. They were instructed to say little or nothing during the seance. At Monck's request the group began by singing hymns: *Shall we Gather at the River* and *Hand in Hand with the Angels*. At the end of the hymns, a hand appeared from underneath the tablecloth and a sharp knock was heard from where Monck's left hand rested. The gas had been lowered but there was enough light to see by.

'The prisoner (Monck) arranged his fairy bells on the centre of the table, and placed the tambourine on top of it. The instruments commenced to move toward him, and Mr Lodge asked him if the articles could move backwards or sideways, and Monck replied that it was best not to ask the spirits to do anything, but to let them do what they pleased. They had to sing again and Monck asked Mr Lodge to turn the gas lower. It was not then possible to see anything. Monck held a scarlet and white tablecloth; the other tablecloth was of a darker colour. There then appeared what Monck called a "materialised hand" from the left-hand corner of the table nearest him. It slowly rose up from beneath the table. There was no light but they could see it. It was about the size of a lady's hand...He took the tambourine off the table, and told them that the hand would take hold of it. The hand appeared to be a wax hand, but she (Ellen) could not distinguish very clearly.

The gas was next turned up a little higher, and Monck asked Mrs Aspinall to take hold of the upper corner of the slate on the tabletop. He put it underneath the table...' Ellen Hepplestone then thought Monck asked Mrs Aspinall if she had hold of one corner, and she said she had. Ellen Hepplestone afterwards heard the scratching of a pencil on the slate. At this point the gas had been lowered again. Monck brought up the slate and gave it to one of the persons present, and the following message was read out, 'Good night, Philemon. Samuel.' He explained that Mr Samuel Wheeler was his spirit guide and that one of the gentlemen present was named Philemon. Ellen thought someone mentioned Philemon's name before the seance took place that night, but she could not be certain. There was another message written on the slate but she could not remember it. It was something in regard to Mr Lodge, but she could not recall the wording. The Chief Constable, reading from his notes, was able to recite this message. It was, 'Oh for a *lodge* in some vast wilderness!'

Apparently, Monck was averse to Mr Lodge being present at the seance, as he knew him to be a mesmerist (one who uses hypnotic powers to spellbind a person). Mr Lockwood, barrister for the defence, asked, 'Has he mesmerised you?' Ellen Hepplestone asked if she had to answer that question as she thought it ungentlemanly.

Lockwood excused her from answering the question and assured her that he would endeavour not to ask questions which she might consider improper.

Ellen Hepplestone continued, 'Mrs Aspinall had a button pulled off her dress and put on the slate. On being asked about it, Mrs Aspinall said she had felt a hand, and a warm hand too, coming underneath the table and over the slate. The gas was again lowered, and Monck intimated they must sing again, or the conditions would be altered. While they were singing...they...heard a sound as if the lid of the piano was being lifted. The room was very dark and the table was near the piano, which was behind the prisoner. There was one note sounded, and then Dr Monck spread his arms out and said that anyone might hold his arms. He asked Mrs Aspinall to sit at the piano to make sure; and then a note sounded, but she could not say whether it was the same note as before. After that Mrs Aspinall and another lady rose to go, having to leave by a train.'

At the end of the sitting Mr Lodge exclaimed to Monck, 'I, for one, must confess that I am not satisfied. I can perceive everything you have done is a trick, and if you will allow me those things and some others that are about you I will show you how they are done – or else will you allow yourself to be searched and let us have a peep into those boxes; and if we can't find that which you call 'a spirit hand' and some other things I shall be convinced, and be a Spiritualist; and of course I will apologise to you in a proper manner if I don't find them.' Lodge repeated the request for a search, which Monck emphatically refused. Dr Monck questioned why George Hepplestone would allow him to be treated in such a manner, but Hepplestone replied that Lodge's question was fair and that Monck had nothing to fear if he were genuine. Still Monck refused to be searched. Instead he struck Mr Lodge on the face then ran to an upstairs room and barred the door. He was asked to apologise for striking Mr Lodge and surrender his props and was promised that if he complied with their requests he would not be detained. Receiving no response, they hurried outside and saw that the bedroom window had been opened and a sheet suspended from the waterspout. They found two boxes in the bedroom and another downstairs. They were found to contain a number of theatrical articles including a piece of linen with a face lightly sketched on it, stuffed kid gloves with elastic attached to them, invisible thread, thin wire, a musical box and a long rod divisible into lengths. Dr Monck 'was adjudged guilty' and was taken to the House of Correction at Wakefield to serve three calendar months with hard labour.

'Spirit' Exhibition

In 1924 an exhibition took place in Leeds of 'spirit' photographs loaned by Sir Arthur Conan Doyle to the Spiritualist Church, New York Road. One of the photographs revealed the image of a wizened old man sporting a long white beard who had died ten days *before* the photo was taken. His face appeared between his daughter and granddaughter. Most of the photographs were images of shadowy faces wrapped in a fine muslin-type material, which was taken to be the person's aura floating amongst fairy lights and clouds.

Unwelcome Guests

An outwardly ordinary new bungalow in Stanbury village, close to Haworth, har-

Fake Victorian photograph of Bro. Andrew Morris with his 'spirit guide' (photo Ian Dewhirst M.B.E.)

boured malevolent spirits. The unlucky couple first to own the property had their possessions strewn around its rooms and smashed. Objects rose into the air and danced in front of the terrified occupants. Plagued by emergent apparitions, the couple contacted members of the Keighley Spiritualist Church at Heber Street. Investigations took place revealing that the bungalow was infested with several manifestations. What these consisted of was never revealed to the general public.

Great Revival?

The number of deaths during the First World War caused loved ones to seek the help of spiritualists in the hope of contacting their dead. Those who practised spiritualism were constantly at risk of persecution until the abolition of the Witchcraft Act passed in 1951. In circulating their publications they had depended on the goodwill of those in authority. In 1973 spiritualists were free to publish widely and hoped to create a great revival and attract new members to carry on the work.

Chapter 4

Restless Souls

'Ghosts white, ghosts black,
come to haunt you after the midnight hour sounds.' *M.C.*

Mournful Ghost of Cockhill

'Girl's Ordeal of Terror' proclaimed the *Keighley News* in 1930. A young Welsh girl had been out walking alone on Cockhill Moor. When about a mile distant from the village she saw 'a white shape, ghostly and creepy' near the hillside path. In a state of panic she ran towards Denholme, not stopping until she reached the safety of the Black Bull Inn.

A Mr Smith who happened to be in the Black Bull at the time said he too had seen the white spectre on the moors when out walking his puppy one evening. The night had been bright and he had seen what he described as, 'a figure of a man pushing his way against the wind.' Mr Smith called out a greeting to the stranger. The wind carried back the sound of a mournful voice crying, 'Lost! Lost! Lost!'

The Revd James Whalley of Todmorden thought he'd heard an 'unnatural sound' as he walked across Cockhill in the 19th century. In *The Wild Moor* he wrote, 'My hair, methinks almost stood on end; my eyes...did not decrease in magnitude. My heart beat, my breast heaved! My half consciousness returning – "Whence," said I, "did those unnatural and mysterious sounds issue?"...I have never heard of any ghosts visiting "the wild moor". If I fail to solve this mystery, I shall become a believer in the art and science of hobgoblins and frightful apparitions. I caught a glimpse and the next moment a distant view, of the "ghost", and then to my entire satisfaction, joy, and comfort I solved the problem and unravelled the mystery. I will, therefore, reveal to all the believers and unbelievers in the art of science of hobgoblins and apparitions, what the "spectre" was, whose "call" I certainly heard, and whose form I truly saw...it was neither more nor less than a *timid grouse,* and not a daring ghost from the invisible world.'

Hawksworth Hall's Dark Phantoms

The hall stands between Baildon and Rombalds Moor, near Bradford. A nameless African boy was once in service at Hawksworth Hall but was murdered by the butler long ago. He is said to haunt the place. He creeps into a bedroom and leaves behind an imprint of his tiny hand upon a pillow. Amongst his ghostly companions is a wandering monk, held captive in days of yore, who hovers close to the little monks' stairwell and a Grey Lady. A large black hound slinks around the hall on wild, stormy nights, seemingly compelled to guard some dark secret belonging to the hall.

My! What larks at Hawksworth Hall

Secret Rooms

Builders renovating Hawksworth Hall during the 1960s discovered three secret priest holes. The first was found in an attic above a bedroom. It was 1.5 metres deep and was located at the back of the bedroom, below the chimney breast. A smaller hide came to light beneath the first hole when an electrician lifted a wooden floorboard during the course of his work. Hides such as this were often used as double blinds in times of Catholic persecution during the reign of Elizabeth I. Access to a third priest's bolthole was found near the fireplace in the Oak Room on the first floor. King James I once slept in the room when on a 'knightly expedition'. Many a priest died of hunger whilst secreted in hides such as these (furnished with only a bed and table-altar) if the owner of the property was detained elsewhere. He was often forced to use light sparingly. He would leave and return only in the dead of night to avoid detection. Apparently an arm from a ceiling pendant in the Oak Room (dated 1611) breaks off prior to an English King or Queen's death. There is a story of a secret tunnel beneath the hall that led to either Esholt Nunnery or to the Hawksworths' kin at Calverley village.

Member of Fawkes Family Weds Protestant

Elizabeth Fawkes of Hawksworth Hall wed Robert Farrer of Halifax. In 1549 he became Bishop of St David's in Wales. When Queen Mary came to the throne he refused to renounce his Protestant faith and was burnt at the stake at Caermarthen Market in March 1555. He endured death by fire without once flinching. His charred body was finally beaten down with a staff into the dying flames.

Old White Horse Inn, Bingley

This rambling, white-painted building was documented as early as 1530 but probably dates back to the 13th century. The mark of a double cross connects the old coaching inn to the Knights of St John. The oak-panelled room was once used for dispensing justice. Charles Wesley preached his brand of religion from three mounting steps outside the inn. The spirit of an 18th-century customer who dropped dead close to the fireplace in the main lounge haunts the inn. Customers have complained of a cold spot here on numerous occasions.

Tenants Flee

A rented house in Leeds creaked and groaned so much that its terror-stricken residents fled. The occupants complained to the estate agent of doors opening and sash windows closing themselves at all times of the day and night. Intrigued, the agent decided to investigate matters. It wasn't long before he too witnessed the strange goings-on. But after feeling the house tremble and hearing several loud creaking and groaning noises he discovered that the haunting was nothing more sinister than the sub-soil slipping due to a new road that had recently opened.

Cinema Ghost

An all-night vigil was organised by Mrs Joyce Coulter in 1977 to prove or disprove the presence of a ghost at the picture house. An apparition of an elderly, grey-haired lady or man had been seen sitting in the main box by some of the customers.

The first owner of the cinema, built close to Crosshills, near to Skipton's defunct railway station, was Charlie Nuttall. After Nuttall died a handyman by the name of Alf was appointed to take care of the building. In later years the cinema was used for a time as a bingo hall.

Mr Phillips and Mr Atkinson purchased the old cinema in 1976. The building underwent extensive renovations. Independently of each other both Phillips and Atkinson heard 'someone repeatedly mowing a lawn with an old pusher.' This happened time and again yet no rational explanation could be found. On Christmas Eve Mr Atkinson went down to the basement to start up the heating for the afternoon matinée. A pool of water on the floor drew his attention to a pile of rusty old nuts and bolts, which had been removed from Edwardian pipework. Further strange incidents occurred and a chain was removed twice from the film projector. Often whilst walking towards the main box Mr Phillips could hear the sound of footfalls following him. Each time he turned to look there was no one there. One day a man called at the cinema to read the gas meter but found the outside doors firmly bolted. On peering through a window, he 'saw someone drinking out of a cup' near the main box. Although Phillips and Atkinson were in Leeds at the time attending to business matters, the man insisted one of them had purposely locked him out, even though the cinema doors had been shut from the outside. Mrs Coulter's all-night vigil at the picture house failed to turn up any phantoms. The old cinema has been converted to Hanson's Furnishers, open late on Wednesday and Thursday for late night viewing...

Keighley Picture House

Archie, once the organist at this cinema on North Street, Keighley, reputedly still haunts it. His repertoire includes the sudden slamming of doors and touching cinema-goers.

Old Hall, Hall Ings

There were far more nocturnal visitations by ghosts, boggards and unearthly creatures in more superstitious times. Closer investigation might well have revealed that some of the 'hauntings' were nothing more sinister than an overactive imagination. An ancient hall once standing at Hall Ings, Bradford was supposedly haunted. A one-legged man keeping a stall near St George's Hall noticed that a ghostly form appeared at an upstairs window at each full moon. Passing workers from Messrs Wood and Walker would regularly gather together in trepidation to observe the weird form. From the foot of Bridge Street crowds gaped in wonder at this marvellous spectacle. Eventually, a conjurer rented the house and gleefully announced to all that the ghost was nothing more than a damp piece of wallpaper peeling from the wall and flapping in a draught from the broken window. The full moon's silvery light cast spooky shadows on to the loose paper, thus explaining the ghostly moving images on the wall.

The Ghost of Paper Hall

The hall was erected at Barkerend Road, Church Bank by an unknown builder – although some believe that William Rookes erected the hall at about the time of the second siege of Bradford. Unfortunately, this is not substantiated by a list of his properties, which fails to include the building. Nobody knows how or why Paper Hall gained its title but the ghost of an admiral supposedly haunts it. Beneath the building, in an underground passage leading to the parish church, the admiral took his own life

Paper Hall, the oldest building in Bradford, has been the scene of several hauntings
(picture: Jake Newiss)

with a sword. In 1884 the resident blacksmith said the apparition possessed, 'A pair of large staring eyes belonging to a face of ghastly aspect and is sometimes seen gazing fixedly out of a window, while at the dead of night mysterious noises are heard as of a wooden-legged man stamping around...dot and carry one, dot and carry one.' A quest to discover the whereabouts of the subterranean passage revealed nothing more than a hole about half a metre deep.

The fabric of Paper Hall began its slow decline in the 1800s. By 1970 the property was in a dreadful state – nothing but a mere shadow of its former glory. Thankfully, the council preserved the hall for posterity and extensive renovations took place.

In more recent times an innocent passer-by has seen a figure dressed in white armour standing outside the building, 'whistling a happy tune and swaying to and fro, holding a spear in his hand.'

Walk of the Dead

In the middle of the 19th century a remarkable letter from T. Chester arrived at the offices of the *Bradford Observer*. Addressed to the editor and entitled 'Walks with a Stranger' it began, 'An old man walks the streets at night and early dawn...the old man never stops anyone, stares straight ahead turning neither right or left. With eyes of burning red. Five feet tall aged about sixty wearing a seedy black costume, hair a dingy grey, wearing a greasy battered hat. Always walks with his hands firmly tucked in his pockets and his neck pulled down into his high collar.'

Chester's attention had been drawn to the stranger's existence when playing whist at the home of a Mrs Pintletoe. Nobody knew where the mysterious stranger lived or where he came from. Mr Chester resolved to get to the bottom of the mystery and follow the gentleman, but being elderly and stout was not in a position to do so himself. Consequently he employed a 'shoeblack' for the sum of sixpence, but the boy gave up after stalking the stranger for some miles. Mr Chester was none the wiser, excepting that the boy had heard the old man mutter, 'Five miles to see a clock and then find it stopped.'

The man was seen wandering in Well Street, near the schoolhouse well, at two one morning. Three hours later Chester's son saw the old boy lurking in Tyrell Street and heard him utter mysteriously. 'Ten drunken men, ten children starving to death, forty dogs surfeited with dainties and the widows of daughters ruined for want of bread.'

A further instalment appeared in the *Observer* a week later. Mr Chester wrote that at about 8.30am, whilst he was reading his newspaper, a young man burst wildly into his room looking pale and frightened. Jim Chaffer had followed the old stranger the previous evening. Chester offered him a tot of brandy to calm his nerves before discovering the cause of his anxiety.

Chaffer had followed the old man to the Mechanics' Institute at the corner of Leeds Road and Well Street where he heard him say, after doffing his hat, 'To the kind endeavours of good labour.' He continued on his nocturnal journey past Peel Monument, down Market Street and Bowling Green. As a preacher approached the man uttered the words, 'Pity he neglects his family and murders his wife.' Chaffer passed him at the bottom end of Ivegate where some half-starved ragged boys were selling fruit. It was then that Chaffer looked directly into the face of the stranger and saw that his eyes were filled with tears.

The stranger walked along Ivegate to the Adelphi but disappeared just as the Exchange clock struck the hour of nine. Chaffer retraced his steps to Market Street, where he hung around until he heard the sound of the old church clock striking twelve. Just as he was about to give up hope of seeing his quarry again, he saw him walking along Church Bank.

Convinced he was returning to his home Chaffer tagged behind him as he turned up Otley Road and past Riddihough's Hotel, opposite the cemetery. Here he crossed the road and climbed over the wall of the cemetery. The young man, resolved to follow at whatever cost, began to cross the road behind him. For the first time the old man stopped and looked back. Chaffer told Chester. 'I felt the effect of that last look creep over me like the feeling must be that comes over the prey of a boa-constrictor when it knows death. The old man waved his hand at me to go back. I staggered to the wall, sat down and wiped the perspiration from my brow then looked for him, but he had gone. I walked to my home. I went to bed. I could not sleep. The look was always before me. The piercing red eyes. At first light I got up and the first person I saw going out on my business was the little old man, with the same step, same gait, same mutterings. I had composed myself to the task of telling you Mr Chester, quietly and faithfully and had overcome my nervousness when just now, as I was about to enter your house, the old man brushed past me again and said, audibly "Pity he marked his own grave." Now Mr Chester I fear something dreadful is going to happen to me, and I am very sorry I partook to follow him.' Chester said he had received a warning from a Fenian never to speak to the stranger again or by the name of the three holy Manchester martyrs, it would be the worse for him.

Billy Pintletoe wrote to the paper a few days later. He said that his friend Jim Chaffer was potty for they had both been in the Blazing Bowl playing pool until midnight on the evening in question. Afterwards they had gone to the home of a Mr Tilt, who had lost all his money in a company that had blown up. Mrs Tilt had almost brained Jim Chaffer with a stick in the darkness—thinking it was her erring husband. Billy and Jim discovered their friend talking with Boulder, Shinder Pilks and a man called Sottle at Boulder's lodgings. After a time Jim left Billy to go to Chester's house to tell him the best tale he could about the stranger.

Jim Chaffer hotly retorted in the following week's edition that Billy Pintletoe didn't know he had followed the old man that night. He maintained the stranger *had* walked into their midst when Billy was fast asleep over the spittoon. He went on to say that two timepieces on the mantelshelf had just struck five when Boulder's bedroom door flew open to show the old stranger with three half-starved children in tow. 'Give them warmth and shelter,' he implored the men. Boulder and Sottle told him to take them to the workhouse. The old man directed his reply to Boulder. 'The boy is yours...yours and the mother is now a floating corpse in the river Humber.' With that he picked up the boy and went out with the beggars. Billy had been unconscious the whole time and had to be brought round with iced water.

The final newspaper instalment arrived at the office in April. Mr Chester claimed he had met the old stranger in a Bradford park. Sitting down beside Chester he warned him to, 'Seek not to know for direful will be your knowledge. What I am I cannot tell but what I have been – listen. A phantom of Nemesis, a murder undiscovered, a bad deed dropped upon the past, and spring into a man. I am a magician behold!' He reached into his pocket and held up a glass. Chester's eyes transfixed as a vision of his life appeared before him, and as the vision faded so did the old stranger!

Reader, make of this tale what you will.

Bradfordians Frightened

In September 1926 a national newspaper carried a story concerning a ghostly apparition haunting the streets of Bradford at twilight. Bierley's council estate and Manchester Road seemed to be its most popular haunts for over a year. A woman looking out of her window received the shock of her life when a hooded creature stared back at her from the gathering darkness. The populace became so alarmed that the local CID was brought in to search every nook and cranny in an attempt to flush out the unwanted visitor. Their diligence was rewarded when the ghost was spotted on a rooftop above a brewery, but it immediately vanished. Bierley Cemetery, whose first burial was that of an infant, Harry Smith of Mill Street, Low Moor, in January 1903, appeared to be its favourite stomping ground.

Shady Ghosts

The offices of the *Telegraph & Argus* were contacted on 15 June 1927 by an official from a tank manufacturer operating from Bradford's old manor house near Bowling Ironworks. The distressed official explained that he had gone into the downstairs washroom when working late one evening and almost immediately felt a strong creepy presence invade the room, causing his hair to stand on end. He said, 'I turned, but could not see anything.' In darker times the gallows stood nearby on Cinder Hill, its gruesome frame silhouetted against the Bradford skyline.

Suspicious Haunting

In 1831 death visited Boggard Farm, Bierley. Old Mrs Kay was taken to the first Congregational chapel in the district, Red Chapel, Scott Yard, Cleckheaton, where she was laid to rest. Although only a distant relative, Mr Frith, a neighbouring farmer, inherited Boggard Farm together with the surrounding land. Not long after the Frith family had taken up residence at the farm they heard ghostly sounds of rustling silk skirts accompanied by heavy stamping on the stairs. Eerie noises issued from a kitchen cupboard and pots and pans inside rattled and clattered in a most alarming manner. Windows flew open, rattled then snapped shut. Blinds were pulled up and let down. Bolts and chains on outside doors rattled day and night. Other noises were described by the terrified inhabitants as 'sounding like someone emptying out sacks of corn and throwing a large bag of hard peas across the floor'. A disembodied voice said to resemble that of Mrs Kay uttered loud moans and groans throughout the hours of darkness, often speaking in some foreign gibberish.

Curious tourists flocked to the farmstead in the hope of a good sighting. All were refused admittance until a gentleman arrived at Boggard from Leeds and begged the family to permit him to stay in the haunted room, where the eldest son normally slept, for one night. At midnight the shadow of a ghost appeared to the sound of the most frightful wailing, and by morning their guest had fled.

Hoping to expose the family as fakes, two sceptical Wesleyan ministers took it upon themselves to spend a night in the boggard chamber. The ministers' respective flocks jostled outside in the hope of witnessing their leaders emerge wretched from what they believed must surely be the pit of hell. They were not disappointed. As dusk gave way to darkness the ministers swore they saw the form of a stooping old woman standing in the centre of the room. Upon nearing the form it vaporised, and the ministers also disappeared!.

Revd Benjamin Frith, an Independent minister (no relation) of Manor House, Hartshead Moor, Cleckheaton, also came with the fervent desire to rid the suffering family of their torturous demons and to solve the mystery. The distinguished reverend gentleman prepared to give the old lady's restless spirit the benefit of his divinity and took care to address the ghost of Mrs Kay by name. 'In the name of the Father, Son and Holy Ghost, who art thou? If thou be the spirit of Mrs Kay, make thyself known by rapping on a chair.' Encouragingly, he received a response and so continued, 'Hast thou the power of speech?' But silence was his only answer.

One paying guest bécame famous in boggard lore. He stayed in the room for a whole month and although he did not see any apparitions, he did hear a number of unaccountable noises and twice discharged his gun in their direction in the hope of *killing* the ghost. The hauntings continued for eighteen months before ceasing of their own accord. The case of Mrs Kay remains unsolved.

Old Silent Inn, Stanbury

Known by the sign of the eagle, legend tells of those within its walls harbouring Bonnie Prince Charlie in 1745. Sworn to silence, those who frequented The Eagle were true to their word and remained silent even though there was a huge reward for the Pretender's capture. A fierce local hillbilly family by the name of Carless captured the prince but he managed to escape. The Eagle thereafter became the Old Silent. The inn ceased trading in 1926 and served as a farmstead until the late 1960s. Writer Halliwell Sutcliffe used the inn as a backdrop in his work *Ricroft of Withins*. A residents'-only licence was granted and the Old Silent opened as a hotel in 1968. A full licence was eventually approved and the old inn was once again restored to village life.

Several ghosts are known to inhabit its rooms. At the dead of night a former landlady who was well known for her fondness of cats appears, dressed in a dark-hooded cloak. She sometimes strokes the heads of sleeping guests. On windless nights the soft tinkle of a bell can often be heard across the moors, calling the ghostly cats. Landlady

Mrs Brogan told the *Keighley News* in 1972, 'I hear the bells. They tinkle in the distance, like fairy bells. They're lovely. If they were to stop I'd miss them.'

A family from Lancashire complained of poltergeist activity during 1990 when they saw a glass leap of its own accord across their room. In 1993 men working at the inn witnessed a ghostly figure, causing them to drop their tools and run away. A cleaner working in upstairs bedrooms complained of a meddlesome presence interfering with her daily work. The Old Silent featured in a BBC documentary 'Haunted Hostelries of England'.

The Old Silent, Stanbury, where the ghost of a former landlady is said to stroke the heads of unsuspecting sleeping guests.

Ghost of Emily Brontë?

Halliwell Sutcliffe writes in his book *By Moor and Fell,* 'Thoughts throng in on one while standing quiet in Haworth main street here, with the ghosts of the near past...It is Emily whose presence seems at times to overshadow Haworth...we see her climb up and up, until her figure, slight against the sunset red, dips over the moor-crest and is lost.' Sutcliffe's brooding image of Haworth tells of Emily's ghost passing by the parsonage on its lonely journey over a rough trackway leading to Top Withins. It is along this path that sightseers pass Emily's favourite waterfall and where the ruin of Deanside Farm comes into view. Once the home of two brothers, Will and Jim Jobbings, who earned a living by doing odd jobs. the farm was known locally as 'T Jobbin Spot'. Sightings of Emily traversing the moorland track produced the following account, 'A tall, thin ghost of a girl dressed in everyday clothes her head bowed as if lost in some deep thought.' A lady dressed in white of unknown origin has also been seen from time to time on the track leading from Stanbury to Top Withins. Perhaps this ghost is far older in its years than is supposed for Emily Brontë may have drawn from the story of the sad phantom when she wrote of Cathy's ghost in *Wuthering Heights*. A young boy standing close to the Brontë waterfall (trickle) claimed he saw a ghostly couple clasped in each other's arms out on the wild moorland.

Northerner II produced the following humorous account which can be found in the pages of the *Yorkshire Post* from 3 October 1972, '...folk who had seen Emily's ghost slouching over the moors would run back screaming to Keighley, faint dead away and have to be brought back by special restoratives. Indeed Keighley Corporation rendered a humane service to the inhabitants of Brontëland when they arranged for a first-aid post to be set up on the edge of the moors to revive people who had seen Emily. The standard treatment for the shock of this experience was a dose from a bottle labelled 'Emily Brontë Mixture' commonly referred to as 'Em and B'. The scheme broke down alas, when casualties became so numerous that any day of the week you would see a long queue of screaming patients outside the first-aid post, and the cost of treating them imposed an intolerable burden on the Corporation.'

Haunting of the Toby Jug

On the anniversary of Emily Brontë's death in the winter of 1974, two mediums and twelve of their followers gathered together by the light of three flickering candles. Purposeful and intent, they sat around a table in the dimly lit back room of the Toby Jug Restaurant. With baited breath they waited expectantly for the ghost of Emily to appear. Their imaginations fired by recent sightings, some of the number had travelled many miles to be a part of the seance. The owner of the Toby Jug, Keith Ackeroyd, and his assistant, John Roebuck, had both sighted the ghost, which they believed to be Emily Brontë. Dressed in a long skirt and holding a basket on each arm the apparition had appeared to them in a 'sort of greyish haze.' According to those who had seen the vision, Emily was particularly active on the anniversary of her death – 19th December. The *Keighley News* reported Mr Ackeroyd's description of a typical Emily visitation. 'Hearing a faint rustling sound, I turned and saw this figure smiling and giggling. She walked across the room to where the stairs used to climb up to the bedroom. I ran up the new stairs and there she was chuckling in the bedroom. Then she went downstairs and out into the street.' Upon reading this account in the newspaper, a sceptic Mr Preston, a lifelong resident of Haworth, commented, 'The description doesn't fit any of the Brontës. They were a gloomy lot, and Emily was the gloomiest of all.' Revd Ashdown was asked if he would perform an exorcism at the Toby Jug in 1974 because Mr Ackeroyd wished to market the property. The exorcism never took place and the property was eventually sold complete with its ghostly resident. Since changing the name of the Toby Jug Restaurant to The Weavers there have been no further manifestations.

Apparently, the ghost of Anne Brontë, whose remains are interred on a windswept seaside hilltop, has, according to Mrs Gladys Topping, attached itself to Mirfield's demolished Blake Hall's wooden staircase. This is now resident in America! Anne

Brontë used her knowledge of Blake Hall when describing Wildfell in her novel *The Tenant of Wildfell Hall.*

Death in the Heaton Family

Author Halliwell Sutcliffe describes a typical Heaton funeral. 'It was on the hillside opposite, I remember that I stood one winter's day – a raw day, with sorrow in the wind, and a thin blue winding sheet of snow on field and heath – and saw a burial party wind slowly down the road. They were carrying John Heaton of Ponden Hall... to the moorside graveyard.' Revd J. Wade, Rector of Haworth, performed the funeral service held at the hall. Wade, who was responsible for tearing down the old Brontë church, was the last person to pray with the dying Heaton. The burial service took place at Scartop Chapel where Wesleyan Minister Revd J.C. Greaves conducted the latter part of the service. The choir sang *Vital Spark*, and at the graveside one of John Heaton's own tunes was sung to the hymn beginning 'Hark, the voice divides the sky'.

Thomas Heaton returns

On visiting Pondon House early in the New Year of 1898, a cousin of Thomas Heaton's who knew him to be away was most surprised to see him taking a walk in the garden. Thomas was easily recognised by his long beard and favourite grey suit. His cousin called out to him but received no answer. Seeking out Heaton's older brother, Robert, she related her odd encounter. Upon hearing the tale Robert fell silent. Throughout his long life Robert Heaton, a down-to-earth Yorkshire yeoman, believed solidly in the Heaton family legend that the imminent death of one of their number would be heralded by a ghostly vision of the person who was about to die. 'The Headless Man', alias Greybeard, would also appear in this lonely valley but only when disaster was about to strike the family.

'Rest in Pace'

Within a short time the prophecy was fulfilled. In February Thomas Heaton expired, aged eighty-two years. Weakened by grief, just eight days later on 3 March 1898 Robert followed his beloved brother Thomas Midgley Heaton to the moorland cemetery at Stanbury. In the south aisle of Haworth Church is a stained-glass window dedicated to the memory of this family. The Heatons were renowned for their lavish arvils (funeral biddings). Robert's funeral service took place at his ancestral home and was conducted by Revd J.C. Hirst.

Their cousin, Miss Hannah Knowles Heaton, a direct descendant who had once lived at Ponden House, died in 1934. A lark perched upon a nearby headstone sung sweetly as her coffin was lowered into the earth. A keen walker even in her eighties, she travelled on foot to visit friends at Laneshawbridge, Lancashire – a distance of seven miles! It is thanks to Miss Heaton that carefully stored family documents were handed to Keighley Library for safekeeping. Amongst the old documents is a summons directed to Robert Heaton to attend the coronation of Charles I to receive from him a knighthood. Robert refused and was forced to pay a fine of £10. The ill-fated Earl of Strafford, who was later beheaded, signed the receipt.

It was this Robert who on 23 December 1640 married Anne, daughter of Nicholas Scarborough of Glusburn Hall, Lancashire, at Burnley Parish Church. She was the granddaughter of Robert Nowell of Read Hall, Whalley. Nowell, a well-known magistrate, played an important role in the trials and deaths of the infamous Pendle Witches.

Pondon Hall at Pondon, once the home of the Heaton family
(The Keighley News)

Brontë Connection

The Brontë sisters were known to visit the shy, musical Heaton brothers (Robert, William, John, Thomas and Michael) at Ponden Hall during the spring and summer months. The house appears as Thrushcross Grange in Brontë writings. The girls often strolled together around the gardens, stopping to rest awhile under the massive beech- and Spanish chestnut-lined avenues (now submerged by Pondon Reservoir). At other times they could be found browsing through the brothers' extensive library of rare and valuable books, which served no doubt to fire the sisters' already fertile imaginations. The Heatons were rumoured to have owned a first folio of Shakespeare. Robert Heaton left this book to be kept at Ponden Hall, which used to be called 'The Scotchman's Arm', for the use of his sons and their future heirs. An inscription above the door reads:

THE

Old houfe

(now standing) was

built by Robert Heaton

for his son Michael

Anno Domini 1634.

The old Porch and Peat

Houfe was built by his

Grandson Robert

Heaton a.d 1680.

The prefent Building

Was Rebuilt by his

Defcendant R.H. 1801.

Greybeard Haunting

After sunset, light cast from a ghostly lantern was often seen wavering along a narrow, high-walled garden above Ponden Hall. It was held by the harbinger of doom – Greybeard the changeling. Before death he was known as Henry Casson, a ne'er-do-well who married Michael Heaton's widow, Anne, shortly after Heaton was killed in the Civil War. Casson had also fought in this war. After the wedding he wasted no time in procuring the family estates for himself. Anne bore him one son, named John Casson. Robert Heaton (Michael's son), the true heir to the Heaton estate, was totally ignored by his ambitious and greedy stepfather. Anne eventually managed to rid herself of him and retrieve her title. Poor Michael, though, was forced to hand over to his stepfather the sum of £13 – a small fortune in those days – as payment for his own household furniture!

Locals sometimes gathered at the end of winding Ponden Road to watch Greybeard form himself into a flaming barrel and roll down the hill past the hall, finally coming to rest at the bee 'hive holes'. An occultist (Abraham Sunderland?) was summoned from Stanbury to deal with the phenomenon. At length he was rewarded for his patience one bitter winter's day when the phantom appeared before him. He carefully lit a rush candle. Holding the light aloft in his left hand he waved the Book of Black Art in his right whist chanting the following spell, 'Niver come nigh th' oed house again till tha's seen this rush light burn to th' end.' The Stanbury occultist swallowed the candle and the spell was complete. Greybeard threw his lantern to the ground then howled as he fled across the fields. He was never seen again.

Branwell Brontë used the story of Greybeard to illustrate his tale *Percy* in 1837. He wrote, 'The Darkwell Gytrash was known by its form of an old dwarfish and hideous man, as often seen without a head as with one moving at dark along the naked fields which spread round the aged house.'

Shepherd sees Strange Sight

Accompanied by his dog Towser, Job Triffit, a simple-minded shepherd, watched ghostly visitations when out tending his flock. Once when looking over towards Ponden Waters he saw a barrel dancing 'in t beck-hoil, an' t' scarecrow wor stood on t' stoan brig wi booath arms stretched aht loike a rantypowle.'

'T' Boggard Hoil'

Contained within the pages of an aged book of black art is a reference to Blackhorse Marsh, high up on Haworth Moor. Situated in this place, not far from Tom Stell's seat, is Grovel Dyke, where you may find 't' boggard hoil'. Emily Brontë in *Wuthering Heights* renames it 'Blackhorse Marsh'. It had long been the case that local children would not play there. Any human being found wandering in this place might fall victim to the dreadful boggard, which concealed itself in the water, waiting to swallow up any living thing it could. At nearby Oakworth another boggard was thought to reside at a farm known as 'T' Boggard Laithe'.

Working Ghost

Through the passing centuries the Manor House at Haworth has undergone many changes. The original building peeps out from the side, overshadowed now by a large extension. A former inhabitant of the manor killed herself in an upstairs room. She has often been seen going about her earthly housework duties in a matter-of-fact fashion. Those who have seen her ghost say she seems completely unaware that she no longer inhabits the earth. Today she may be kept very busy as the old manor is now a hotel.

Weeping Ghost

Emily Brontë related the following tale to Mrs Gaskell. A wealthy Haworth wool manufacturer had married off one of his daughters to another wealthy manufacturer who lived somewhere beyond Keighley. A younger sister aged about fifteen – an innocent – was sent to attend the young bride who was expecting her first child. A few months later the husband returned the girl, now pregnant with his illegitimate child, to Haworth. On learning of her condition the girl's father and sisters cruelly rebuked her for having brought shame upon the family name. The poor girl was locked away in a room until her father came to a decision about her future.

Mrs Gaskell wrote of it in Charlotte's autobiography. 'Only her mother, and she was reported to be a stern woman, had some pity on her. The tale went that passers-by on the high-road at night time saw the mother and young daughter walking in the garden, weeping long after the household had gone to bed. Nay, more; it was whispered that they walked and wept there still, when Miss Brontë told me the tale – though both had mouldered in their graves. The wild whispers of this story added that the cruel father, maddened perhaps by the disgrace which had fallen upon a religious family, offered a sum of money to any one who would marry his poor fallen daughter; that a husband was found, who bore her away from Haworth, and broke her heart, so she died while even yet a child.' Mrs Gaskell writes elsewhere that the family home stood near the high road to Haworth. Its grounds were noted as having the very first greenhouse in the district.

Evidently the family was a large one, and for a short period of time the Brontë sisters visited them. The Brontës were very likely to have personally known the pregnant girl. Descendants of the wool manufacturer are supposedly cursed to fail in business and health to assuage the young girl's sufferings. Staunch Baptists, the Greenwoods of Bridge House, Haworth often invited the Brontë girls to tea. Was this the family Emily had spoken of to Mrs Gaskell?

Phantom Coach

By the side of a narrow, winding road high up on Haworth moor stands an old former coach house. The solid building lent itself to conversion from its former use into a residential dwelling. In 1968 a couple living there heard the thunder of horses' hooves. On stepping outside they beheld a phantom stagecoach drawn by two horses. It came to a halt in front of them and ghostly visitors alighted. A gentleman sporting an old-fashioned top hat escorted a lady wearing a crinoline dress through the wall of the coach house, where a door had originally been, then faded from view.

Monk Crosses Path

Ensconced in their usual corner of the Black Bull one dark stormy night, Haworth characters Big Tommy Wilkinson and Harry-the-Hat began discussing old village tales. Others gathered round, entertained by the strange stories that they had to tell while the wind whistled loudly through the leaves of the graveyard trees outside. Time passed and as the hour of midnight approached the storytellers bid the company good-night. Setting off up Main Street, weaving their way somewhat unsteadily homeward, the two stumbled past the King's Arms and the Old White Lion. Having reached the point where the road narrows, they saw to their amazement the unmistakable form of a ghostly monk gliding silently across the road. Unable to move they watched as the apparition disappeared into a solid stone cottage wall across the way. Being first to recover his senses, Harry gravely warned Tommy to 'keep his mouth shut otherwise they would be the laughing stock of all Haworth'.

Sinister Rustlings

In the pages of *The Wild Moor* the Revd James Whalley relates the following tale. 'Not many years ago a house in the best street of —— (Haworth) was uninhabited, because it was believed to be haunted, and by it young people walked at night with quickened pace and beating heart. The rustling silk gown of a lady had sometimes been heard moving to and fro in the third storey, by the trembling listeners at the foot of the second flight of stairs.'

Brontës out Ghost Hunting

Many have wondered why it was that at least two of the famous Brontë girls were seen coming 'down from Barnside', a somewhat remote area situated between Cowling and Laneshawbridge. Could they have heard the following stories of murder and hauntings? Charlotte at least was here for she describes the view from Barnside looking out towards Boulsworth Hill when she writes, '...the evening star hung over the brow of Boulshill...the farm fields stretched away between.'

Barnside Murder

During the late 1700s a peculiar family by the name of Hartley rented Barnside Farm, Laneshawbridge from Mr John Clayton. The mother, an eccentric, gained the title of Wolf Woman because her face was covered with coarse black hair and each of her yellowed fingernails was long and twisted. She shared the farmstead with an infant and a teenage son, Christopher, who courted pretty Hannah Corbridge, a well-liked local girl. On Sunday, the 19 January 1789 Hannah mysteriously disappeared after last being seen with her beau. A fruitless search was made for the heavily pregnant girl and a constable was brought to search Barnside Farm. The body of the murder victim was at that time secreted in a box full of oat dust, but the mother concealed the fact by sitting on it while feeding the infant breast milk. Hannah's worried relatives consulted a

Todmorden wise man. He told them they would find her mutilated body hidden near Barnside Hall, but warned them not to go near the area as Hannah would come back to haunt them. Instead, they stood on rising ground near Emmott Hall pointing out the direction the searchers should take. The girl's work apron was found sticking through the earth in the place which the wise man predicted. Hannah's remains were deposited at Newchurch-in-Pendle on 29 January 1789.

A week to the day later Hartley was arrested in Flookborough and transported back to Colne. It transpired that Hannah had been poisoned by a piece of parkin cake specially baked by Hartley's mother. When this failed to take effect, Christopher Hartley callously tried to hack off her head. He dragged Hannah's lifeless, bloody body back to Barnside and hid it inside the oaken box until nightfall. Then he moved it to a field named Northings close by Barnside Hall. He was sentenced to die on the gallows at Lancaster on 28 August 1789.

Hannah Haunts Farmstead
Barnside Farm remained abandoned for many years for it was said that the restless spirit of Hannah Corbridge wistfully searched the empty rooms for her heartless lover. Many visited the deserted site out of morbid curiosity, hoping to catch a brief glimpse of the ghost. Eventually a man called Tillotson tenanted the old farmstead and the wailing spectral waif was seen no more. The present owners of Barnside Farm, who have lived there for thirty-five years, report that they have never yet seen the ghost of the murdered girl.

Bloodied Stones
Barnside Hall was eventually demolished. Some of the stones were carted away to Laneshawbridge, where they were used to mend crumbling stonework. Soon after this work was completed the inhabitants of the village noticed that the stones brought from the hall appeared to be dripping with blood. Curious villagers gathered round to witness the spectacle. Most convinced themselves it was the blood of the murder victim for it was well known that after hiding the body Hartley had wiped the blood from his hands on the stones. Sightings of Hannah have been reported at nearby Earl Hall. She usually appeared in a room at the farmstead around midnight. In past years a farmer wishing to rid himself of this unwanted guest called in a Roman Catholic priest. He began to light a host of candles, but before he could complete his task Hannah flew down the chimney in the guise of a haycock. In priestish tongue the holy man ordered her to appear in her human form. This she did, holding forth an outstretched hand containing a tiny child. Throughout the proceedings the priest uttered the relevant exorcism words. As he spoke the room grew dim for one candle after another died out until there was only one small candle. The priest warned the spirit she might never appear again while a candle burned. Grasping the glowing candle the good man swallowed it light and all, thus preventing it from burning away and Hannah disappeared. From time to time Hannah's ghost has been seen wandering the lonely moors she so loved in life.

Brontës Seek Ghosts?
As they had a deep interest in the supernatural the Brontës are sure to have heard the

Earl Hall, near Barnside, where the ghost of murder victim Hannah Cobridge has been seen on a number of occasions

ghost stories of Barnside and ghost-ridden Wycoller Hall. A 1779 diary records the latter having at least one fearsome haunting. The Brontë sisters were seen tramping from Barnside to Wycoller via Laneshawbridge on the same day. Perhaps it was their natural curiosity that caused them to actively seek out knowledge of dark tales, murder and hauntings.

Wycoller Hall

The ancient seat of Wycoller (Wic-alr) lies between Keighley Moor and Coomb Hill. The once wealthy Cuncliffe family arrived at this remote place after losing their ancestral home at Billington in the days of the Commonwealth. Thought to have been built around 1550 by the Hartley family, Wycoller Hall has fallen into ruin and is reputedly haunted by a number of Cuncliffe ghosts.

Bloody Murder

Many years ago a young girl living in the village related the story of the ghostly horseman who rode through her village in a tempest on the same evening each year. This is her account. 'One of the Cuncliffes they say murdered his wife. For that reason he was doomed to pay an annual visit to the room in which the murder was committed...he used to come attired in the costume of the early Stuart period, the trappings of his horse being of an uncouth description. I never really knew whether he came from Stanbury, Laneshawbridge, Colne, Widdop or Trawden quarter; but the night of his visit never failed to be dark and wild and sometimes there was lightening and thunder.

Haunted Wycoller Hall, visited by a bevy of ghostly apparitions

When the wind howled the loudest, and everybody was as still as a mouse, locked up for fear in his own house, he would come dashing past our windows, and we could tell his horse was so ragefully hot that he may as my brother said he did have snorted fire from his nostrils. After crossing the narrow bridge he stopped presently at the hall door, and then, the rider dismounting, would make his way up the broad oaken stairs which led to the death room. A woman's blood curdling scream, followed by an awful dying groan, would next be heard. Later the spectre-man would come downstairs, re-mount, and gallop back the way he came.'

The ghost is said to arrive via the narrow Slab Bridge in front of the hall. By all accounts the image of this particular ghost is almost transparent. This Cuncliffe murdered his wife with a dog whip after flying into a jealous rage when seeing her in the arms of a lover. But the 'lover' turned out to be his innocent wife's long-lost brother. Each year on the anniversary of the murder Cuncliffe's ghost is forced to re-enact the hideous crime.

Last 'Writes'

As Colne man Frank Slater lay abed dying in 1918, he composed a lengthy poem about the murder entitled *The Spectre Horseman*. The final verse runs thus:

'On Hallow's Eve, when brown October dies,
And drear November bids her storms rise,
When stormy blasts without do roar,
With shutters fast and locked the door,
In memory of the virtuous dead
Let this legend then be read.'

Hunter Cuncliffe

In the days of Charles II, Squire Cuncliffe was engaged in his favourite sport of fox-hunting when his quarry ran through the gates of the hall, into the house and upstairs to his delicate wife's bedchamber. Following behind the fox on his white hunter, furiously blowing his hunting horn, and followed by a pack of hounds in hot pursuit, Cuncliffe crashed through the hall. His wife died from shock as the triumphant huntsman held the dead fox aloft in his bloodied hands. They say the broad, oaken stairs bore the marks of horse's hooves long after the dreadful event took place, and the ghost of his wife still cries at the spectral fox-hunt.

Squire Game to the Last

Henry Owen Cuncliffe died at the hall, aged sixty-six years, on 8 November 1818, after watching a cockfight in his bedchamber. Mirrors were fixed to the ceiling so he could observe the combat because he was too weak to sit up. In the excitement of watching the fight his heart gave way. A picture was painted depicting the scene and is entitled *Game to theLast*. Henry Owen Cuncliffe was laid to rest in Colne Church. His death marked the end of the Cuncliffe family. After his passing the hall remained empty, due to the heavy debts he had amassed during his lifetime. Within two decades the hall had crumbled, becoming a lonely and desolate place. Charlotte Brontë explored Wycoller and other 'old ruins and old halls situated amongst older hills and woods'. It was from her knowledge of Wycoller Hall that she imagined Mr Rochester's Ferndene Manor as described in *Jane Eyre*.

Woman in Black

Black Bess or Old Bess dresses in black silk widow's weeds and has been seen haunting the grounds of the ruined hall since the 18th century. She waits anxiously for the return of her husband – a seafaring Cuncliffe lost at sea in the 1600s. Another tale informs us that Black Bess was really a West Indian girl whom one of the Cuncliffes wed. On the way back to England he regretted the marriage and tossed her overboard, whereupon she drowned. Her spirit followed him back to Wycoller, where to this day she still searches for her murderous husband.

In 1948 Mr Bracewell, who had lived in the medieval village nearly all of his life, said, 'The last we heard of Mrs Cuncliffe's ghost was before the war when my son, Wesley, stayed up one night to wait for it. At two o'clock (am) he heard footsteps and thought I was joining him. He called for me but I was at home in bed. He didn't stay long after that.' Some years later Black Bess was seen standing silently on the Packhorse Bridge by two burly workmen. They spoke to her but she just faded away. About 1867, a couple from the village of Trawden were alone together in an upstairs chamber of the hall when they suddenly heard footsteps climbing the staircase. Frightened by the noise, they clung to each other. The footsteps grew nearer and they could hear the rustling of a woman's silk dress. Suddenly the door opened and there stood a lady dressed in black. Ignoring the lovers, she looked around the room and departed without a single word.

Crime Committed

In 1500 Robert Cuncliffe of Billington was banned from the county for a 'felony against the wife of Eli Wood.'

Strange Presence

Pretty Wycoller House, built by Richard Hartley, was home to the Dewhurst family until 1957. The family were often troubled by peculiar noises, footsteps, lighted candles inexplicably snuffed out in draught-proof rooms and doors creaking open of their own accord. Unsuspecting persons felt an invisible push when entering a particular unoccupied room. A niece, Shirley Wilkinson, saw a vision of a woman dressed in vivid blue pass down the stairs. The Dewhursts' young daughter was frightened by 'A man wearing two caps – one round and one square one on top – and a long black cloak...' The source of the malignant activity remains unsolved. The local café is from time to time at night visited by a ghostly feline.

Druid Worship?

Further up the dene from Wycoller, the oldest bridge (Bank House Bridge) looks like a tree trunk spanning the stream and resting on stones placed at either side. The reason for its existence is not known for the stream is easily accessed at this point. It is said that a druidical place of worship was close by. Lowlands Bridge, on the Colne side, served as an arch in the cellar of Wycoller Hall until it was carefully dismantled and placed in its present position.

Cursed painting at Streeton Hall displayed by licensees Ellis Bottomley and Clayton Smith (picture: The Keighley News)

Mysterious Happenings

A picture of sheep grazing on a hillside was commissioned at the turn of the 19th century to commemorate the memory of a child burnt to death in an upstairs room at Steeton Hall, Keighley. Local lore says the building will be destroyed by fire should the artwork ever be removed. Whitbread Brewery ordered its removal during renovations a decade ago. Shortly afterwards a fire did start, causing a good deal of damage. Needless to say the canvas was very quickly returned to its rightful position.

The haunted room where the ill-fated infant died now accommodates paying visitors, some of whom have complained of hearing a small child sobbing and the sound of breaking glass. The sound of hurried footsteps on the staircase long after twilight has also been heard. Lights mysteriously switch on and off at will.

It is said that should an animal horn housed at the hall be removed, it would cause the whole building to crumble. Should the horn ever be blown the ghosts of past residents will return to haunt the hall. A subterranean passage beneath Steeton Hall allegedly connects to St Stephen's Church across the way. Sometimes the rattle and clank of chains can be heard in cellars that once served as prison cells.

Bar staff complained of pictures flying off the walls and glasses being thrown about when someone new joined their team. Apparently the original owner of Steeton Hall vowed never to allow alcohol on the premises. A member of staff said, 'Whenever someone ordered a tonic the ghost used to burst the glass – this seemed to happen most Sundays.' Perhaps the ghost is religious.

Chapter 5

Ancient Customs

'In some countries the bride is crowned by the matrons with a
garland of prickles, and so delivered unto her husband, that he might
know he hath tied himself to a thorny pleasure!'
– a 16th-century insight into marriage

Old Wedding Customs

After a wedding ceremony in Stanbury it was customary for the party to indulge in a
hen-drinking session at the nearest inn. Male guests sported brightly-coloured ribbons
in their hats. Clad only in trousers, they raced each other along the highway. The first
runner to break a ribbon stretched across the road was deemed
to be the winner.

Bingley's weddings were a more sedate affair. Before
and after the tying of the knot the wedding party, with a fid-
dler at the head, walked arm in arm
through the town. When a couple married in Wilsden the
custom was for the village
women to tie up the lych gate
with their apron strings.
The newly wedded cou-
ple were refused leave
to untie the knots until a
toll of half-a-crown
(12½p) was surrendered.
Upon their release they
jumped into a waiting
carriage. Carters in
the know would
draw their wag-
ons across the path
to block the car-
riage's progress.
On payment of a further
half-a-crown the couple were allowed to pass unhin-

Victorian wedding parties on their way to the church
(The Yorkshireman)

dered. Often rope was used to the same effect – several ropes being placed at various intervals. The custom ended when a certain reverend person threatened to engage a policeman.

Other local customs included throwing stockings, rice and slippers as the bride and groom left the church and, in the 1600s, thrashing the bride with old shoes for luck. This took place as the couple returned to their new home after their wedding. Happily, this practice has since died out!

Leeds Hen-Brass Custom
Working-class wedding parties in Leeds retired to the local tavern after a wedding. The happy couple bought the first round as a treat. After this a hat was passed around the company each time the glasses needed filling. This money was known as hen-brass.

Future Spouse
On the Eve of St Agnes an unwed maiden hoping to 'see' her future husband ate stale bread and drank parsley tea. She would then remake her bed with a pair of clean sheets while chanting, 'St Agnes, I pray thee; I, a maid, would married be! So thou my husband show to me.'

Clog and Shoe Weddings
To remove a shoe was a sign that an exchange or sale of property had taken place. The *Book of Deuteronomy* highlights the use of a shoe when a widow's brother refused to marry her. She was expected to 'loose his shoe from off his foot.'

A curious entry in Haworth marriage registers dated 1733 to 1737 chronicles, 'sixteen people were married at Bradford, and by ye Clog, and Shoe in Lancashire, but paid the Minister of Haworth his Dues.' In the forest of Skipton, north of Haworth, matrimony was subject to a singular toll during the reign of Edward II when it was ordained that every bride coming that way should either 'give her left shoe or 3s. 4d (16½p) to the forester of Cookryse, by way of custom or gayclogs.'

None-Go-By, Skipton
Close to Flasby Fell, a substantial property rejoiced in the name of None-go-by. It was used in the time of the Cliffords as a forester's lodge. In those days, as explained, the marriage ceremony drew a toll in the Forest of Skipton. This might account for the oddly named None-go-by (that is, until you've paid!). At one time this house was a beerhouse. The enterprising landlord erected a sign bearing the words,

> 'Let none go by without a call,
> To taste my beer, both strong and small.'

In Craven guests would gather in the couple's bedroom while the happy pair sat on the bed minus their shoes and stockings. The female guests turned their backs to the bed and passed the groom's sock over their right shoulder with their left hand, towards the face of the groom. The female with the straightest aim would be the next to wed.

Skipton Nominy

Tommy Thompson the sexton would recite the *Saying of the nominy* for a small 'consideration' donated by a newly married couple at the door of Skipton Parish Church.

'God prosper long, your nuptials with much peace,
And mutual love betwixt you still increase;
If happy minds and pious hearts unite,
Your present love will future times delight.
Christ pour upon you things that needful be,
And crown your nuptials with felicity!
I wish you as much health, wealth, silver, gold,
As apples in an orchard may be told.
I wish that you may never disagree,
Till wolves and lambs do join in unity!'

A Wibsey Wedding

Wibseyites carried a bundle of cloth behind a couple about to wed in church. The material was passed between the wedding party until it reached the church door. Wedding races, with a blessing and a kiss from the bride for the winner, were practised in Wibsey until the turn of the 20th century. Those who were superstitious would be sure to marry early in the week.

'Monday for wealth,
Tuesday for health,
Wednesday the best day of all;
Thursday for losses,
Friday for crosses,
And Saturday no luck at all.'

Catching a Husband, Stanbury Moor

Horsfall Turner described Ponden Kirk (Penistone Crag of Emily Brontë's *Wuthering Heights*) as 'an upright rock, which some have connected with worship of Druids'. The Kirk waterfall is about a mile distant from the ruinous Top Withins.

If an unmarried woman or man wished to find a spouse they should squeeze themselves through a gap only slighter wider than half a metre at Ponden Kirk—but only on Midsummer's Eve night. The enquirer would be sure find their new spouse before the year was over. Unfortunately, this action could not always be relied upon and a country farmer named Griffe complained that, 'Once when he was a raw lad, he came here with a lass and she had crept through the hole, yet she did not marry him.' Ponden Kirk is known to local inhabitants as 'the place where they wed odd uns'. Not far from Ponden Rock is a spring named Robin Hood's Well. A saunter to this area accompanied by her husband Arthur Bell Nicholls in spring 1855 proved to be pregnant Charlotte Brontë's last outing. Soon afterwards she developed a fatal fever and died.

New Moon, New Husband

A Yorkshire maiden in pursuit of a partner went into a field in search of a stone held fast in the earth. There, bathed in moonlight, she would kneel down upon the stone and recite the words,

'All hail, new moon, all hail to thee,
I prithee, good moon, reveal to me
This night, who shall my true love be,
Who he is, and what he wears,
And what he does all months and years.'

She then had to retrace her footsteps in a backward manner until encountering a stile and go to bed without speaking a word to anyone.

New Babe

It was customary to offer a newborn child four gifts: silver or a penny for luck, salt for life, a candle to light the infant's way and an egg to symbolise future fertility. It was also believed that fairies would steal an unbaptised child unless it was carefully watched. It was essential that a baby should cry during its baptism or it was deemed too good to live. Ann Goodgion, a Skipton midwife, died in 1632. She had delivered 920 children!

Candlemas Day

These old sayings attempt to forecast the weather on 2 February:

'If Candlemas Day be fair and bright
Winter will have another fight.
If dull and nipping,
Winter is not long for sitting.'

Or:

'If Candlemas be bright and fair
There's half the winter to come and mair.
If Candlemas Day be cloudy and black
Then away wi' owd winter astride o' its back.'

Men Knit, Women Work

Manure was hung on either side of a horse in square boxes or crates in 'hotts' and taken to the fields. Accompanied by a helper, a woman let down the underside of the hott to discharge manure on the land. Brockett's glossary declares, 'that between the confines of Yorkshire and Westmoreland, it was common for the men to employ themselves in knitting, while the women were engaged in servile employment of carrying these 'hotts' upon their backs.'

Funeral Customs

Until 1823, torchlit funerals were commonplace in Yorkshire. At one time it was quite usual for a noted Airedale dignitary to be buried in this manner, and sometimes over one hundred torches would light the way to the graveside. Likewise, the removal of corpses took place under the cover of darkness. Relatives and friends used candles and torches as they watched over the coffin at night before a body was committed to the earth. Candles were supposed to stave off spirits of darkness from the corpse's earthbound spirit. Windows were opened in the room where the dead lay to ensure their souls could fly upwards to escape the demons waiting to entrap them. Coffins in the

Middle Ages were rare. Corpses were normally wound up in a linen winding sheet or sometimes lead. Those belonging to a religious body were buried in their own garb. Parish coffins served as a benevolent gesture to the poor of the district. After the funeral cortège departed the churchyard, the body would be removed from the box and tipped unceremoniously on to the rotting corpses already contained in a pauper's graves. The parish coffin would be returned to the church and presented for re-use until its deterioration was so apparent it could not be respectfully delivered to the mourners.

Destitute persons, stillborn babies and sometimes suicides were interred free of charge on the north side of the churchyard – where 'Owd Nick' and his demon helpers lurked in dark corners. A custom derived from foreign influences was practised in West Yorkshire and continued until recent times. Not widely understood, the adopted alien custom was to place a coin in the mouth prior to interment to ensure the departed was solvent and could pay the ferryman's demands to convey their soul over the shadowy Styx.

There was a custom of handing out white gloves to unmarried maidens, which was the case at Emily Brontë's funeral. Before the days of photography it was common practice to take hair from the corpse to fashion plaited remembrance bracelets and brooches to hand out to family and friends. The children's game of hopscotch was originally a funeral ceremony. It symbolised the soul leaving the body.

Phantom Funerals

When carrying a corpse to Haworth cemetery Stanbury folk sang an old song:

'Am I doomed to die,
To lay this body down.'

Should a young maiden be doomed to die before the end of the year it was believed she would see her own funeral procession pass through the bedroom and a corpse would sit on the bed beside her. Reports of phantom funeral processions have been passed down throughout the ages.

Bury Me by Torchlight

'We attend them with lamps and torches, because being delivered from this life of Darkness, they are gone to the true light.' St Chrysostom AD400.

When James Kitchingman sold off Allerton Hall, Chapeltown, his ancestral seat, to Leeds merchant Josiah Oates in 1755 it was the oldest house in the district. For over four hundred years almost every member of the Kitchingman family who died there had been carried by torchlight, in the old Roman way, from the hall to St Peter's Church, Leeds. It was customary for the family to light a great chandelier of thirty-six branches that was kept especially for each occasions. Robert Kitchingman expired on 17 May 1716 after reaching 100 years. For nine days Robert's corpse lay in a room hung with black sheeting and a velvet pall together with escutcheons. A hundred torches lighted his last journey to the grave – one candle commemorating each year of his life. The mourners were handed a pair of gloves each, a scarf, biscuits and a sack. £50 was doled out in small amounts to the poor of the parish standing in the chapel yard at the time of his interment. A few months later Robert's wife Mary received the same honours in death as her husband.

Removal by Lamplight

The burial plot of a Wesleyan minister, Revd Matthew Lumb, was a piece of ground in front of the chapel in the centre of Otley town where he had delivered his hellfire sermons. At his burial in 1846 his corpse was assured of eternal undisturbed rest. But by the turn of the century the chapel, bereft of local support, became defunct and the churchyard was appropriated for commercial use. Lund's corpse had to be removed and to avoid sightseers the deed was executed in the early hours of 12 December 1906. Exhumed in shadowy light cast from hand-held lanterns, the coffin and its contents were carried to Otley Cemetery.

Grave Errors at Keighley

Those wishing to remove human remains must first submit an application to the Home Office. This procedure requires the applicant to present evidence that the body can be disinterred without any unusual difficulty and would not cause disturbance to any other remains. On 4 December 1917 the Home Office received such a notice to disinter the body of an unclaimed corpse committed to a pauper's grave at Utley. The woman was found drowned on the 8 October 1917. A relative claiming the body wished it to rest in the family grave.

Burials at Skipton

Until the year 1803, when a woman died giving birth to her firstborn her corpse was taken out in a coffin covered by a white sheet. Four females carried the deceased to the churchyard, where the body was interred at midnight. When an unmarried maiden died young girls walked slowly before the corpse carrying sweet garlands. The flowers were then hung in Skipton Church on the rood screen set between the choir and nave until they withered and died. These hooks remained inside the church until they were taken down in 1853. The custom was also practised in Kildwick, Carleton, and Gargrave.

Pitchfork Mourners

Funerals held in Stanbury were usually grand affairs. Before the mourners left the deceased's home for the church, a tray with a drink, a biscuit and mourning card was left out for the deceased. As soon as the hired bawler arrived the coffin was taken up and on receipt of one-shilling-per-head (5p), the procession solemnly wound its way to the church. The bawler heading the cortège would strike a solemn note with his pitchfork and, following his lead, the mourners would sing hymns. On reaching the churchyard the pallbearers would rest the coffin under the lych gate to await the minister's arrival. After the burial the mourners enjoyed a good funeral tea (included in their shilling payment) and caught up with local gossip at a nearby inn.

Funerals were lucrative affairs in Keighley, a chance for both the chief mourner and undertaker to improve their finances. On the death of a loved one those who adhered to tradition would distribute cards throughout the neighbourhood inviting all

A Victorian hearse. Notice the horses' heads adorned with black ostrich plumes *(The Keighley News)*

and sundry to attend the funeral at a shilling per head. The recipient of an invitation would feel obliged to attend the service as it was considered very bad form not to do so. On entering the parlour the mourner was invited to view the corpse, which lay on display in an open coffin. The principal mourner sat on a chair by the corpse's head, holding out a collection bowl. Those who donated were rewarded with a glass of sherry or wine and cake.

To sustain mourners after a funeral in earlier times, a dole of bread known as an arvil was handed out. In the 1850s in Market Street, Keighley, Rebecca Buckley operated a thriving business making grave clothes for corpses.

T'owd Way

One superstitious old man, when on his deathbed at Steeton in Craven, '...gave commandment concerning his bones,' according to J.H. Dixon. He wanted everything to be done 'i' t'owd way'. Everyone 'must brew plenty of drink and bake plenty of pudding cake and cut it thick, and hand it round at least three times, everyone must eat and drink their fill.' The old man, lying in his coffin, was to be 'decked in his shroud with violet, pansy, columbine and daisies with all the old rites and observances about his dust.' After observing the old man's last wishes the mourners were to carry his corpse to Bolton as they sang old funeral songs along the way. One custom that may also have been observed at the old man's funeral was wafting flames from a small fire. This was often done in Craven to purify corpses before burial.

The Bradford Horn

Huntsmen procuring a wild boar's tongue from an animal in Cliffe Wood were, on production of the trophy, granted part of an expanse of Hornblow land at Great Horton named Hunt Yard. The charter stipulated that 'the huntsman and his heirs for ever, should be presented on St Martimus Day, annually, at Bradford and by the names of Rishworth hold a day of the hunting kind; and after blowing three blasts on a horn should cry aloud, "Come, heir of Rishworth, come hold my dog whilst I blow three blasts of my horn to pay my Martinmass rent withall."' The Northrop family was supposed to have owned the Hornblow lands for centuries until the Rishworths earned it.

Mr Rhodes presented the Bradford Horn to Bradford Corporation and its image has been incorporated into Bradford's coat of arms. It was Mr Rhode's intention that the horn should be put on public display in the new town hall building, but no provision for its storage had been made. The relic was in the possession of Sir Titus Salt for a time. For many years it lay forgotten in the cellar of the old Grammar School. When it was re-discovered it was sent to Cartwright Hall but it is now in the Lord Mayor's Chamber at Bradford Town Hall. In 1812 or 1813 Richard Fawcett had the mouthpiece repaired, binding it with silver to prevent the horn from splitting.

Bingley Hunting Horn

Bingley also had an old hunting horn. It was last known to be in the possession of a Mrs Horatio Scott Wood of Woodcliffe. The horn had belonged to her late husband's ancestor – huntsman Jeremiah Scott, late of Gawthorpe Hall, Bingley. The great-grandson of old 'Jer', Mr E.K. Scott of London, described to the Bingley Rotary Club his ancestor's hunting exploits. 'A pack of hounds was kept in the town in the early part of the century. They were what are known as "trencher fed", that is each person maintained his own dog. "Jer Scott", as he was familiarly called, used to come down into the Main Street, and with several blasts of his horn gather all the hounds together for a spin over the moors.'

A poem about the Otley fox chase was composed circa 1851:

'On the following week to the former old spot,
Bold Reynard was taken by the orders of Scott;
The morning was fair, and scores on the plain
Had the pleasure of seeing bold Reynard again.
Tally Ho!
Squires Outersides, Ferrand, Cowgill and Scott,
And Knowles (the brave huntsman must not be forgot),
Each pursued the Winn fox till they could do
No good,
So they left him for pity in Squire Fox's wood.
Tally Ho!'

Market Customs

Markets held by travelling traders were usually held on a Sunday. Dancing, games and sometimes fairs took place within the confines of the churchyard. Edward I endeavoured to end the practice but the custom refused to die, carrying on until Elizabeth I caused merchants to set their wares out *after* the morning church service. Baildon was supposed to have had a market before Otley received its charter granted by King Athelstan. Its market cross (demoted to a lamp post in 1891) was but a plain stone column 14ft high standing on two squared steps next to the obligatory town stocks at Town Gate.

Sweeping Out the Old Year

This custom might have been expected to lose its charm and significance and might naturally have been forgotten. However, complaints were received in 1868 that gangs of drunken young men (hobbledehoys) in the streets of Bradford were taking advantage of the ancient custom by using brooms and other implements to terrify innocent passers-by on New Year's Eve.

Pray, Give us a Collop

Older acquaintances have told me Collop Monday was when children knocked on doors asking for rashers of bacon, supposedly to see them through the coming fast period. An entry in a Keighley Wesleyan Infant Day School Book sheds further light on the subject. 'Today is what people in the neighbourhood call Collop Monday. It is the custom for children to go about from house to house begging "collops" or pieces of bacon. In consequence there are several away from school.' Obviously the lure of a nice bit of fatty bacon was much stronger than that of schoolwork!

The boys preferred Thursday and Friday of this week for they could wink at and kiss the girl of their choice. Apparently, Saturday of this week was known as 'mucky Saturday' and children were permitted to go unwashed.

Pancake Tuesday

Every man and maide doe take their turne,
And tosse their *pancakes* up for feare they burne;
And all the kitchen doth with laughter sound,
To see the *pancakes* fall upon the ground.
Anon.

On Shrove Tuesday fathers and older brothers made whips and tops for children to play with. The origin of Shrove Tuesday harks back to 1406 when it was a day set aside for the Apprentices' Holiday. The Pancake Bell would sound at noon and apprentices could expect a half day's leave. In later times employers tried to end the tradition and of one such attempt an apprentice said, 'The bosses used to lock the doors to try to keep us in. But there were always those who would scramble through the windows.'

Catholics were absolved from all sin on Shrove Tuesday and the church bell would call them to worship in the days before Henry's Reformation. The Bingley bell sounded at precisely 11am each Pancake Day. This was one day in the year when every soul in Bingley 'claimed thirteen hours of freedom'. Would-be husbands were warned to take note of their future wives' pancake tossing, for a girl who was unable to throw a pancake failed to make a good wife.

Need-Fire

At the onset of foot and mouth disease in cattle, the farmer lit a 'need-fire' by rubbing together two small pieces of wood. The friction caused the wood to burn, igniting a prepared bonfire. The infected cattle were driven through the smoke of the fire to drive away the infection.

Feast Customs

Bramley folk who had left the village made a point of returning once a year to attend the 'The Clash', to meet up with old friends and neighbours, revelling in any new hot gossip. The feast became so popular that it rivalled the ordinary feast of Bramley. Thorpe Infants' School at Idle was forced to close when Victorian children refused to attend, preferring instead to go to the Idle Feast.

Feast of the Boar

In 1859, a sexton digging a new grave in Bingley Cemetery on the south-west side of the churchyard disturbed an arrangement of ceremonial objects. A portion of a boar's skull was found, thought to have been buried by the Vikings who held what was known as the Feast of the Boar. The skull had been covered over by a flat stone measuring 1 metre by 75cms.

Every autumn parkin pigs are made and sold at baker's shops all around the Aire Valley. The pig is a reminder of a sacred animal – the wild boar – an offering eaten at the festival of the sun god Freyr. Bingley's October fair was the time when parkin pig was eaten.

Farewell Feast

When the feast in nearby Baildon ended its days, a mock funeral was carried out. Melancholy-faced Billy Stead, dressed in mourning attire, carried a placard to the church announcing the death. He also carried with him a number of bones.

Ox Roasting

On 26 July 1862 *Keighley News*, then in its infancy, published a story entitled 'Keighley Feast: Roasting of an Ox whole'. The following is the newspaper's account of a costly mishap that occurred in the course of food preparation for the great feast day. 'It is Keighley Parish Feast on Sunday and a butcher of the name of Joseph Throupe, of Britannia Street, Halifax Road, has been catering for the John Bulls of the town; but the eye of the conservatives of public health, being directed to the carcass he had slain, it was seized and conveyed to the Town Field, and was roasted whole in the presence of a large concourse of people, last evening, between eight and nine o'clock. The cooks were all dressed in blue, and not being experienced men cooks, it was burnt to a cinder; consequently the good people of Keighley will have less supply of beef than they might have had. It is rumoured that the kind butcher will have to pay for this roast rather than be paid. It is an occurrence, the like of which has not taken place in Keighley in memory of the oldest chronicler.'

It was perhaps fortuitous for Keighley townsfolk that the carcass was burnt to a cinder as not long afterwards the paper published another report under the banner of

'Seizure of Bad Meat. Last night Mr John Sharp, inspector of nuisances for the Keighley district accompanied by Police-Supt. Gill, visited the residence of Joseph Throupe, butcher of Britannia Street, Keighley. They requested admission to inspect the premises as they had been informed that he had a carcass of bad meat in his possession. The request was refused, but he seeing that they were determined to enter opened the door. They found the carcass of a cow that had been killed at Harden, near Bingley, and which they considered was not fit food for man or beast. They at once put it into a

Annual festivities and merrymaking at Shipley Glen *(The Yorkshireman)*

cart and took it to the King's Arms Inn on Church Green. A respectable jury was at once summoned and met at a quarter to eight to view the carcass, and afterwards retired into the King's Arms Inn, where they were met by J.G. Sugden Esq., magistrate, and Mr R. Hodgson, magistrate's clerk. The jury was unanimously of the opinion that the carcass was not fit...ordered that it should be burnt forthwith, which was afterwards done in a field belonging to Mr Medcalf at the top of Lawkholme. This was the first beast known to have been seized at Keighley.'

Excited crowds gathered together to partake of the great ox roasting of 1887. Brightly patriotic coloured posters invited one and all:

QUEEN'S JUBILEE OX-ROASTING.

This is to give notice that on ye Saturday, ye 25th day of June, in the year of Our Lord one thousand eight hundred and eighty-seven, that is ye 50th year of Her Majesty's reign, We, the loyal inhabitants of ye borough of Keighley, being anxious to commemorate this memorable event, will roast an ox in honour of Her Majesty's Jubilee, and that all ye loyal inhabitants of ye said borough are hereby earnestly requested to witness the same, which will be holden in a field kindly lent by Mr William Sellers, situate on ye road leading to ye old Town of Skipton and ye road commonly called Lawkholme Lane, which leadeth to ye River and ye are hereby told that same ox-roasting will be divided amongst ye poor of ye town. Ye sum of threepence each will be charged for admission to ye ground for ye benefit of ye Cottage Hospital.

GOD SAVE THE QUEEN.

The head of the ox will be stuffed, mounted and balloted for. Tickets 6d. each.

Haworth Feast

From the manuscript pages of preacher Oliver Heywood, dated 1680. 'On the Lord's day, July 12, there was a rushbearing at Howarth and their Tyde (as they call it) on wch multitudes of people meet, feast, drink and play, and commit many outrages in revellings, in rantings, riding, without any fear of restraint...oh dreadful! The like was seen at Bramly the same day...Lord stop this outragious folly.'

Slaughter Days

Prior to 1807 Leeds butchers only killed cows on two days of the week – Sunday and Monday. Thus the flesh was freshly cut for the Tuesday market and lasted until the Saturday market. The custom was abandoned because cow meat in the summer months soon turned rancid. The meat was often sold on to the public even though much of it was unfit for human consumption.

Ancient Corn Custom

An old chronicle sets down the following corn rite, 'The origin of this custom is very remote. In ancient times each family ground its own corn in hand-mills. When water-mills were invented, their introduction was eagerly desired, and no one being found to build then in some poor districts, the King was petitioned to erect mills in various places, to which he consented, on condition that the inhabitants would bind themselves and their heirs forever, to grind at such mills, on the terms then agreed on.'

The last sheaf of corn cut, when the harvest moon was fullest, was carefully stored until the following crop gathering to ensure a good supply of corn and bring good luck throughout the coming year. On the last day of hay harvest it was customary in Craven for men to don grotesque masks and play tricks at the churn-supper.

Witches' Bird

The mischievous magpie was thought to be in league with the Devil and it was an ill omen indeed if a single bird were seen. To avoid repercussions a Cravenite would make a cross in the air or remove their hat while at the same time repeating the rhyme,

'I cross one magpie,
And one magpie cross me;
May the devil take the magpie
And God take me.'

Or

'One for sorrow, two for mirth
Three for a weddin', four for a birth,
Five for heaven, six for hell,
Seven the de'ils ain sell.'

Midsummer Party

Two centuries past this ancient midsummer custom was practised throughout the West Riding: all newcomers to the district within the preceding twelve months were expected to present cheese, bread, ale and an invitation to a midsummer party to their neighbours.

Exley Head Bullring

For over 150 years Oakworth attracted gamblers because the village boasted a bullring. Queen Elizabeth I ordered Thursdays should be apportioned to the 'growling of the dogs, the bellowing of the bulls and the roaring of the bears as they worried each other…On the opening of this sublime amusement (?), the bull is fastened to a stake by a chain which extends to about fifteen yards in length, and terminates in a very strong leather collar passing round his neck, his horns being previously muffled at the points with a composition of tow, tallow, and melted pitch. The attack then commenced with dreadful noises of different kinds – bellowings, hootings, huzzaings, and whatever can work the poor animal into a state of fury; hats, &c., are aimed at him in front, and he is punctured with sharpe stakes, and irritated with repeated twists of the tail behind. The irritation being judged sufficient, a single bull-dog is first let loose upon the prey, and if he be found incapable of pinning him by the nose to the ground, he is soon assisted by a second, and even a third; and when these are tired or gored other bull-dogs, howling and impatient of control, are let loose in their turn, till the poor exhausted captive faints beneath the protracted attack, and falls victim to a sport as barbarous as ever disgraced the race of man.'

Keighley folk would feast on the bull's flesh after the awful debacle was over. Believing the meat to be contaminated from the teeth of bulldogs, butchers kept a lighted candle over the carcass to 'cure it'. Last used in 1794, the bullring drew enlisting army officers with their animals. Their aim was to encourage young men to take the King's shilling (5p). In 1970 the stone-walled enclosure, at Dyke Top opposite Wheathead Lane, was filled in. A similar bullring was situated in the town of Bingley, opposite Gawthorp's basket shop, Main Street. An old resident, Mr Willie Hird, born in early 1800, could just remember the last bull baiting episode in the town.

Bull Baiting

Skipton's musty old constables' accounts record bull baiting customs in the town—the bullring was fixed outside the Bay Horse Inn. The town clerk received 1s. (5p) per annum for 'keeping charge of the bull rope'. Other entries included:

1680, Oct. 4. Presented this day by Robert Goodgion, one of ye jury, that John Michell, of Skipton, in sum'r last killed one bull and did not bait him, contrary to ye paine, for which wee fine him according to ye paine.

1734, Oct. 2. Paid for keeping ye bull rope 1s. 0d.

1752, May 5. We, the jurymen, do amerce Samuel Goodgion and Benjamin Shires each the sum of 3s. 4d. for exposing to sale in the market-place within the manor bull beefe not being baited.'

Outlawed

It wasn't until 1835 that the 'keeping of any house, pit or other place for baiting or fighting any bull, bear, dog or other animal' was at last banned by an Act of Parliament.

Bishop Blaize, Bradford

The patron saint of woolcombers, St Blaize, was believed to have invented the art of woolcombing. He also healed sick animals and human beings by the power of simple prayer. On the 3 February each year, certain churches invoke the spirit of Bishop Blaize to bring about miracle cures for the affliction of the throat. A priest chants Blaize's prayer as he holds two candles shaped in the sign of St Andrew's cross over the diseased throat while at the same time pronouncing the words, 'Blaize, the martyr and servant of Jesus Christ, commands thee to pass up or down.' Another prayer runs, 'May God through the intercession of St Blaize preserve you from that disease and every evil.' The Rosminian Fathers of Charity introduced the cure in 1835.

For the relief of toothache or diseased cattle, believers were urged to light a candle and repeat the following charm:

'Then followeth good Sir Blaize, who doth a waxen Candell give;
And holy water to his men, whereby they safely live,
I divers Barrels oft have seene, drawn out of water cleare,
Through one small blessed bone of this same holy Martyr heare:
And caryed thence to other townes and cities farre away.
Each superstition doth require such earnest kinde of play.'

Bishop Blaize, Patron Saint of Bradford woolcombers

Blaize was murdered in AD316. Seven holy women anointed themselves with his blood. His statue stands above the main entrance of Bradford's Wool Exchange, erected in 1867. He clutches the implement of his torture in his hand—an iron comb. It became the custom in England to light fires on prominent hilltops in honour of Blaize's memory. In Bradford it was customary to hold Bishop Blaize Festivals at septennial intervals. On Thursday, 3 February 1825 – a year before the much hated power loom was introduced, Bradford 'gave up its heart and soul' to the festivities. Seven to eight thousand people were employed in the woolcombing industry at this time. Shops and factories closed for a whole day (excepting public houses). Legions of people poured into Bradford from the outlying towns and villages to join in the fun.

The upper crust met at the Talbot while the commercial classes converged on old-world hostelries such as the Bull's Head, where the crowds were thickest waiting for the procession to begin. At 8am when 'the streets were already bursting with spectators' the festival began to the sound of 'marshalling bands of music, and the "ordering up" of the important personages who had to assume the characters of the Bishop, King, Queen, Jason, &c.' They moved on towards Kirkgate after King Richard delivered the lines:

    'Hail to the day, whose kind auspicious rays
    Deign'd first to smile on famous Bishop Blaize.'
    'To the great author of our combing trade...
    For England's commerce, and for George's sway,
    Each loyal subject gives a load "Huzzah! Huzzah!"'

At the end of the day 'Life's a Bumper' was heartily sung.

In 1833 a further Blaize festival was planned but was spoiled when Chartists posted bills around the streets of Bradford announcing:

BISHOP BLAIZE

Whereas, a number of evil-disposed persons lately assembled, and wilfully and maliciously Burked The Venerable and Reverend Father in God,

BISHOP BLAIZE.

It has been determined by a number of his Friends, out of Respect to his Memory, to give his Remains public and honourable Burial, on the Third day of February next. The Band and funeral Procession to meet at the Piece Hall Gates precisely at Ten O' clock in the Forenoon, and it is requested that as many people as possible who gain their Livelihood by the exercise of his Invention, will, out of gratitude to the Founder of the Trade of Bradford, follow his Remains to the grave. A Committee is appointed to receive contributions to defray the expenses.

The Committee Room, Talbot Inn, January 1832.

Those in the worsted trade continued to keep the Bishop's anniversary alive by dining together once a year. Bishop Blaize once again took up his position in the Bradford procession on the 9 September 1870, starting from Lister Park. 1873 was Bradford's final attempt to revive this old custom and on this occasion the Buttershaw Brass Band headed the parade. Keighley citizens celebrated the Bishop Blaize festival in 1819.

Bishop Blaize, His Ghost

'Midnight, as lying in silence alone,
Lost in deep, sleepless thought in my bed,
I heard my name called in sepulchral tone,
And a light round my chamber was shed...
"What art thou?" I sung out, not in a little dread,
"So untimely, thy business wants?"
"I am Blaize, the Lord Bishop," he solemnly said,
"The clerical, primitive scud."'

Stephen Fawcett 1868.

Chapter 6

Church and Religion

'Where e'er we tread, 'tis haunted holy ground.' *Anon*

Light

In uncertain times churches served as sanctuary from the perils of war. Their towers were used as fire beacons to warn of impending danger. Sometimes the tower was the only means by which the wayfarer in peaceful periods could pick his way through dark and lonely places to his intended destination. One such beacon tower can be seen at St Ives, Bingley.

Leeds Parish Church

When the old church at the bottom of Kirkgate was pulled apart in 1838 several interesting relics came to light. A number of broken, sculptured stone Anglo-Saxon

Effigy of a Stainton knight unearthed by workmen beneath Leeds Parish Church

crosses were found – the tallest was 4 metres high and bore a runic inscription of Cuni (King) Onlaf, dated about 950. Beneath the communion table was a brass plate inscribed with the name of Thomas Darrell, Vicar of Leeds, who knocked at the door of heaven in 1469. A mural dedicated to the Hardewycke family was uncovered behind the altarpiece. Workmen lifting the choir floor were amazed to find a wonderful limestone effigy dressed in chain mail and plated kneecaps. It was complete with a shield and a knight's sword but its legs below the knee were missing. The shield provided a clue to the knight's identity, revealing him to be one of the Stainton or Steynton family who lived around 1300.

An interesting event occurred here on 25 December 1787 when a couple arrived to be married. However, the bride came out married to a different suitor!

Papist Body Thrown Over Wall

In Leeds Parish Church's burial register of 1584, written in a quaint, faded hand, is the following curious account. 'Rychard Lumbye, of Chappilltoune, being a Papist, not comyng to the churche the space of xij years, being indyeted at the gen'all and peace sessions, vpo the statue, pscuted as the....of Papists; excommunicate, Dyed at Chappilltoune the third day of December, and was by hys kynsfolk and neighbours brought towards the churche to be buryed, but at the churche yerd gate stopped by the vicar and churchwardeners; the corps remained till the tenthe day of the same month at night, and hys friends could not gett lycens to burye hym, going to York for yt purpose, hys said corps was in the night conveyed to the south east side of the churche and thrown over the wall among the nettles, and buryed.'

Just how many bodies were interred in unconsecrated ground, their souls perhaps forever in torment, one cannot tell. In 1685 the practice still continued. The parish registers reveal, 'John Thompson, dying at Hillows Bancke, was excommunict'd and was brought into the churche yaerde, and ther left in hys wynding shete, the fift day of August, and afts. buryed by some of his friends in the nettles under the churche wall, out of the common place of buryall.'

Persecution in Craven

In the reign of Elizabeth I, Catholics were forced to surrender wealth gathered over many centuries. Priests were compelled to renounce their faith or face execution. Families refusing to attend Protestant churches were fined up to £390 per year, and a £100 fine was levied on those who failed to have their child baptised in the Protestant faith within a month of birth. Paid informers spied on Catholics at every turn. According to an account in St Andrew's church records of 1604, Nicholas Duckworth of Keighley, his wife and a female guest were reported for practising Catholicism. Hauled before the judges they were fined heavily. Harbouring a priest or attempting to convert a person to Catholicism carried the death penalty. In 1631 there were thought to be 1000 Catholic priests in hiding, falling to 800 in 1669. There was a Catholic revival in Shipley, near Bradford, in 1851 and meetings were held in a rented room at a local inn. Revd Henry Walker became the first priest in 1863. The clubroom at The Fleece, Bingley was used for Sunday Mass in 1870.

Middleton Lodge, Ilkley

Prior to 17 February 1835, Benedictine monks stored Keighley baptism records at Middleton Lodge. A figure of a ghostly, black-robed monk has been seen climbing the oak stairs and seeking sanctuary in a secret chapel nearby. The Fathers of the Passionist Order purchased the property in 1922, forbidding entry to females.

Relics of Otley Church

Patronised by the Fairfax, Fawkes, Vavasour and Palme families, the church, built from both Saxon and Norman remains, was restored in 1851 and again during 1868. Below the south doorway are two stone coffins, each is covered by a heavy slab and one has a simple carving of a Roman solider. In the churchyard a tunnel-shaped stone monument was erected in memory of thirty-odd navvies. They lost their lives when excavating the Bramhope Tunnel end of the Leeds to Thirsk railway line between 1845 and 1849. The inscription reads, 'I am a stranger and a sojourner with you, give me possession of a burying place with you, that I may bury my dead out of my sight.'

Dead Catholics Eaten

'1609, March 8 Thomas Goodgion, a recusant and excommunicate, died the viiith day. Mr Wilde refused to burie him.'

On the 8 March 1609, Thomas Goodgion died. He remained a staunch Roman Catholic to the end so Revd Wilde refused to bury him in consecrated ground. Instead, the corpse was flung into a common ditch. Pigs uprooted the body and ate it. *The Liverpool Catholic Almanac* of 1899 tells us that in, '1611 a bitter storm of persecution extended itself in these parts to the bodies of the deceased Catholics. The (now Protestant) churches in all places denied them burial. Some were laid in fields, some in gardens, and others in highways as it chanced – one of those being interred in a common land, had her corpse pulled out by the hogs and used accordingly.' Skipton's new Roman Catholic cemetery was consecrated on 4 July 1872.

Skipton Church once interred the dead within its walls but W.H. Dawson, in his *Loose Leaves of Craven* 1891, says that, 'so unhealthy did the church become owing to the presence of innumerable graves, that it was found necessary – years ago – to place a thick layer of concrete over the entire floor in order to keep down the obnoxious and fatal effluvia.'

Magic Church at Holy Croft?

Holy Croft or 'Haley Croft' near Exley Head was once the home of Catholic priests. An anonymous author, inspired perhaps by some ancient legend, composed a poem. These few lines printed at Halifax in 1817 lay in obscurity for many years.

'Their speed soon brought them to the place,
Where ancient people say,
That popish priests did once reside,
Read, meditate, and pray,
Tradition says here stood a church,
Which by some magic hands,
Was in an evening snatch'd from thence,
And placed where it now stands.'

Lane Methodist Church, Silsden Moor

Chapel Church, Silsden Moor has been deemed a property of national historical and architectural interest. The ground on which the chapel is built was long owned by the powerful Clifford family of Skipton Castle and rented out at 2s 6d. (12½p) per year before being handed over to Methodist worshippers in 1948. The building, set up high on the moors, opened as a chapel on 12 May 1887 and ceased to be used for religious worship in 1974. A time capsule was found containing memorabilia from the Victorian era.

The three-hundred-year-old building was sold off to Mr and Mrs Hoyle. Whilst scraping layers of old whitewash from the kitchen walls they found a curious hand-painted inscription dated 1689, complete with a drawing of what appears to be a mythical winged creature and three birds of the air. The ancient text between two pillars reads:

'Let all bitterness and wrath and anger and clamour and evil speaking be put away from you all malice and be ye bind one to another tender-hearted forgiving one another even as God for Christ's sake hath forgiven you.'

The initials I.W.M.W. appear at the side of painting. The new owners believed an altar existed below the text. A tiny, twisted, ecclesiastical staircase to the left of the inscription appears to confirm this idea. The Hoyles thought the first residents might have had close connections with the canons of Bolton Abbey. The old place was once used as a Chapel of Ease, where a monk would attend remote parishioners. Some childish drawings on a wall were autographed by Elizabeth and Margaret in 1704.

The Quaker Movement

During 1652 George Fox, founder of the Quaker movement, was drawn to a place of pagan worship in the heart of witch country at Pendle Hill, Lancashire. He claimed to have received a great and wondrous vision which foretold of the coming of our Lord.

James Naylor of East Ardsley was converted to the faith in 1655. Imprisoned for believing he was the Messiah and for believing he had the power to heal the sick and bring alive the dead, he was taken from Exeter prison to Bristol. His disciples followed, chanting, 'Holy, holy, holy, Lord God of Sabbath'. After a ten-day trial, Parliament ordered that Naylor was to be branded on his forehead with a large 'B' for blasphemy, that his tongue be bored, and that he be publicly whipped and then pilloried before being imprisoned.

Keighley Quakers Persecuted

'Sarah Hurd on Sunday 7 March 1674 in a very disorderly and seditious manner rom'd into the Church of Bradford in time of divine service, and did then and there by some indecent and clamorous speeches disturb the minister in his prayer and the whole congregation in their devotion. She was a Quakeress.' J. Horsfall Turner 1888

One of the very early Quaker burial places is at Horton Croft, Bradford. In Stanbury, where forty-five interments took place between 1656 and 1718, a modern cross has been incorporated into the boundary wall of this tiny green expanse (opposite the village school), informing the curious onlooker of the site usage. To the left of the burial ground is a walled-up doorway that once led into an upper room where the Friends would sometimes hold covert meetings. A stranger recently set up his tent on the green. As one villager exclaimed with a smile, 'I bet he didn't know he spent the night on a burial ground.'

The Society of Friends' activities were not accepted as part of Keighley society, and those in authority viewed the sect with grave suspicion. In 1660 the town constable, John Denbigh, sent a mob of thugs to terrorise Quakers preaching to the villagers of Laycock. They set about the Friends with clubs, bill and staves. Two Quakers, Joseph Jessop and William Clayton, and twenty more were delivered by the mob to the constable and then taken before Charles Fairfax—Justice of the Peace at Menston. On refusing to abandon their religion they were each sentenced to six weeks in prison. Denbigh profited from the arrests by 24s. (£1.20p)—his fee for conveying the prisoners to jail. The founder of Keighley Grammar School, John Drake, had a grandfather and father who were staunch Quakers and who suffered for the cause. They were incarcerated in York Prison for a time for refusing to take the oath of allegiance.

At Guisburn sessions in 1682 several Keighley Quakers were summoned to appear before the magistrates to give a bond and money for their good behaviour. The men refused and were taken to York Castle for four months until they were released at the general sessions held at Pontefract. After spending two years in York Gaol for his religious beliefs, Quaker Richard Shackleton was finally granted a licence in 1696 to open his home in Harden as a Friends' Meeting House. Shackleton married Sarah Briggs of Guard House and Calversyke Hill, Keighley. In later years their son Roger, in defence of the Quaker cause, 'prepared an address to the Secretary of State on behalf of the Quakers'. This manuscript is housed at the British Museum. The Briggs families are interred in a small Quaker cemetery off West Lane, Keighley.

David Hall, preaching in 1711, wrote, 'after some time had concern to go into the streets of Skipton and Keighley on Market-day to warn people to repentance and amendment to life.' Hall may well have appreciated William Darney's poetic verse about the town. 'In Keighley, by thy own right Hand, a church is planted there; O help them SAVIOUR all to stand, thy Goodness to declare.' Hall was excommunicated at Skipton in 1714 for 'teaching a school without license'.

The old Quaker meeting house on Mill Street, Keighley was erected in 1709 and conveyed to Thomas Blakey, Thomas Murgatroyd, Thomas Brigg and Richard Waddington for five thousand years at a 'peppercorn rent if demanded' in 1712. It was the oldest building remaining in Keighley to be used for religious activities up until the time of the Westgate Clearance programme of the 1930s. Six summers later the foundations of the new Friends' Meeting House were laid. This small building stands at the junction of North Street and Strawberry Street.

A small burial place for Bradford Quakers was located past Todwell Farm, near Quaker Lane and Southfield Lane, one of the oldest thoroughfares in Horton. The first interment was Thomas Hudson in 1656; the last John Appleyard of Bowling in 1699.

Elizabeth, daughter of the persecuted preacher John Winn, was laid to rest here among twenty-five religious companions.

Quaker Prophet

Jervas Storr, a Quaker gentleman of Leeds, died in 1805. He was a charitable fellow and gave away most of his handsome income to the poor and needy, calling personally at their hovels. Storr always wore a square habit and coarse clothing. To those in need he must have 'looked like an ancient prophet' handing them manna from heaven.

Homestead Erected on Burial Site

Matthew Wright, who suffered imprisonment for his religious convictions at Wakefield in 1653, donated a plot of land at Goodmansend to Bradford's Quakers. He was the first to be buried in it in 1672. Quarryman John Hardy bought the cemetery from the Quakers in 1830, dug up the bodies and promptly built his new home on the site! The name 'Goodmansend' originates from the time when the ancient home of holy men, which was said to be in a decayed and ruinous condition in 1695, stood on the site. Vicar Lane was the path they trod from the vicarage to the parish church.

Old Bell Chapel, Thornton

'The corpse being set into the ground while the preacher repeated a prayer for the dead man's soul. Those gathered let the corpse into the grave and desired his spirit to go in peace.'

Searching for the old Episcopal chapel of ease and its graveyard, my friend and I followed the B6145 Thornton road towards Denholme, about four miles from Bradford's busy town centre, until reaching the large edifice of St James's, Thornton (the village of thorns). On getting out of the car and peeping over a stone wall we were rewarded with the sight of the ruins. Brontë's Old Bell Chapel, dedicated to St James and situated above Pinchbeck Valley, and 17th-century Thornton Hall added a peaceful backdrop to this bramble-covered, neglected cemetery. The monuments record old-fashioned, biblical names. One story tells of an infant – a girl – who was almost christened Lucifer until the clergy intervened!

The pale winter light was just beginning to fade when we first glimpsed the poetic ruins as we walked down the straight but rugged path cut through the churchyard. The top part of the bell tower still exists though the bell has long since gone from it. Only fragmented memories remain in the guise of the fast-crumbling epitaphs of past generations once living and working at Thornton, World's End and beyond. The village of Thornton was made up of just six houses in 1711.

Thornton Characters'

The Puritan minister Revd Joseph Thwaites held the living at Thornton for forty-five years. He took a firm stand against the low morals of the villagers and the large number of excommunications and caused a resolution to be passed in 1787. The rules were that 'no publican shall sell beer, &c., after 10pm on weekdays, the feast day excepted, nor shall they sell beer before 12am on the Sunday, nor between two and four, nor after

The Old Bell Chapel, Thornton, where some of the Brontë children were baptised *(The Yorkshireman)*

eight pm except to travellers. All persons found tippling to be "presented" before the magistrates...'

In Patrick Brontë's day there were but three and twenty dwellings including several inns. One of them, T'Owd Bull's Heed, was on Kipping Lane at 't'top o' t'than' and run by William Riley. It was frequented by Kate 'Divine' and Tom 'Godly'. Patrick Brontë used a room at this inn as a substitute church while work at the Old Bell Chapel was being carried out. Another inn went by the sign of the Black Horse. Here James Pickles offered hungry devotees of the church a basin full of broth and a hearty pint of ale for three pennies each seventh day. The Bull was eventually demolished in 1929, passing into the realms of history to make way for a modern road. There was also the Sun and Star, fondly referred to as T' Coffin End. When customers of The Sky got out of hand, muffin maker Charlotte Holder – Thornton's very own strongwoman – knocked the troublemakers' heads together as hard as the village stonemason brothers, Jonathan and Daniel Ackroyd, could have done!

The Brontë family lived in Market Street. Over their front door is a stone inscribed J.A.S. with the date of 1802. They are the initials of John and Sarah Ashworth. Elsewhere, Mally Adams must have kept a tiny grocery and spice shop as her whole stock was valued at about half-a-crown (12½p) and she could only afford to display an orange and a kipper alternatively in the window! David Blunt, the 'honest' fish hawker, plied his wares in the street. He called out, 'Fresh fish!' But after clinching the sale he would mutter, 'Wor once.' The village artist was once observed carrying a cod down Kipping Lane. The artist had just sold one of his works and to celebrate he purchased the largest fish he could find. The fish was so large that its head trailed upon the roadway.

Puritan Listers

Joseph was born to Edward and Sarah Lister (née Hill) at Bradford on 17 June 1627, the fifth child in a family of six. He was the first to write of the persistent lady ghost at Bolling Hall who had begged the Earl of Newcastle to spare the lives of Bradford folk. Joseph and his crippled son Accepted Lister (known affectionately as 'Ceppy) lie buried and forgotten beneath fierce brambles in the shadow of the ruined church. Both father and son were well loved in Thornton. When 'Ceppy preached there 'scarcely ever was a dry cheek'. 'Ceppy delivered his last sermon, taken from Hebrew IV, 1, at Kipping. After suffering much pain, 'ye Lord took him home, ffeb. 24th in ye night betwixt 12 and 2 a clock.' He was interred near the south wall on 28 February 1709 and given this epitaph reads.

'HERE LYETH THE BODY OF
MR ACCEPTED LISTER,
MINISTER OF THE GOSPEL,
WHO CHANGED THIS FRAIL LIFE FOR A BETTER,
FEBRUARY THE 25TH 1708-9.
Anno aetatis 38,
AFTER HE HAD BY HIS OWN ABUNDANT LABOURS
VERIFIED HIS OWN MOTTO – 'Impendam et expendor'

Translated, his motto reads, 'I will spend my strength, and be willing to be spent (in the cause of Christ).'

Joseph Lister died on 11 March 1709 aged eighty-one years and was carried to the grave of his son three days later. Thornton villagers felt 'it was then a mournful time with the poor broken'.

The stone tablet provides a clue to the builder of Thornton's Old Bell Chapel

Brontë Connection

Five of the seven Brontë children were christened at St James's (otherwise known as the Old Bell Chapel), now in a ruinous state. At the east end of the church is a lovely, high, vaulted window. To the left-hand side of the wall are three stones informing the inquisitive onlooker that, 'This. Chappel. Was. Bvilded. by / / / e Freemason. In. the. Yeare. Of. Ovr. Lorde. 1612.' It is a mystery why the name was deliberately defaced. Perhaps the builder did something to upset the clergy who sought revenge by employing another mason to erase his name from the tablet forever. But the mason may have left a clue as to the identity of the builder's name – four upright strokes and the letter 'e'.

A second and third stone record further dates of 1587 and 1756. At the rear of the church are three plain, stone, Celtic-type heads set high into the wall – probably to dispel any malignant spirit trying to sneak its way into the back of the vestry. Incidentally, the new St James's Church, built in the Early English style, has a foundation stone which was 'laid with Masonic honours' in August 1872.

A small, low doorway below the date stones leads into a tiny room where the roof is beginning to break away as ivy twines and spreads itself over the ancient stones. This portion was the vestry where registers were signed. It was here that Patrick Brontë, his wife Maria, the Fennels and Revd Morgan stood after Emily's christening in August 1818. Remarkably, the baptism entry for Emily stands out from all other entries – written in strong ink by Morgan's firm hand. A tiny window frames the bramble-covered gravestones, transforming the sombre view into a pretty picture in summertime.

In a photograph taken of the vestry wall I fancied I could make out the features of a number of men, women and children – waiting and watching – their faces projecting through the rubble of the stone wall. This gave me quite a start when I saw it and I immediately resolved never to go there alone.

The church was, by all accounts, a plain, bleak building when in use and must be prettier now in its demise than it has ever been – for it was likened to a great barn of a place 'dark and cave-like, mouldering away'. A description of the interior of the Bell Chapel and its equally ancient inhabitants was written by Francis Leyland *after* Patrick Brontë's renovations. 'Two galleries hide the windows almost from view, and cast a gloom over the interior of the edifice. The area under the pews, and in the aisles, is paved with gravestones, and a foetid, musty smell floats through the damp and mouldering interior.'

The 1679 octagonal font was discarded for awhile, cast aside in some outdoor corner until being moved into the new St James's Church for safekeeping. One can only wonder why tourists have not yet clamoured for special Brontë baptisms. Here, too, lies the old bell, now peacefully sleeping in a corner of the church – no longer calling worshippers to Sunday prayer. When the congregation built a new chapel it abandoned this outdated religious pile to crumble away to dust.

Letter to Wordsworth

Mystery surrounds a number of verses found written on the inside leaf of the Old Bell Chapel register for 1807 to 1822. At first it was believed that Patrick Brontë had penned the poem, but on closer examination researchers thought it to be the work of Thomas Atkinson (pre-1815). Branwell Brontë laid claim to the lines when he sent the following to the poet Wordsworth on the 19 January 1837. He wrote, 'What I send to you is but the prefatory scene of a much longer subject. The fifth verse of which runs thus:

So, I can read my title clear
To mansions in the skies,
And let me bid farewell to Fear
And wipe my weeping eyes.'

Here lies the mystery. Where did Branwell find these lines? They were first set down in a spidery hand long before his birth and he was no more than a baby when his family left Thornton.

Thornton Quakers

The Quakers worshipped in secret in a barn attached to Kippax House. The penalties risked were beatings, imprisonment or worse.

Held to Ransom

In 1643 a testament *Crumbs of Comfort* and a seven-year-old boy were forcefully removed from the home of Edward Parker of Brownsholme, Lancashire and taken to a Roundhead garrison in Thornton until a ransom of £13 was paid for the boy's safe return.

A Barren Place for Religion

'We are eddicated in wer hearts, an' that's hall 'at God wants.'
– a Bradford preacher

Preacher Oliver Heywood travelled to Keighley with the purpose of calling on his friend Richard Wilkinson. Taking advantage of an opportunity to preach, he delivered an impromptu sermon on Thursday, 19 November 1672. Retiring to his lodgings he wrote, 'I preacht and tho it to be a barren place for religion yet there were a great number assembled and oh how was my heart wonderfully drawne out in prayer for the conversion of some soul! and many there were strangely affected who knows what good may be done in that ignorant profane place! when I was preaching, one that heard me, all on a sudden cryed, out "A fl_ for him, what dost thou sit preaching there!" and opened the door and run away, and we saw him not again. I inquired after who he was, they told me he was one West of Keighley who was a great professor in the Antinomian way, then a Quaker, married two wives at one time, but now fallen off into drunkenness and horrible debauchery, – two great Antinomians heard me that day.'

John Wright listened intently to the sermon and sought Heywood out. Eager to notch up a convert, Heywood counselled Wright for a gruelling five hours before withdrawing to enter in his diary, 'I perceive he (Wright) is an halfe witted man.'

Church Built from Salvage

In 1719 the Presbyterians moved to the north corner of Murgatroyd's croft on Chapel Lane, Horton. Abraham Sharp, the celebrated mathematician of Horton Hall, was one of the trustees. He described himself as a Protestant Dissenter from the Church of England. Sharp's elder brother, Thomas, had opened his home to worshippers of the faith in 1672. The initials T.S. were scratched on a pane of glass in the room allotted for worship.

The new edifice known as Toad Lane Chapelmade use of materials from Howley Hall, Batley, which was erected in 1590 by Sir John Savile (the first honorary alderman of Leeds). In 1730 it was 'at the instigation of a faithless agent, blown up with gunpowder by order of the Earl of Cardigan.' The remains, Mrs Gaskell tells us, were but a step away from the home of Charlotte Brontë's friend and companion, Miss Wooler. The pair had, no doubt, explored the arched cellars, which were still intact in 1860. The total cost of second-hand building materials brought from the hall amounted to £340.3s.5d. The gates from Howley Hall were eventually removed to the home of Arthur Briggs of Cragg Royd, Rawden.

Payments for Materials from Howley Hall

Pd. for Hooley (Howley) windows... £3. 0. 0d

Pd. for 14 loads of ye same leading to Bradford, at 5s. per load... £3. 10s. 0d

Charges at Hooley when best ceiling was taken down... £0. 0. 10d.

Paid for six pilasters at Hooley... £0. 9s. 0d.

Paid John Cocker for Hooley gates leading... £2. 5s. 0d

All-Seeing Eye

Brethren from the Leeds Provincial Grand Lodge of Freemasons gathered together at Holy Trinity Church, Boar Lane, Leeds on 14 October 1857 to inaugurate the memorial window dedicated to Charles Lee, a drysalter of the town. 'The window measures nine feet six inches in length, by four feet eight inches in width, and the head is semicircular. In the centre is a figure of Sanctus Johannes, the patron saint of the order, who holds the bible in his right hand, and the square in his left. He is entering the porch way of the temple, on each side of which are two pillars supporting the royal arch, with the monogram J.H.S. forming the keystone. Above the figure is a circular compartment with the 'All Seeing Eye,' the holy bible opened at 2 Chronicles, and the square and compasses laid thereon. Below the figure are three medallions; the centre one contains the initials of the deceased 'C.L.'; the other two are the jewels of the offices he held, viz.: Provincial superintendent of R.A. Masons, and Deputy Provincial Grand Master of West Yorkshire. The floor of the porch is laid with mosaic pavement, and the working tools are grouped thereon. The window is surrounded by a border composed of an endless chain, and radiating ribbon of blue and red, and encircling the border are the words 'Let there be light, and there was light' also 'Brotherly love, relief, and truth.' In the

Masonic All-Seeing Eye in Window of Holy Trinity Church

bottom of the window there is a handsome slab of black marble, on which is engraved in gold letters the following inscription: – 'In affectionate remembrance of personal worth and Masonic services, the brethren of the province of West Yorkshire. He departed this life on sixth of November 1856, in the 62nd year...His remains are interred in the family vault in Addel church yard.'

Holy Trinity Church was built from stone extracted from Black Moor and donated by Mr Killingbeck prior to 1722. The church lost its original spire during a tremendous hurricane in 1841.

Heretics and Wild Enthusiasts

After the Reformation, papists were rejected and cast out of the church. They were deemed false prophets and teachers, bent on seducing others away from government and church beliefs. The new authority stated those who gathered with Christ must promote the true interests of religion and the welfare of men's souls.

Dawson commented in his *Loose Leaves of Craven* 1891, 'It is worthy to note that Methodism had created a deep impression in the neighbourhood of Skipton before Wesley came to that town. Fourteen years earlier something like a religious mania appears to have occurred, and with it the name of Methodism is connected in a singular and not altogether agreeable manner. I find that among the persons "presented" for excommunication, or lighter judgement, at the Archdeacon's Court at Silsden in 1752 were three zealots who are referred to thus: -

"Ag't Judith Steel, a Heretick and wild Enthusiast, for pretending to be a prophetess inspir'd and without sin, riotously assembling numbers of weak followers in the night time, taking confessions and pretending to forgive them their sins or absolve them, giving occasion of scandal to one well-established faith, and most holy religion."- In this case "The judge admonished Steel to frequent her chapel & and to behave for the future better, & dismisst her without paying any ffees."

"Against Thomas Sawley, another Heretick and wild Enthusiast, for publickley and impiously declaring that all the clergy of the Church of England are the devil's servants, and that all that follow them are certainly damn'd, even his own mother, saying that unless she turn'd Methodist she had no more chance to be sav'd than a cat in hell." – In this case "Sawley appear'd and deny'd the charge; and (the Court) admonished him to behave better for the future & and dismissed him."

"Against John Leach another Heretick and wild Enthusiast for frequently and wickedly declaring that all the persons buried in Silsden Chapel yard are certainly gone to the devil, and that none but the Methodists can be saved, giving great offence to our whole congregation; all these seem a general spawn of Rome."'

A Methody Window Curiosity

John Whitley of Toils Farm, Eldwick, Bingley, a convert of Mr Skirrow (founder of the Bingley Baptists), welcomed John Wesley amongst other Wesleyan ministers as a guest to his farm between 1761 and 1784. (John Nicholson, the Airedale poet, once lived here.) Later owned by the two Miss Compton Stansfields of Esholt Hall, the farm was rented out to a Mr Greenwood and during his tenancy several curiously etched windowpanes were removed by order of the Compton Stansfields. In being taken from its original setting the most significant etched pane was accidentally cracked down the centre. Believed by the sisters to have been executed by the hand of John Wesley, the glass bears a portrait head of a man resembling him and is engraved with strange ciphers and the date 1675. In 1905 the pane was passed to a Wesleyan – Mr Severs. His research shows that John Wesley did not do the engraving as Wesley employed the Byrom style of shorthand. The ciphers scratched into the glass were of the Williamson's system, first adopted in 1775. The deciphered words read, 'God is love, and he that dwelleth in love dwelleth in God, and God in him.' It was signed Samuel Smith. The signature is in the same handwriting as the text but using an earlier system – that of Aulay McCanlay which dates from 1747. Smith was a circuit preacher in 1776. The transcribed verse, in direct opposition to Wesleyan teachings, advises the reader thus:

'Man, thy years are ever sliding,
Brightest hours have no abiding,
Use the golden moments well.
Life is wasting,
Death is hasting,
Death consigns to heaven or hell.'

Other shorthand warnings read, 'Octr. 1776, Prepare to meet thy god.' and 'Death, Judgement, Heaven and Hell.' 'Prepare to meet thy God.' and 'Amos', dated 9 April 1809, were written by J. Denton, circuit minister. These special etchings were finally placed in a secure glass frame and placed in the Wesleyan Chapel at Eldwick. Possibly from the same period, another etched pane can be found in an old house in the village of Brough, East Yorkshire. In one of its ground floor windows is a beautifully worked miniature portrait of a minister. It appears to have been the fashion throughout Yorkshire for religious men doing the circuit to leave their marks on glass.

Kirkstall Abbey

Henry de Lacey, believing he was dying, promised God if his life were spared he would build an abbey. His prayers were answered and Lacey, true to his word, on 8 May 1147 sent a prior and twelve white monks to Barnoldswick to build an abbey. However, the monks were unhappy there. After much ado the abbot's mind turned to the River Aire, where he knew of a band of hermits living on its riverbanks. The monks left for Kirkstall, Leeds on 20 May 1152.

The abbot persuaded the hermit's leader, Seleth, to join the Cistercian monks. Seleth believed he had been guided from his native southern England in 1100 by the voice of the Virgin Mary. She had said, 'Arise, Seleth; go into a province of York, and seek diligently, in a valley called Airedale for a certain place called Kirkstall, for there shalt provide future habit for thy brethren, wherein to serve my Son.' And so the commencement of Kirkstall Abbey (Christall Abbye) began.

Abbey Destroyed

The abbey fared well until taken by Henry VIII during the Reformation. It was not long before the holy pile fell into ruin. During 1583 gritstone was removed for re-use as building materials in Kirkstall and Leeds. Stone steps were carted from the abbey to 'Griece, on the west-syde of the bridge at Ledes'. It was rumoured that some of the abbey's stone was taken to East Riddlesden Hall at Keighley and used in the rebuilding of one of the barns during the occupation of the Rishworths or Murgatroyds. The abbey granary, which had been built from sturdy slate brought from Elland, Halifax some five hundred years before, survived intact until it was pulled down in 1741. Five years later the monks' abandoned dormitory gave way and tumbled to the ground.

Pipe Mystery

In 1779, two sides of the tower and a section of a third fell down. A few pipes were found in the plasterwork. Dr Whitaker points out that the tower was built before tobacco had arrived in England, 'from which we have to infer that some substitute for tobacco was then in use.'

A scientist named Balabanova believes that a vanished species of tobacco plant grew in European countries and Africa long before Columbus made his South American discovery.

Lonely Vigil

'It is said the evil that men do lives after them, the good is oft interred with their bones; yet not of these of monks can it be said that the good bequeathed is held in no defence, and their services remain unrequited by Time.' Jonnie Grey 1891'

A lone monk is said to walk within the walls of the dilapidated cloister, keeping his silent vigil even on the wildest and darkest of nights. He is doomed to visit his own grave and those of his fellow monks in the Chapter House – a small burial ground to the east of the church accessed from the cloister by a vaulted passage on the south side.

Abbey House is still home to an elderly abbot whose unquiet spirit has been seen wandering the rooms from time to time after the midnight hour.

Ghostly Guardians

The abbot's treasure is supposed to be hidden somewhere amongst the abbey ruins and guarded by two animal ghosts – that of a black cock and a black horse. Many moons ago a tired old workman labouring in the fields at harvest time wandered into the abbey grounds at noon to escape the heat of the day. Creeping into the stables he was surprised to see a large hole in the floor. Looking down he saw what he described as a 'great houseplace', a room lit by a roaring fire. Letting himself down, he soon realised he was not alone. As he turned a spectral horse raced towards him. At that exact moment a fearsome, shiny black cock beat its wings and 'catched him fair clip ower t'head' before alighting on top of a chest.

Undeterred, the old man felt easy riches were within his grasp. He called out the words, 'Brass in t'kist, I'll open and find.' However, the guardians of the treasure forced the old codger to retreat. Throwing his body to the ground, the last thing he heard was the cock crow. He awoke to find himself stretched out on the floor of the barn. The hole had vanished forever and no matter how hard he tried he 'nivver fun yon hoile ageean.' The gold is still waiting to be claimed.

Beneath Newlaithes Hall at Newlay, demolished in 1964, were cellars boasting

Empty Medieval stone coffins in the Chapter House at haunted Kirkstall Abbey, Leeds

Norman arches dating from the 12th century and a subterranean tunnel dug by the monks. This underground passage was said to lead directly to Kirkstall Abbey. Could this have been the tunnel found by the old man?

Accidental Deaths?

The following was written by Thomas Gent in 1733. 'Three men, two of them Brethren, Wrights or Carpenters by their Profession, coming through the Abbey, seem'd to be offended, that the Stone of the Altar lay in their Way. Whether they were in liquor, and strove vainly to remove it, I cannot say; but some of the Inhabitants of *Bramley* (for I Ask'd more than one) afforded me, that they were the rash inconsiderate Persons, who broke the said Stone, as indeed now it appears. Not long after, these two Brethren, crossing the River, were both drowned. An old Man, living at *Bramley*, named *Richard Bullmer*, much given to fishing, told me positively, That he had sought for 'em about three Weeks in *Are*, almost as far as *Leeds*, and at last they were found in the Water, near one another, over-against that Part of the Church, where the Altar-Stone was laid. The other person, as I have been inform'd since, came to a very untimely End...Vengeance will pursue those who...defile the Place where God has been worshipp'd.'

Wives

'The monk waxed fat, And issuing shorn and sleek, Would twist his girdle tight and pat the girls upon the cheek.'

Henry VIII discovered that some of the Kirkstall monks had taken wives, some more than one. These monks were hanged.

Mary Maid of the Inn

John Booth of Shipley relates the story of Mary who worked in a pot or beerhouse named Hark to Rover on the old road near Vesper Lane, close by the abbey walls. This watering hole was a known resort for every kind of low life and highwaymen.

'One stormy night, as two travellers sat at the inn, each having exhausted their news, the conversation was directed to the abbey and the stormy night and Mary's heroism, when a bet was made by one of them that she dare not go and bring back from the nave a slip of elder tree growing there. Mary, however, did go, but having nearly reached the tree, she heard a low indistinct dialogue; at the same time as something black fell towards her, which afterwards proved to be a hat. Going toward to the place where the conversation was proceeding, she saw from behind a pillar two men bearing a dead body. As they were passing the place where she stood the moonlight shone on the face of one of the bearers. Mary fell senseless; one of the murderers was her intended husband. When she recovered from the swoon into which she had fallen it was found that she had lost, forever, the gift of reason.'

Brontë Proposal

It is thought that Patrick Brontë proposed to Miss Maria Branwell in the romantic medieval setting of Kirkstall Abbey, a place he was fond of, and thus began the Brontë story. An oil painting of the abbey adorned the walls of the Brontë parsonage, perhaps a memento of the day Maria accepted Patrick's offer of marriage.

Grange Discovered

The monks owned land at Bramley Fell, where they built a grange at Swinnow. During the building of Pudsey railway in 1877 workers uncovered foundations of a building said to be the hitherto unknown situation of the grange. The 13th-century building's stones were $1\frac{1}{4}$ metres long and $\frac{1}{2}$ metre thick. They were cemented together so well that workmen were forced to cut through rather than try to remove the stone in one go.

An Act of God

A new church at Kirkstall, built in the 13th-century style and dedicated to St Stephen, was virtually destroyed by lightening in 1833. Large stones burst from the newly constructed walls – the steeple 'shattered to atoms'. Loud, thunderous cracks were heard in the upper part of the church roof before it was rent asunder.

Oastler Connection

On 22 August 1861 Richard Oastler, hero of the Ten Hour Act, died whilst on his way to the spa town of Harrogate. Members of the Short Time Committee carried him to his final resting place at St Stephen's graveyard, where he joined his wife and two children. His good friend Parson Bull read the burial service. On the eve of his death Oastler appeared as a ghost before the son of Mr Walker at Bolling Hall, Bradford – thereby fulfilling a promise made to the young man to prove there was life after death!

Oldest Methodist

Mary Waterhouse of Wilsden, 103 years old, was loudly bewailing the evil temptations of the Devil. A neighbour, George Varley, who happened to hear her said, 'Take no notice of the Devil cos' he's nowt more than a gurt liar, luk what he promised Christ, he promised him the kingdom of the world yet the liar didn't have a stone to call his own.'

Ancient Ivegate

Bradford's Ivegate or Avegate, a steep medieval thoroughfare, takes its name from the tiny chapel or cell dedicated to the Holy Trinity and the virgin St Sitha, the Patron Saint of laundresses, built here in the 15th century. Harry Speight thought 'there might be some connection with our medieval chapel in Ivegate (Saint Hiev) and the mysteriously named Black Abbey, (probably White Abbey) which are separated from each other by a very ancient direct thoroughfare of one mile.'

Lang Kirk

Kildwick appears to the passer-by to be locked in a time warp. But its pretty stone houses lying content at the foot of a hill belie its contact with the outside world and its attendant problems. A serious famine during 1314 caused residents to eat the flesh of dogs and rodents. Driven by acute hunger, some even consumed their own children. If not carefully watched strangers stole children away and feasted on their flesh in some dark, hidden recess of the parish.

Cravenite Martyr Priest William Spencer who returned to Craven in 1584 was executed on 24 September 1589 at York alongside his friend Father Spencer for refusing to give up his Roman Catholic ways. Government spy Titus Oates reported him to the authorities.

The old bridge was first erected by the Prior of Bolton to serve the church, but it also leads to haunted Kildwick Hall and the White Lion Inn. The Prior of Bolton Abbey owned the church until two clothiers, Thomas Drake of Halifax and Robert Wilkinson of Bradford, purchased it sometime after the Dissolution. They, in turn, sold at a profit to the Currer family who were to make Kildwick their home for almost two centuries.

The first mention of a church appears in the 1066 survey. In the 12th century a church was built in stone. Throughout the centuries changes have taken place – a door here, a wall there – until gaining the name of 'Lang Kirk' on account of the building becoming so elongated. During restoration a number of broken pre-Norman preaching or burial crosses were found.

Antiquities

Upon entering the church, ahead of you lies a 15th-century church chest made from a quarter bole of solid oak. It has three hefty locking clasps and was once used to house churchwardens' accounts and various important church documents. The chest has the appearance of a sturdy coffin. Behind the chest is the white effigy of Sir Robert de Stiverton who passed from this world in 1307. His hands are clasped in fervent prayer and his faithful dog rests at his feet. He became Lord of Steeton, knighted by Edward I for his part in the Scots invasion, and travelled twice to the Holy Lands. His dusty bones rest at Bolton Priory. Look carefully and you will see the effigy - moulded by the hands of medieval craftsmen - has not escaped the work of the graffiti artist. A window in the north aisle contains the arms of the de Stiverton family.

The octagonal font standing by the south doorway has survived since the 15th century. Unfortunately the original font cover given by the Canons of Bolton Priory in the 16th century was broken up and turned into a dozen chairs before being auctioned off to the highest bidder. The south aisle boasts a walled-up priest's door. Looking upwards there is a stone lintel bearing the carved cross of St Andrew. To each side are two Maltese Crosses linking the crusader's stone to a Knight Templar living in the 14th century. Within a recess in a wall is a basin bowl re-discovered in 1901. This was where religious vessels were cleansed after services. It is thought this spot may be an indication of a side altar chapel or the high altar of the much earlier church. A picture recognised as George and the Dragon was found hidden under plasterwork. The old weathervane seated on top of the tower was a gift from W. Curwen of Steeton in 1709. Money was raised by public subscription to renew it in 1828. The registers began in 1575 and show how this little 'paradise' compared to the outside world. There are numerous entries of death by 'peste', childbirth fatalities were commonplace and the sexton whipped dogs. An hourglass was purchased in 1673 to allow the parson to time his sermons.

Marble effigy of Sir Robert de Stiverton, who died in 1307, at Kildwick Church near Skipton.

The church was once infested with bats in the belfry and old churchwardens' accounts tell us that on 5 November 1746, 1s. 6d. (7½p) was 'Paid to the Ringers for Ringing on Oct 9th. Being the Thanksgiving Day after the Rebellion.'

Brontë Connection
The cottage nearest the inn was the home of parish clerk John Hartley Tillotson. Before moving to Kildwick he was apprenticed to a Haworth stonemason. For some reason one of his jobs was to walk to Keighley railway station to collect certain famous literary parcels from a London publisher addressed in the Brontë girls' pseudonyms.

Organ Monument
John Laycock was a handloom weaver but switched trades to become an organ maker. He often wore the leather from his shoes when walking to Leeds and back from his home at Glusburn near Skipton to hear his beloved organ music played in the parish church. When he died his passion in life became his monument in death. His gravestone in Kildwick churchyard is in the image of the first model organ he ever made.

Witchfinder Visits Craven
In 1634 quick-witted John Webster, curate of the church, denounced a boy, Edmund Robinson, brought out from the Forest of Pendle by two minders – one of whom was his father. The boy's orders were to seek out and denounce witches attending church on the Sabbath (in reality they were taking gag money from the so-called witches). Webster was not taken in by them and threw them out in disgust.

Suicide?

Two graves are situated by the chancel. One belongs to Roger Coates who, folklore insists, killed himself rather than be taken by Royalist soldiers.

'Here lieth interred the body
of Roger Coates of Kildwick Grange
who departed this life
upon the 7th day of March
in the 42 year of his Age
Anno Domini 1660.'

There is, however, no real evidence to support this story since he was buried in the chancel after being given a Christian burial service. His home, Kildwick Grange, was erected by the toil of monkish hands. One room may have been used as a private church.

Unanswered Prayers?

A churchwarden went to the parson of Kildwick Church one Saturday evening to ask if he would pray for the Lord to send rain. The good parson replied, 'To be sure I will; but it will be no use while the wind stays in this quarter.'

Punishment

More than forty people have been publicly whipped here – while naked!. The village stocks, last tenanted between 1858 and 1860, lie directly below the churchyard and above the White Lion Inn so miscreants often found themselves between the Devil's broth and Godly sobriety. A henpecked husband's last tribute to his departed wife, carved on a tombstone in the churchyard, runs,

'Here lies my wife, poor Molly, let her lie,
She finds repose at last, and so do I.'

Who Goes There?

It was the first time my companion and I had visited the church of Kildwick. Thrilled with the splendour and quietness of the place we immediately set about exploring its many nooks and crannies. Having my back to the entrance whilst employed in taking a careful pencil rubbing of graffiti on de Stiverton's effigy, I distinctly heard the church door creak open then shut with a resounding bang. Turning around I called out to my friend, thinking she had gone outside without telling me. But she called back from the opposite end of the church. Both of us (being the only ones in the building) had clearly heard the door open and close but no one had entered. My companion asked me if I had heard the organ playing a few musical chords...

Strange to say that this has happened each time we have entered a church together. Here at Kildwick, once at St Mary's, Newchurch-in-Pendle and St Stephen's, Steeton where I was sure we had been locked in for the door refused to yield in my panic!

Heaven's Doorway

The Norman entrance porch to Adel Church, where the image of Satan sits, has been compared to St John's version of the doorway to heaven in *Revelations 4.* 'After these things I saw, and behold is a door opened to heaven...and there was a rainbow round about the throne...and round about the throne, four living creatures full of eyes before and behind. And the first creature was like a lion, and the second creature like a calf, and the third creature had a face as a man, and the fourth creature was like a flying eagle.'

The octagonal-shaped font was removed from the church in 1801, rediscovered five decades later and reinstalled. The replacement font, described as 'more like a sundial', found its way to Leeds General Infirmary and was placed inside the entrance hall. The identity of the church founder is a mystery. However, it is on record that Ralph Pagenal gave the church of St John, Addle to the Priory of Holy Trinity, York in the reign of William II.

In the middle of the 1600s Adel Church was to be demolished and another built in the centre of the parish. Thankfully, the order was not carried out and the building survived. Some claimed that Adel Church once stood at Black Hill (a Roman town?) and was used as a Roman temple, thus explaining the square stone walls. A Saxon wheel cross was found amongst Roman artefacts. An outcrop of rocks at Adel inspired Henry Moore in his work. Lepers from Otley were refused entrance to the church and had, instead, to listen from the outer side of the leper or squint window situated near ground level.

Relics of Priory Church, Bolton Abbey

Richard Moone, the last Prior of this Augustinian abbey, employed a guild of masons to rebuild the central tower in 1520. The tower had collapsed in 1490. But this work was only three-quarters complete at the time of the Dissolution. Now a statue of a lonely pilgrim holding a staff in his right hand welcomes visitors. Whitaker says the nave of the church was spared after the Dissolution for the use of the Saxon Cure.

Sir G.E. Street was employed to restore the church in 1864. A rare 13th-century sealed altar stone carved with the five wounds of Christ was found in the porch, being used as part of a pavement. It has a hollow centre where some unknown sacred relic had once been preserved and sealed with a sliver of stone or brass. On entering the church, to the left is a pillar bearing the marks of three consecration crosses – this was where the Bishop tapped the walls with his staff during the consecration service. The original choir screen is now in Skipton Parish Church. There were no seats for the congregation until Street made his restorations. The parish registers date from 1603.

A selection of panel paintings by George Bottomley, a Keighley artist, on the western face of the tower wall were curtained over in 1935 on the instructions of the Duchess of Devonshire because the paintings were not to her taste. It is said that Queen Victoria commissioned the artist to supply her with a painting after hearing of his work here. An arched chamber situated beneath the organ area is stacked high with human bones from graves opened up during restoration works.

Upright Burials

A writer known only as R.W.K. tells that in 1862 there were at the east end 'seven large rough stones, about seven feet long, laid side by side, and raised originally about twenty inches above the floor; these cover the vaults of the Claphams, of Beamsley.'

Legend has it that there were nineteen upright coffins held within the Clapham's tomb. Here, by tradition, the Lords of Beamsley were buried upright.

'There face by face, and hand by hand
The Claphams and the Mauleverers stand;
And in his place amongst son and sire
Is John de Clapham, that fierce esquire;
A valiant man, and a name of dread
In ruthless wars of the White and Red;
Who dragged Earl Pembroke from Banbury Church,
And smote off his head, on the stones of the porch.'

An anonymous rhyme on the same subject advises:

'Pass, pass who will, yon chantry door,
And through the chink in the fractured floor
Look down, and see a grisly sight,
A vault where the bodies are buried upright!
There, face to face, and hand by hand,
The Claphams and Mauleverers stand.'

R.W.K also observed that, 'there remain, however, only three brass plates of the Morleys, who purchased the estate, that nearest the wall being fixed to the prostrate altar stone of the chantry.' The three brass plaques are inscribed as follows:

'*Here lies ye body*
Of Elizabeth the Only wife of Josias Morley, Gent.
Who departed this Life ye 13th day of
Mar. 1715, aged 77 years And three months.'

'*Here lieth the Body*
Of Josias Morley
Of Scale House Gent.
Who departed This life the 6th Day of October
Anno Dom. 1731.'

'*Here lyeth the Body*
Of Mrs Ann Morley
Relict of Mr Josias Morley,
late of Scale House,
Deceased, Who departed this life
the 21st day of November 1746, Aged 61.'

It appears that Dr Whitaker did not know the location of the entrance to the vault so, looking in the wrong place, found only one coffin standing upright on his visit to the priory. This coffin belonged to one of the Morley family (descendants of the Mauleverers). Whitaker wrote in his *History of Craven*, 'Perhaps this unnatural position of the bodies has caused them and their coffins to collapse, in consequence of which they may have been removed.' An old custodian of the abbey, Mr Hustwick, told the Revd Robert Collyer in 1871 that he employed workmen at a cost of £3 to dig out the Clapham vault. When the vault was opened, 'there were the coffins sure enough, standing upright, just as the old folk used to say they were.'

Skeletons and Graveyards

To the north of the high altar, a skeleton was pulled from a recess below the canopy of a tomb. A brass plaque had the Lombardic letters 'N.E.V.I.' inscribed upon it. The bones are thought to belong to Lady Margaret Nevill, who was interred here in 1318. In 1670 the eminent Dr Johnstone journeyed to the priory and claimed to have seen the 'effigy of Lady Romille beneath the canopy'. The memorial cross of Lord Frederick Cavendish, who was assassinated in Ireland, stands in the graveyard. The stone was hewn from a Bradford quarry and the design was copied by Palmer & Brindley of London from runic stones at Bingley and Ilkley in 1882. A red stone gravemarker belonging to Thomas Crake has a crudely carved angelic being, complete with wings, guarding jealously over its prostrate tenant.

River Hauntings

They say a pure white horse rides the swirls of the River Wharfe each May Day morn. Beware, though, for the horse is the harbinger of death. It was on one such May Day that three of the Mauleverers children, Jeanette, Annette and May, ventured out from their home. They were hoping to watch the coming of the White Horse and a fairy spirit at the Strid – a narrow gorge where the Boy of Egremond was supposed to have drowned, causing his mother 'endless sorrow'. All three girls were found dead in the river. A sign near the Strid warns of the danger as many bodies have been sucked down into the murky depths of the water over the years. In the summer of 1864, brave heart Christopher Bailey of Keighley used a ladder to climb down 8 metres and managed to remain submerged for almost three minutes. He noticed that although the surface flowed quick but smooth, below the waters were 'continually whirring and boiling'. Nearby is a rock bearing the initials of H. Gill, postman between Skipton and Bolton Abbey around 1860.

Abbey Hauntings

Medieval monks are said to haunt the ruins of the 12th-century priory, drawn perhaps by the atmospheric sound of monks' voices on a recording of a plain chant. A musical monk has been known on occasion to play the organ and ring bells.

Monks have been seen at the gatehouse, in the grounds of the priory, walking in the old choir and loitering in the churchyard. They have been seen disappearing into walls a metre or more thick. A coal merchant once stopped his lorry on the road nearby convinced he had run over a pedestrian. Of course, there was no body for the figure had simply vanished. A monk described as wearing a grey hood draped over his head and shoulders and a dark undergarment reaching to his ankles was seen by the Marquis of Hartington as a youngster. The boy said he had gone to bed just before midnight when he saw the figure of an aged, grey-haired monk. He ran to tell someone and fetch a lantern, but by the time he had returned the figure had vanished. Children living at Bolton Bridge knew one monkish ghost as 'Punch' because of his pointed black hat. The Black Canon's footsteps have been heard moving about the rectory floor and have often been mistaken for a real person by unwary visitors! The smell of incense and honey mead sometimes wafts around the rectory rooms. The Revd James MacNab set down a full account of his personal experiences of visitations from long-dead monks in 1911. Charles Cavendish saw a monk in the 1920s. Even King George V, when visiting the Duke of Devonshire, took a great interest in the hauntings of Bolton Priory. In 1965 a figure attired in a long black cassock, a cloak and flat hat approached a frightened man near the gatehouse. The month of July appears to be the most likely time to see a Bolton Abbey ghost.

Next Stop – Bolton Abbey
In fact, there never was an abbey. The religious foundation here is a priory. The local railway station built in the 1880s was named Bolton Abbey and the parish is now known by this name.

St Mary's Church, Carlton

There was a chapel here in AD1120, and a list of vicars exists reaching back to 1292. St Mary's was restored in 1858 and all the gravestones in the nave were covered over in the process. However, the vicar, Revd Morris, made a faithful copy of the inscriptions. The oldest gravestone in the churchyard is dated 1667.The registers of St Mary's begin in 1538 and are said to be some of the oldest surviving registers in the country. John Calvert the churchwarden sets out the process of giving out apprenticeships in the church account book.

'2 April, 1777, That Hez. Swire doth agree to take a Female apprentice as soon as one shall be found, and in the same apparel that the said apprentice shall have and wear; instead of Will Sagar his present apprentice who is afflicted with the Evil.'

Chapter 7

Epitaphs and Cemeteries

'Life's little stage is a small eminence, Inch high th grave above.'
Edward Young

Bradford Legends

'At dead of night, when lunar shone
Cold, still, and blue o'er Bradford town,
And still the lurries roar,
I lay in lone and sleepless pain,
And mused on life – so short and vain –
And friends long gone to come again,
And cheer me once more.
Then with a groan, I turn'd my head,
And saw a form beside my bed –
A putrid thing, sans life and soul,
With sightless gaze and visage foul,
Wrapped in a mouldy shroud,
Pray, what art thou, in fun'ral cowl?
I asked art thou from some graveyard stole?'

A Vision of Death, Stephen Fawcett 1872

Fawcett was born in 1806 in Burley. He mastered several foreign languages and wrote poetry. Bradford chronicler William Cudworth believed Fawcett to rank high among the best of local poets. He said Stephen Fawcett 'possessed humour, but it was of the grim kind'. His last hour on earth was spent in the company of John Laycock and friends in the White Abbey area of Bradford in the Yuletide month of 1876. Fawcett left Laycock's house about 9.30pm, promising he would return soon. An hour later his corpse was found stiff and cold, only metres away from where his 'voice was last heard', in a backyard at Rebecca Street, City Road. Stephen Fawcett's death at seventy-five was probably caused by malnutrition. The 'Bard and Philosopher's' remains were carried from Rebecca Street to the Wesleyan Chapel Cemetery Allerton on 14 December. Only part of Rebecca Street remains today.

Suicide Burials, Bradford

Suicides were not allowed a Christian burial service so a stake was pushed through the heart and they were buried quietly near Deadman's or Dead Lane (Vicar Lane) in the dead of night. The stake custom was probably performed to stop the suicide's restless spirit from wandering the earth. Thankfully, the practice was outlawed in 1823 by an Act of Parliament decreeing that all those who had taken their own lives should be buried in the churchyard between the hours of 9pm and 12 midnight *without* Christian

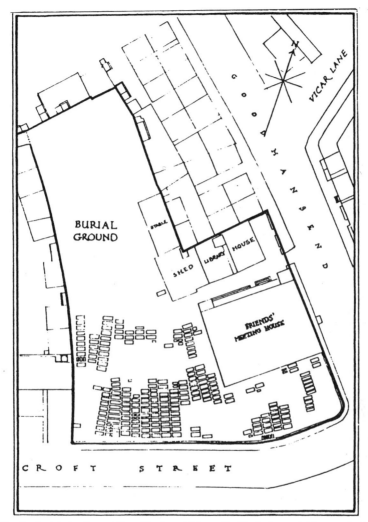

Map of Quaker burial site close to Vicar (Deadman's) Lane, Bradford where suicides were buried in the dead of night (The Religious Society of Friends, Bradford)

burial rites. The last recorded individual to be buried in the manner described was a murderer by the name of John Morland.

Dead Beat?

A curious entry in Skipton burial registers for 19 December 1618 reads, 'John Jackson, a taylor, of Leedes, was wounded at Skipton, and there dyed and was buried after the coroner had satt on him.'

'Burial' of St Lawrence

The 10 August is the anniversary of St Lawrence – the day on which the old parish feast was celebrated. This unfortunate saint was roasted alive in AD258. Three days before the saint's death he gave away all his possessions to the poor. He even sold gold and silver belonging to the church, giving the proceeds to the blind, infirm, orphans and widows. When the prefect of Rome discovered what he had done he had him girded to a metal griddle over hot coals. During the early 1830s Bingley woolcombers blamed the saint for the bad luck they were suffering and so devised a cunning plan to avenge themselves for the evil caused by the curse of St Lawrence.

The woolcombers set about constructing a rough, wooden coffin and an effigy of the offending saint was shoved unceremoniously into the box. During the hours of darkness they carried the coffin and its 'corpse' to some lonely spot on Bailey Hill. A hole was dug and amid loud oaths from the pseudo mourners the 'body' was laid to rest. One of those present was a small boy by the name of Thomas Longbottom. In Bingley anyone caught idling would be told, 'I see Leng Lawence has gotten howd on tha.'

Idle Curiosities

Graves

In the churchyard at Holy Trinity Church, Idle, leaning against a wall, is a gravestone dedicated to Jeremiah Brooke of Idle. It records his life thus:

'A Mariner, on the troubled seas of life,
Who had many tossings,
And many fierce struggles,
With its tempest billows
Until at length, he welcomed Christ,
The great Captain of his salvation
And on the 29th Day of December 1857,
He was enabled to cast anchor
In the article of Death,
And enter the haven of eternal repose
After a voyage of 57 years.'

His word of warning, and admonition to those he has left behind is, 'Welcome the same Captain, for there are storms on life's dark waters.'

Idle Saint

In Idle churchyard, a headstone bought by the sexton had its face turned against the light. The inscription read:

'In Memory of Lorenzo de Barnes, who died Dec. 20th 1842 – He was a native of the United States, an Elder in the Church of the Latter Day Saints, a member of the High Priest's Quorum in Zion's Camp in the year 1834. He was one of the first Gospel Messengers from Novou who has found a grave in foreign land. Lorenzo was just thirty years old when on a Mission to England, Fell Asleep in the Lord at Idle.

Sleep on Lorenzo erelong from this
The conquered grave shall yield its captive prey;
Then with thy Quorum shalt thou reign in bliss.
As a king and priest to an internal day.'

The Home Secretary gave approval for Lorenzo's remains to be exhumedat midnight. This was done in 1853. A Thackley man named Waterhouse was given the fright of his life when the sexton offered him a lift on the cart carrying the coffin. The poor man fled, convinced he had seen a boggard on the road.

The Mormon's bones were transported to Salt Lake City, America. The Latter Day Saints worshipped at Bradford Road, Idle. Their meeting place at Mount Zion Chapel (near Ogden's Croft, where five cottages were erected by a friendly society that met at Idle's haunted White Swan) was situated on the left of Hampton Place. It was eventually converted into four cottages. In 1840 a pamphlet appeared entitled *A Poetical Sermon, preycht to t' White Heathens o' Wibsa, ther native tongue, be a Latter Day Saint.* Pat McKay, the Catholic priest, was furious when he encountered Mormon brethren at Idle Green and shouted a few less than Godly words at them. Horsfall Turner wrote a poem about the incident.

State of Graveyard

In 1876 *The Yorkshireman* published this account of the state of the graveyard. 'There has been more idling at Idle. There is a church at Idle and there is also a churchyard, where many of the "rude forefathers of a hamlet" are supposed to sleep. Thus can be said with certainty but the church authorities have ventured much further. The other day leave was obtained to erect a tombstone over the grave of a person who had been dead several years, but, on coming to search for the grave it was not to be found. The gravediggers dug here and there, but, each time they were in the wrong place, and the right grave, we believe, has not been found. This style of numbering the dead is truly "idle" and opens up a very grave question.'

Bottoms Up!

There is an unusual beer-barrel tombstone in Kirkheaton cemetery near Huddersfield. Apparently the fellow was such a heavy drinker all his life that his widow decided the only epitaph left to raise was a beer barrel! Symbolism was heavily relied upon in the days when the most of the populace could neither read nor write. Emblems and signs such as an hourglass or sands of time, the All Seeing Eye, coiled serpents forming a circle to represent eternity, God's hand extending from a heavenly cloud and the scythe of the Grim Reaper are typical. Crossbones and skulls depicting the departed person as a skeleton were always popular motifs. 17th-century examples of these gruesome memorials with hidden meanings can be seen inside Bradford Parish Church.

A Grave Observation

Here a spokesman expresses the thoughts of Keighley Town Council on the preservation of social history through churchyard conservation, 'I don't think a wall would be much good, for them that wer' inside couldn't get aht and them that wer' ahtside didn't want a be in.'

CONVENIENT.

SCENE: *A Cemetery near Bradford.*

Talkative Gravedigger (to Casual Bystander) : **Ay, them theare graves ower yonder is sort o' public graves. Ye pay what ye can afford an' they chucks ye in 'em onnyhah like. Nah, thease here graves, heré, is private ones. Ye buy 'em, an' they're yer awn propertty, an' ye hev all ready an' nice an' handy like. I like these private graves best, mysen —** *ye can* **put** *yer missis in or owt ye've got, an' theare ye are ye knaw !*

Grave humour *(The Yorkshireman)*

Widely-travelled Corpse

In the early hours of 10 September 1868 the remains of Bradfordian Sarah Holroyd, who had emigrated to Atlanta, Georgia, arrived in Yorkshire by train. This unusual cargo was addressed to Mr C.A. Dixon, agent, Bradford. Miss Holroyd was finally laid to rest at Bierley churchyard after a journey of 4000 miles.

Forgotten Gravestones

A number of antiquated headstones came to light during excavations at St Andrew's Church, Keighley. They had been hidden under eighteen inches of sod and soil. The oldest gravestone found was dated 1690. To the east of the vestry door a stone read:

'Noe riott that brought this human's frame decay, A true consumption took this man away, Called William Denigh, in Kighley, aged Nintty three, that lived and died in peace and unity, Who departed this life June 30th 1710.'

Carved skull in Bradford Parish Church

John Driver, a sergeant for twenty-one years in the 54th Regiment of Foot, died in 1815. His epitaph reads, 'He served the King in earthly things, and now he serves the King of Kings.' Another gravestone (Calvert) proclaimed, 'Fair science smiled not on his youth yet spur'd by industry and truth too useful knowledge attained and friendship with superiors gained.' An inscription on the gravestone of Jeremiah Fowlds of Keighley, an early freemason, who expired in 1820 reads, 'Masonic secrets long to him known, a Templar's order did his merits crown.'

Mortuary Inn

This haunted old farmstead at Newlay, now known as Abbey Inn, was once used as a mortuary. Bodies in coffins waited to be collected for burial and were stored right outside the inn's toilets. Customers answering the call of nature were often forced to squeeze past them.

Waiting Patiently

The body of Betty Jowett reposes at Thornton. She was the wife of Jonathan Jowett of Foreside and departed this life September 19 1854, when she was 70.

'In the most Holie and most High
I have reposed my trust;
And now, I wait for the Trumpets
To call me from the dust.'

Pointing to Heaven

Pick your way carefully through the tangled undergrowth (a feat which must almost be impossible during summertime) to the far side of Thornton graveyard. Here a granite pole 6 metres high can be seen posed over the Shackleton family plot. A hand attached to the top has its index finger pointing heavenwards, seemingly in competition with the new church tower.

Abandoned Cemeteries

Hidden away behind Acres Mill on King Street, a tiny Swedenborgian or New Jerusalem burial ground lies overgrown and abandoned. The society was formed in Keighley in 1789. The New Jerusalem Church (now demolished) was erected in 1805. Above the doorway were the words, 'All religion hath relation to Life, and the Life of Religion is to do good.' Modern industrial units eventually swallowed up the church and its graveyard. Only two gravestones remained in the little churchyard in 1937, both belonging to the Maud family. One bore the inscription 'Abraham Maud 1810.'

The Bethel Chapel stood next to the old lodging house on Turkey Street, at the bottom end of West Lane, Keighley. A faded document once lodged at the old Bethel Chapel shows plans for the extension of the burial ground. It states that in September 1827 the congregation paid five shillings (25p) out of their own pockets for each yard of land. The principal members of the church, in consideration of the undertaking, agreed on the 30 October 1829, 'That no one shall be allowed to bury their dead in our burial ground who do not hold sittings in the chapel, or who have not subscribed towards the liquidation of the debt, unless they pay a certain sum of money for their grave or graves (which money is not yet specified) and which money shall always go towards clearing off the debt on the ground until the whole is clear, and when this shall be the case, the said money shall be added to the minister's salary. Persons are not included in the resolution who are members, or who are regular hearers who are so poor as not to be able either to subscribe or to pay any sittings.'

Mr Joseph Shaw, the first pastor of Bethel Chapel in 1813, moved to Slack Lane six years afterwards. He and his flock built the Zion Chapel or Shaw's Chapel. The pastor refused nothing but blows when he needed contributions for building works. He was once heard to remark when offered a single penny piece that 'it would buy a penn'orth o' nails'.

Upper Green Congregational Chapel, Westgate, was the oldest Nonconformist chapel building in Keighley. A deed belonging to the chapel is dated 15 April 1752 and mentions a Thomas Leach of Bridlington leasing, 'all the tenement then used as a chapel or place of religious worship for Protestant Dissenters, commonly called Presbyterians...' In 1760 the chapel was sold to John Clapham of Utley House and Thomas Brigg of Keighley for twelve guineas (£12 60p). The chapel was situated next door to the 17th-century Friends' Meeting House. Upper Green had its own little burial ground in the chapel courtyard. A memorial stone for the Revd David Dewhirst, who died September 13, 1824, in his 60th year, and was a minister at the Independent Chapel, Keighley, for more than 30 years, was kept in the ground-floor room. The graveyard was home to Grace Pickard, late of Exley Head, and Joseph Keighley of Utley. About one hundred bodies from Upper Green were removed. The following notice chiselled in stone was once displayed near to the chapel, 'The people called Quakers have a right of way through this yard.'

Those in Turkey Street burial grounds were plucked from their resting places and disturbed from their deathly slumbers to make way for road widening. They were re-interred at Utley cemetery in 1964. The burials had originally taken place between the years of 1816 and 1865. John Town, the founder of the Baptist cause in Keighley, was buried in Turkey Street around August 1824. Joseph Tuley the famous pig-breeder body also rested here.

Shunning the sacraments of the parish church, Quaker Thomas Brigg (1633 to 1707) was determined to avoid burial within its graveyard. To this end he purchased a strip of land in front of The Gables, a row of Gothic-style houses at Calversyke Hill, Keighley. In this little burial ground known as Briggs Sepulchre the bones of the wealthy Briggs family and some Quaker friends rest beneath twenty or so plain head-stones.

Not far from Mill Street there was yet another burial ground. Only dusty records hold testament to its ever having existed.

The gaiety and lights of the old Britannia Hall, Keighley, erected in 1850, once spilled out over an old, town centre graveyard tenanted by sombre headstones, grassy mounds and high railings. The defunct burial ground was purchased by the New Britannia Lodge of Oddfellows and sold at an optimum price when new building and road schemes were approved. Morrison's supermarket car park stretches over the site of old bones.

Notice of Intent

In order to alert interested parties such as relatives or friends of the deceased, the Disused Burial Ground Act 1981 and the Pastoral Measure 1983 require public notice to be given of any intent to exhume bodies from graves in consecrated ground. For example, the *Keighley News* reported that eighty-five bodies interred between the years of 1740 and 1885 were, 'Listed for removal and cremation from St Andrew's grave-yard.' A seven-day notice of intent was issued to known relatives, informing them of the proposed removal of their ancestors so that an extension could be added to the church. The funerary deposits were carefully collected and afterwards interred in a different section of the graveyard.

North Bierley Cemetery

This Bradford cemetery was consecrated 16 October 1902. A number of reverend gentlemen, watched by a large crowd of curious onlookers, slowly walked halfway around the extensive piece of allotted land chanting the 16th psalm, 'Preserve me, O God, for in thee have I put my trust'. The reading of the 'Sentence of Consecration' and prayers followed, 'O Lord God, who has made us for Thyself, and in...setting apart this portion of land as God's Acre, wherein the bodies of those whom we love may lie in peace...Amen.' The religious gathering left the cemetery singing the hymn 'Brief Life is here our Portion.'

FAST AND LOOSE.

The blushless maid, with laugh and dash,
O'er life's rude stage doth bound,
No deed too foolish or too rash,
Her haunts forbidden ground ;
But Death with horrid joy looks on,
He knows the way she goes,
That her career will soon be gone,
And he'll the curtain close.

An artistic view of death *(The Yorkshireman)*

Stone Coffin

During repairs to Leeds Parish Church in July 1809, a seven-hundred-year-old coffin was brought up out of the ground beneath the entrance to the bell chamber. It had been chiselled from a large block of solid stone and made airtight. This sort of coffin had been favoured during the 12th and 13th centuries. Within the coffin lay a full-sized skeleton, the owner of which must have been an individual of wealth and high standing during his lifetime. There were beside it 'some other bones' belonging to two other human bodies.

Haworth's Washday Blues

Until 1847 Haworth washerwomen hung out their washing in the time-honoured tradition – using Haworth's tombstone monuments as clothes dryers. Then Arthur Bell Nicholls came along and forcefully ejected them and their clothes props from the confines of the churchyard.

Saxon Coffin

In 1849 workmen at Edwin Eddison's Addle Mill Farm, Leeds hit upon a perfect Roman or Saxon stone coffin measuring more than 2 metres long. The coffin was buried 60cms beneath the surface. The contents revealed nothing but a small amount of black mould.

Glass Beads, Leeds

On 26 September 1823, workmen employed in the making of a new roadway from Hunslett to Bellisle stumbled across, 'a stone coffin containing some thigh, leg, and arm bones, under a covering of plaster, which when removed, exhibited the cast of a human body, with the impression of linen which had enveloped it. The face appeared to have been covered in semicircular glass, which was partially decomposed; the skull had perished, but the teeth remained in excellent preservation. A considerable number of glass beads were found in the coffin, of various colours and sizes; but, though the coffin and its contents were carefully washed, no coin or inscription was found to fix the date of interment. Mr Blenkinsop took charge of the coffin, which appeared to be of the Bramley Fall stone, and was covered with a lid five inches thick.'

Farewell Performance

Playing at the Theatre Royal, Bradford on Friday, 13 October 1905, the famous actor Sir Henry Irving (born in 1838, real name John Henry Brodribb) died in a chair in an ante-room at the Midland Hotel just one hour after his brilliant performance of Lord Tennyson's *Becket*. His last words to a captivated audience were, 'Into thy hands, O Lord, into thy hands.' His ghost was supposed to haunt the old theatre. The 'death' chair was carefully marked H.I. and sent to the Garrick Club, London.

CELEBRITIES UP TO DATE.—Mr. HENRY IRVING.

Our artist's idea of how, in his dressing room, the great tragedian nightly works himself into a fit state to "give up the ghost."

Henry Irving's ghost was reputed to haunt a Bradford Theatre *(The Yorkshireman)*

Body Removed

'Aw sud like to see t'man e Denum hooa didn't kno owd Mark.' Doctor Mark Illingworth, a popular village character, died in 1874 in his eighty-eighth year. It was arranged that his remains be interred at the Southgate Baptist burial ground, Denholme, Keighley. Old Mark's last request was made to his son Jonas. He asked for a stone tablet inscribed with the words of Frederick Schiller. Jonas dutifully carried out his father's last wishes. The rememberancer read,

'What went before and what will follow me I regard as two black impenetrable curtains which hang down at the two extremities of human life, and which no living man has yet drawn aside. Many hundreds of generations have already studied them with their torches, guessing anxiously what lies behind. On the curtain of futurity many see their own shadows, the forms of their own passions enlarged and put in motion; they shrink in terror at this image of themselves. Poets, philosophers and founders of States have painted this curtain with their dreams, more smiling than dark as the sky above them was cheerful or gloomy. Many jugglers too, make great profit out of this, our universal curiosity. But their strange mummeries they have set the outstretched fancy in amazement. A deep silence reigns behind this curtain; no one once within will answer those he has left without. All you can hear is the hollow echo of your question, as if you shouted in a corner.'

However, the quotation is incomplete. The last part of the passage continues, 'To the other side of this curtain we are all bound: men grasp hold of it as they pass, trembling, uncertain who may stand within it to receive them. Some unbelieving people there have been, who asserted that this curtain did but make a mockery of men, and that nothing could be seen because nothing was behind it: but to convince these people, the rest have seized them, and pushed them in.'

The headstone caused great consternation amongst the Baptist population of the village. Some of their number formed themselves into a group dubbed by local newspapers as *The Denholme Ten*. This powerful committee were firm in their resolve to have Illingworth's epitaph removed from the gaze of any who strolled through the churchyard. They ordered that the headstone was to be taken down but decided it could remain if faced downwards on the grave. Illingworth's son and his supporters published and distributed several printed pamphlets 'of a calumnious character' including *The Denholme Ten, The Late Mark Illingworth* and *The Denholme Baptists*.

Three years of constant protest fell on deaf ears and the old doctor's stone continued to remain face down upon the earth. Making no secret of their intention to disinter his fathers remains, Jonas Illingworth and his sympathisers left their homes armed with shovels and pickaxes. Meeting at the lych gate they were refused admittance by The Denholme Ten who summoned a constable. Securing a key from a silent well-wisher they gained access via the back gates. A large crowd followed, eager to watch the unusual spectacle. The remains were removed from the hostile environment of Denholme's Southgate Baptist, now dubbed 'a disgrace to the village', and conveyed to the adjoining Wesleyan Reform Chapel under the mantle of darkness. When he was safely re-interred old Mark Illingworth benefited from two more verses added to his headstone,

'Here lies Old Mark, he died in Christ,
Only lived once but was buried twice,
First time he was buried where he was not wanted,
He was re-buried here when the licence was granted.
May Old Mark rest and remain in this ground,
Until the final trumpet sound.
I hope and trust the sound will be,
Arise, Old Mark, and come with me.'

An Account of the Removal of Old Mark's Remains

'On the twentieth of October, Jonas and his men,
They went to the Baptist Chapel to see the Denholme Ten,
They went up to the front gate, but admittance could not find,
So Jonas took his men and they all went behind.
I am come to take my Father up, as you are all aware;
But the Denholme Ten they all declared, Old Mark we cannot spare,
It's not Old Mark that's troubled us, as you can plainly see,
It's the stone that's down upon its face, that don't with us agree.'

The men did, however, retrieve the body and carried it to its new destination. They had some difficulty climbing Pump Hill!

'Of course the men did do their best,
But they had to put him down to rest;
It looked rather strange for a dead man to talk,
But I understand he wanted to walk.
No, said one of the bearers, his name is Old Barb,
You must lie still, Old Doctor, till we get in the yard.'
'They buried Old Mark a second time,
He was buried first time where they did not fancy,
So we brought him here by Old Will and Nancy.
Here lies Old Mark, he died in Christ,
Only lived once, but was buried twice.'

Lost Cemetery

Workers employed in railway construction work near Queens Street, Leeds in 1848 were amazed when they unearthed bone after bone: human skulls, thighs and leg parts were extracted from the soil. It transpired the remains belonged to soldiers who lost their lives during the Civil War. Cannon balls were found lodged in ground near Spring Hill Gardens, between Wellington Street and the Suspension Bridge.

Skipton Epitaph

'Here lies Bob Saunders, who received a thump
Right on the forehead, from the village pump.
He saw bright stars until the end
And many doctors did his cause attend.'

Hanged for Sheep Stealing

In 1790 at Leeds Assizes Will Gowan received the death sentence for sheep rustling but was reprieved at the last moment. Overlooked in a quiet corner of St Michael and All Saints churchyard at Haworth is a very small, flat gravestone covered with green lichen. It is meagrely carved 'J S.1796'. Its occupant was not so lucky as Gowan and was hung on the gallows in York for sheep stealing. Relatives moved his broken body from the prison yard to Haworth by cart and laid him quietly to rest. His grave can be found close to the rear of the famous Black Bull Inn.

Revd Patrick Brontë fought against the death penalty for sheep stealing and other lesser crimes and made his views known to the public in 1830.

Epitaph of a Sheep Stealer

'Who lived by wool and died by hemp;
There nothing would suffice the glutton
But with the fleece to steal the mutton;
Had he but worked and lived uprighter,
He'd ne'er been hung for a sheep-biter.'

A starving Bradford man was transported abroad for seven years for the theft of one sheep. William Smith, a butcher from Leeds, stood trial at York Assizes for the theft of four sheep belonging to farmers Joe and Tom Smith at Rothwell. He was found guilty and went to the gallows on 12 August 1820. A verse etched on the outside wall of the Debtors' Prison by Tom Smith, a sheep stealer who was hanged in the same year as William at York Prison, has been preserved:

This Prison is a House of Care
A Grave for Man Alive
A Touch stone to try a Friend
No place for a Man to Thrive.

Branwell's Final Tribute to a Sister?

'She lay with flowers about her head -
Though formal grave-cloths hid her hair!
Still her lips the smile retain...
They came and pressed the coffin lid
Above my Caroline..
And then, I felt, for ever hid
My sister's face from mine!'

Reflections on Branwell's Death

Charlotte Brontë wrote after the death of her brother, 'Nothing remains of him but a memory of errors and sufferings.'

Grave appears overnight

Alarmed villagers noticed a mysterious wooden grave marker inscribed with the word 'Florence' had appeared in a closed cemetery at Cowling Hill in 1988. The police were alerted, but on investigation found the earth undisturbed. The local undertaker Mr David Brook was unable to find any reference to a burial in this part of the cemetery. All was revealed when Nancy Moor of Cowling solved the mystery. She told the *Keighley News*, 'It is a very old grave, and the family has refurbished it without telling anyone.' Apparently Florence was just a child when she died.

Epitaphs

A memorial, no matter how humble or grand, is a tangible reminder of those gone before us. Early English stonemasons were much taken by monkish paintings and were influenced by the workmanship of foreign carvers. The masons utilised these varied ideas of symbolism when they carved stone tablets honouring the lives of those departed. Early founders of a church were normally buried inside the church walls to the north of the chancel for this side was usually without windows or doorways.

Leeds Parish Church

'In Memory of Ellen, daughter of
George Walker, Joiner and Builder
Of Leeds, who departed this life
Jan'y 8th 1824, Aged 12 years.
Farewell the desire of our eyes,
Till thee we meet above the skies,
Short was thy stay and quick the road,
Death closed thy eyes to see thy God.'

'HERE LIETH
INTERRED THE BODY OF
WILLIAM SMITH,
WHO DIED SEPR 27TH 1784
AGED 67 YEARS
ALSO HIS THREE WIVES
AND HIS TWELVE CHILDREN'

Sunderland Family

'Tis hard to lay to dust those hearts,
That we have loved and known,
That took in all our joys and part,
And made our grief their own.
But one who loved them more than we,
Has called their souls above,
Full well he knew what best would be,
And did it all in love.
Refrain from tears, pray shed no more,
Although your children's gone before;
In love they lived in peace they died,
Their lives were asked but were denied.'

– a sad epitaph to babies Sarah, Hannah, John and Thomas Sunderland of Hermit Hole, Keighley 1832.

A Keighley Soldier's Epitaph

'Here lies a true soldier
Whom all must applaud
Much hardship he suffered
At home and abroad.

But the hardest engagement
He was ever in
Was the battle of self
In the conquest of sin.'

Tom Sutcliffe of Shaw, Haworth

'Died in 1845 aged 19 years
Young man beware as you pass by
As I am now, so you must be.
As you are now so once was I
As I am now so you must be
Therefore prepare to follow me.'

Don, the Faithful Dog

Outside what was once Fred o'Cockhills, otherwise known as the gamekeeper's cottage, a memorial stone testified:

'Here lieth a faithful old dog called Don -
A better, stone was ne'er laid upon;
He was true to his game, and true to his master:
Reader, his equal, I doubt, will not be after,
Died Cockhill, May 1845 aged 13 years.
Shot dead by James Walton, Halifax, 12 years.
Also Betty, sister to above, died Nov., 1846, aged 12 years.'

To Blacksmith Barlow

Died October 29th 1824 at Raw Nook.

'My stithy and my hammer reclined;
My bellows, too, have lost their wind;
My fire's extingu'd, and my forge decay'd,
And in silent dust my vice is laid:
My coal is spent, my stock of iron is gone,
My last nail driven, and my work is done.'

Susannah Vevers, Armley Churchyard, Leeds

'Since she is gone, why should we weep or cry?
It was God's will, give, and try.
The parent's patience, and if good he see.
He can give nine, if that his pleasure be.'

This inscription of 1694 is no longer legible.

Brass Plate Inscription, Leeds

'Here lies his father's eldest son,
Whose name was Edward Waddington;
Close by his grandfather, John Thwaites,
Both snatcht away by cruel fates;
Whom God above, (wee hope), has blest,
To live with Him in endless rest,
Buried the 2nd Janverie 1674.'

Horton Lane Cemetery, Bradford

'A blooming youth cut down by Death
Lies buried beneath these clods;
The Doctor's skill was all in vain
For the command was God's.'

Low Moor Church, Bradford

'Young females all who knew me in my bloom,
I did not think of being cut off so soon;
By Grace Hillam's lies my heart was broke
Do you not think this was a dreadful stroke?'

Dudley Hill Wesleyan Chapel, Bradford

'Hannah Haigh Died
Aged twenty-one years on 30 August 1831.
Daughter of William and Mary Haigh of Bowling, Bradford.
And you can look upon this my tomb
Without remembering all or part, of what I did
And what he's done,
Who sent me here with broken heart,
To such foul deed I'd have you look,
With perfect hatred and despise,
The man who used deceit,
And took my moral virtue as a prize.'

A Curious Epitaph found somewhere in Yorkshire 1885

'AT.HTHIS, ST, oneli Eska TH. ARINE, GR
Ay, chANg'd FRO! Mab Usy li Fe toli feess
CLAy Bye ar Than Del – Ay s Hego The rp
EL fan D Nows He's thrn'd Toea RTH h?
Ersel FyEWEE, PinGfr IE NDSLE t ME
ADVISeab A Te yo URGRIEF an DDRy y
O! UR EyeS forwhatav AI – Isaflo O
Doft Ears WHOk NoWS BUT Ina Runo F.
T Ears In So – Me t'ALL Pit – CHERoRbroa
DPA ns He INHER shopmaYBEAG a IN'

The translation reads thus:

'Beneath this stone lies Katherine Grey,
Chang'd from a busy life into clay;
By earth and clay she got her pelf,
And now she's turned to earth herself.
Ye weeping friends, let me advise,
Abate your grief; and dry your eyes,
For what awaits a flood of tears?
Who knows but in a run of years,
In some tall pitcher or broad pan,
She in her shop may be again.'

St John's Churchyard, Leeds

The tombstone of Sarah Steels who departed this life aged 60 years on August 14 1819 lies behind the old Leeds Charity School.

'Stop gentle reader shed a tear
And think on the one that lies here
While musing on the state of me
Think on the glass that runs for thee
Let not this world your soul betray
But think upon thy dying day.'

Lost Dates

Countries in Europe converted to the new calendar introduced by Pope Gregory XIII 170 years before Britain. This created problems because we were eleven days behind. England finally adopted the Gregorian system when Parliament passed the Act of 24, George II in 1751. Prior to this date the New Year began on 25 March — the first month. Which explains why September, October and November are named after the numbers seven, eight, nine and ten respectively. An example of this can be seen on a Quaker tombstone near Skipton which reads, 'Here lyeth interred the body of Edward Watkinson, of Bradley, who departed this life the sixteenth day of the eleventh month called January, anno 1684.'

The calendar as we now know it began on Thursday, 14 September 1752 — the day after Wednesday the 2 September 1752. Consequently no person was born or died between 2 and 14 of September that year. Because of the English delay in adopting the Gregorian calendar one is apt to be confused by the dating of old gravestones, documents and parish records. For example, December 1691 is followed by January 1691 because the year 1691 ran until March followed by April 1692.

Chapter 8

Tragic and Mysterious Deaths

'Death has no advantage but when it comes as a stranger' *Quarles*

The Unsolved Case of Mr Blum

On Saturday, 12 May 1866, the *Keighley News* headlined a sensational story:

Mysterious Disappearance of a Gentleman

'On Saturday the 28th April, (German born) Mr Blum, the second master at the Bradford High School, disappeared very mysteriously from his accustomed haunts; and, notwithstanding the most diligent inquiries, no trace of him could be found. Various reasons led his friends to suppose that he must have met with foul play – that he was either dead or under compulsory restraint. He was a gentleman of correct habits, regular in the discharge of his professional duties, and never absent from his lodgings at dinnertime without informing his landlady of his intention...'

No Clues

On the day of his disappearance, maths master Israel James Blum attended school as usual between the hours of nine and twelve noon. On leaving the building he met singing master John Anderson. He then called at the shop of Henry Bewzeville Byles, bookseller, 17 Kirkgate, Bradford to pick up the second volume of Charles Dickens' *David Copperfield* and place an order for Babington's *Manuel of Botany*. At 1pm a Mr Cooper spoke with him in Market Street and the two arranged to meet at 7pm that evening outside the Theatre Royal. Blum informed Cooper that he intended to look at *The Times* at the station, then go home for dinner and afterwards do some laboratory experiments back at school. Two minutes after leaving Cooper's company, Blum met Charles Behrens but told him he couldn't stop as he was in a hurry. He headed off down Bridge Street in the direction of the train station where, incidentally, a train left for Liverpool at 1.30pm.

This was the last known sighting of Blum in Bradford. 'He did not take a single article from his lodgings in the morning except the clothes he wore, and he left his things as a man would do who was going to return to them in an hour or two. Inquires were instituted in Leeds, Hull, Manchester, and Liverpool, and the police were stimulated to exert themselves to find him. But no trace was found of the missing gentleman till Monday of last week, when the body (of a man) was discovered by two young girls, Miss Fulton and Esther Davis, at 3.30pm at Hoylake, a village near the mouth of the Mersey...'

Unknown Body Identified

Fisherman Tom Hughes was out shrimping but when the body was discovered he immediately ran to fetch the doctor and PC Garside. The *Chester Chronicle* reported that the body 'was lying in the hollow of a rock, with the back to the wind, the head resting on a ledge, the knees up, the feet crossed, one hand bent near the body, the other at the right side. The face was calm, as if in sleep.' The victim's throat had been sliced twice and there were no hesitation marks present. His great coat was carefully laid out beneath him. The book *David Copperfield* was found at 7pm on Monday by a man named Parr at a place overlooking Redstones. Page 101 was folded.

'An inquest was held on…(2 May at the Royal Hotel, Hoylake), but as the deceased was unknown, and there were no circumstances in connection with the death in possession of the jury, a verdict was returned that he had died by his own hand. The doctor (Dr George Dodd of Upton near Hoylake), who had examined the body, however, said his physiological development would lead to a quite a different conclusion.'

Friends Despair

On Monday worried friends of the deceased placed an advert in the Public Notices column of *The Times* (popularly known as The Thunderer*)* and other newspapers. The date was 7 May, and it was now over a week since the disappearance.

'GENTLEMAN LOST – Mysteriously DISAPPEARED. A GENTLEMAN, living in Bradford, Yorkshire. His friends feel convinced that he has lost his life by accident, or met with foul play. He was last seen on Saturday, 28th April, about 1pm in the afternoon, in Market Street, Bradford. Any INFORMATION will be thankfully received and REWARDED. Address Chief Constable, at Bradford, Yorkshire, or at Leeds, Yorkshire. Description: – Very short (about 5 feet or a little more), slight, fair complexion, dark hair, thin beard, large forehead, dark eyes, near sighted, wore steel spectacles. Had on light overcoat of a reddish brown, dark morning coat and waistcoat, light trousers, ordinary black silk hat (maker Alfred Lee, Bradford), small gold watch (serial no. 7.213), with gold Albert chain, having a key or pendant attached by a steel ring. Quick, active manners and intelligent expression.'

A breakthrough came on 8 May when a telegram was despatched by Leeds policeman Superintendent Mr Hunt to Bradford High School's headmaster Algeanon Foggo. It read, 'Come over immediately. I have received news by post, and have very little doubt as to the identity of the missing gentleman.'

Thanks to the advert in *The Times*, police at Birkenhead contacted West Yorkshire police and delayed burying the unknown corpse. Mr J. Sutcliffe and Monsieur

HATS! HATS!!

ALFRED LEE'S

CELEBRATED HATS

CAN ONLY BE OBTAINED AT HIS ESTABLISHMENT,

52, KIRKGATE, BRADFORD.

These Hats, for Elegance, Durability and Price, cannot be surpassed by any other House in the Trade.

Alfred Lee was the maker of Israel Blum's missing hat (Jones Mercatile Directory, 1865)

Landolphe travelled to Birkenhead and on Tuesday formally identified the body as that of their deceased friend, Mr Blum. 'From the investigations these gentlemen made (having also noticed that the right hand had several abrasions to it), and from circumstances which are known in Bradford, there is grave reason to believe that the verdict of the jury would have been very different could they have had before them all the facts which are now known, for there is no conceivable reason to have led to suicide, while all the circumstances point to the theory of murder. From the arrangements the deceased had made it is certain, in the first place, that he had hurriedly decided to go to Liverpool, and that he contemplated but a short visit. The circumstances, too, of finding the body point too plainly to the suspicion that he met with foul play. It is known that he must have had at least several pounds (£16) on him when he left Bradford, but only 8s. (40p) was found in his pocket, and no purse. His gold watch and chain, also, were missing – all his letters (which he invariably carried with him) and even his spectacles. Again, though a lengthy and careful search was made, no instrument, which could have inflicted the wounds (a small penknife), could be discovered, while he could not possibly, on the supposition of suicide, have thrown it into the deep water. However, the police are now on the alert to search the affair to the bottom. A reward will probably be offered, and it is to be hoped that the apparent murder will be brought to light. The watch is a small gold Geneva lever, with gold face, and numbered 7.213 the gold Albert chain had a seal or other pendant attached by a steel ring. The following extract from a letter, dated the 24 April 1866 addressed by the deceased to a young lady residing in London, to whom he was engaged, affords the only clue to the disappearance of Mr Blum on the day named:

"I had a strange letter from Leeds from a stranger who is staying here on business. He comes from Hamburg, and wishes to see me. As it is impossible for me to go to Leeds until Saturday I must consider meanwhile what to do. A strange thing is it not?"'

The Mystery Deepens

'No trace of the letter here referred to had hitherto been discovered and more than likely *was* in Mr Blum's possession when he left Bradford. It is surmised that the appointment mentioned in the letter may have been altered from Leeds to Liverpool.' During police investigations it transpired that Blum had a brother, a North American soldier and sailor and war veteran Paul Bloomfield, Blomfield or Blumfield. He, like his brother's fiancée, lived in London. Blum had told friends he had met his brother in a Bradford street in 1865 and had walked with him to the train station. Bloomfield, who had returned from Hamburg, was desperate for cash and had been given money by Israel so that he could sail to Australia.

At Hoylake Mr Blum had been seen alive at 2.30pm on Sunday 29 April, apparently sunbathing on the Redstones. At 6pm the same day two sisters on their way to Hoylake Church noted his handsome appearance. William Banks and Elizabeth Parr saw him 15 minutes later close by the church and confirmed that he was wearing both hat and spectacles. The last sighting of him alive was about two hours later, at 8pm, when a woman watched him as he stood on the sand at the back of the now demolished

Royal Hotel. He appeared to be waiting for someone who was late as he repeatedly looked at his pocket watch. If he *had* planned to meet the stranger from Hamburg, had he had received a *second* letter on the day of his disappearance which asked him to carry some identifying feature? Perhaps a volume of *David Copperfield* – the only item he specifically choose to carry with him to Hoylake.

Cover Up?

What exactly did happen to our man Blum? The reward offered was never claimed. The pocket watch and chain were never discovered, nor indeed was the 'murder' weapon. Blum's old school friend Mr J.C.B. Jones of Everton, master of Liverpool College, sent a letter requesting a second inquest to Sir George Grey on 24 May. After receiving the correspondence Sir George directed a Mr Waddington at the Home Office to contact the Chester coroner Henry Churton to ask if he thought the case was that of murder? Sir George personally discussed the case with Bradford headmaster Mr Foggo and Joseph M. Barrett of Leeds on 31 May. Churton, though, stuck to his original opinion that Blum had taken his own life, even though the 'rocks were far too distant from the sands and the water for him to have thrown anything where it could not have been discovered'. He added for good measure that Mr Blum's own father had committed suicide at St Luke's Hospital, London – which he had not. Churton indicated that the person who first found the body might have stolen the gold watch and purse. It seems unlikely that any thief would leave behind a handsome gold and onyx signet ring and gold breast pin. Indeed, the only items taken were those which could identify the body. Since it was almost certain the fisherman who found him couldn't read, why steal paper when he could have gold?

Dr Dodd found Blum's body almost drained of blood, which led him to believe the victim, had been murdered elsewhere before being washed clean. There was no blood to speak of on the rocks and two pairs of bloody gloves were found – three near the body and one on the shoreline at low tide. The victim's clothes were saturated with water yet there had been no high tide. Neither Bradford nor Liverpool police forces were able to locate where Mr Blum had lodged while in the Liverpool area. Bradford's Superintendent Shuttleworth returned from Hoylake without obtaining any new information about the mysterious disappearance of the Bradford schoolmaster.

It later transpired that his brother Paul had stayed at the Brunswick Hotel, Liverpool the previous November but had not been seen since. It was thought he had set sail from Plymouth as an emigrant's steward on the *Charlie Palmer* on the 2 December 1865. A London acquaintance of Paul Bloomfield said that he too was dead but his story lacked credibility – unfortunately we are not told why. The author of the mysterious letter to Blum never came forward.

Was it Murder?

After further investigation the *Chester Chronicle* reported, 'It is a matter of great controversy whether he committed suicide or was murdered. A strong feeling exists in Bradford that he met his death by another's hand.' Artist Mr Lancaster took a photograph of the deceased (a copy of which was sent to the Home Office) before Israel's body was committed to the grave at Hoylake Church.

A Clue in *David Copperfield*?

David Copperfield, which Mr Blum carefully selected to accompany him on his last journey, was first published in several parts from 1849 to 1850. Remarkably, the text contains several parallels with Mr Blum's own circumstances: a new *schoolmaster* arrives at Copperfield's school; *James* Steerforth, Copperfield's *old school chum, dies* in a storm and his body is washed up on the *shoreline;* Steerforth's mother is a rich *widow* living in *London* and Copperfield's closest friends board an *emigrant ship* bound for *Australia.*

THE END OF STEERFORTH

On that part of the shore where Em'ly and I had looked for shells, two children,
I saw Steerforth lying with his head upon his arm.--*Copperfield, p 799*

Harry Furniss's drawing of James Steerforth's body being found on the beach (*David Copperfield*, by Charles Dickens, 1909 American edition)

Subsequent Investigations

Recent investigations into this intriguing unsolved case have revealed nothing. I am informed that no trace of any communication with Sir George appears in the Home Office Daily Registers of Correspondence and no photograph of the victim is registered at the Public Record Office, where the records are stored. Similarly, the Registrar Office at Birkenhead, Merseyside holds no trace of his untimely demise within their death indexes. A professional researcher has also been unsuccessful in locating information about Mr Israel James Blum in national repositories. And so the mystery of why and where Mr Blum met his death deepens, raising more questions than answers. Blum's small, gold-faced Geneva lever pocket watch with its serial number 7.213 may be the last remaining clue to what really happened in 1866.

Servant Girl Beheaded

Leonard Scurr was not only a Minister of Beeston Chapel in the time of Oliver Cromwell, but also an industrious pit owner. He gathered together a good deal of his wealth as he planned to set forth to London to do 'a bit o' business'. He kept his plans a secret, telling only those who needed to know. But the evening before his intended journey, on the 19 January 1678, two thieves crept into his home and murdered every soul within including Mr Scurr's infirm mother. The thieves took delight in beheading an innocent servant girl. The robbers, Holroyd, Littlewood and a woman accomplice, ransacked the house before setting fire to it. Holroyd and the woman immediately escaped to Ireland whilst Littlewood went to ground in the country.

In Ireland the woman flaunted her new attire—a gown and a bright red petticoat belonging to Mrs Scurr. Fate stepped in when a previous servant of the Scurrs recognised the garment and reported them to the law. The couple were arrested and transported to York Castle. It wasn't long before Littlewood too was taken prisoner. The men were convicted at the Lammas Assizes in 1682. Holroyd never repented and was executed on Holbeck Moor, Leeds amid a crowd of thirty thousand. His body was afterwards hung in chains and left to rot. Littlewood somehow gained a reprieve and was never seen or heard of again. The woman, Holroyd's mistress, was never tried for her part in the murders.

Identical Death

Dense fog in Shipley on 4 March 1891 caused Frank Seed to lose his life when he accidentally fell into the Leeds and Liverpool Canal just 30 metres from his lodgings. Two men and a woman tried to save him but couldn't see properly because of the dense fog. The woman, Ellen Hoyle, gave evidence at the inquest that she could just about describe the victim. Later that day she lost her life in the *same* place and in exactly the *same* manner!

Stolen Child

In the summer of 1824 a four-year-old child belonging to William Rodgers of Hunslett near Leeds was stolen away by Charlotte Peck, a vagrant woman who had recently taken up lodgings close to the family. Three long months passed before news of the little boy came. During this time the grief-stricken parents roamed the country in search of him. Newspapers across England carried the tragic story in great detail. Reports of a sighting came from Dover and indicated that the kidnapper was making for France. Peck was finally caught at Swansea in Wales and revealed she had travelled fifteen hundred miles to evade capture. The justice sentenced her to seven years' hard labour at York but she died of grief soon after. The child was restored to his parents but he, too, died soon after his return.

Human Fireball

In 1826 Mrs Hannah Jowett, a ninety–three-year-old who had taught generations of children about Jesus, accidentally burnt herself to death. She was the oldest occupant of the oldest cottage in Wilsden. Her family was out at Sunday service and had last seen the old lady preparing her own devotions to the Lord. As she knelt in prayer Hannah went a little too close to the open fire and her clothes caught alight, turning her into a human fireball.

Heroic Death

Pinhaw Hill was used as a lookout post during the Spanish and Napoleonic wars. It was a link in the chain of warning beacons and guards would take up their posts on Elslack Moor, ready to warn those below should the enemy advance. The start of 1805 was wild and stormy. Cutting winds drove down icy snow. In these Arctic conditions the guards at Pinhaw found their descent blocked. Several days into the blizzard the food supply was exhausted and morale low. Robert Wilson, an honest woolcomber from Sutton, set out alone to collect fresh food supplies. He struggled through snow-drifts to reach Elsack. On his way back to camp with provisions he became disorientated and was lost in the blinding blizzard. He was found frozen to death, the supplies scattered around him, just two hundred metres from his comrades. An entry in the local parish register reads, 'Robert Wilson, woolcomber found dead in the snow at Pinah.' A memorial stone commemorates the place where he fell and is inscribed with the words, 'Here was found dead the body of Robert Wilson, one of the beacon guards, who died 29th January, 1805, aged 59 years.' During the Second World War, on the 16 September 1940, a German plane dropped half-a-dozen incendiary bombs on Pinhaw Moor and only narrowly missed Wilson's memorial stone.

Death in Snow Storm

James Whalley based the following account on an old tale. 'In those days the ancient inhabitants of the moorland district heaped on their large fire-places (large enough to roast ox) heavy logs of wood, with big cakes of turf cut off "the wild moor"...As the flakes of snow were gathering on the narrow, antiquated windows, and the winds were shaking the grey old trees, and whistling through the large key-hole of the ancient British oak door, the patriarch of the family, drawing his great grandfather's chair nearer to the roaring fire, began his evening story...

"It was a severe rigorous and angry winter's night, like that described when a brave-hearted young man was lost on "the wild moor." No whitewashed stones were there that day, to indicate to the adventurous pedestrian the beaten path. The dark curtain of night fell before the young man's eyes, and neither moon nor stars appeared. It was the darkest and blackest of nights. He wandered up and down to find his missed way and lost track, but all in vain. Eventually, he sank so far into one of the morasses, that he could not extricate himself. On the following day, one of the inhabitants of the moorland district crossing "the wild moor" beheld, at a considerable distance, in one of the marshes, an unaccountable object, resembling a human being. He approached nearer and nearer to the unknown creature, and well-nigh fainted when he descried a human being, stiff, cold, and lifeless, standing in a ghastly and upright position!"'

Frozen to Death

An ancient road known as 't'stairs' meanders over the moors past Marsh, through Old

Oxenhope and Leeshaw then on to Crimsworth Dene, eventually joining the road at the quaint village of Peckett Well. High up and exposed, the old road was often impossible to pass in inclement weather.

Ben Foster's Untimely End

Between 1813 and 1814 a new road was cut by local contractor Hiram Craven (he constructed the Ouse Bridge at York). It was a more direct and broad route so 't'stairs' was abandoned in favour of the new Cockhill route. Emily Brontë describes this very road in the third chapter of *Wuthering Heights*.

On 4 February 1831, yarn manufacturer Ben Foster set out from Denholme to Crimsworth Dene to deliver yarn and warp 'lasting' pieces to handloom weavers. With his horse Jumper harnessed to the cart and his faithful dog Shep following behind, he took leave of his business partner and brother, Henry. As he used the Craven road up to three times a week Foster felt confident that he would return home by nightfall if he concluded his business just before twilight. But by then the weather had turned wild and dangerous. A deep blanket of snow had already covered the moors; its surface whipped up into drifts by an unrelenting wind under a heavy, snow-laden sky. Foster began his return journey against his friends' advice. He missed his right turn on Cockhill Summit, an eerie road to travel alone at the best of times. Slicing through fresh snow, the wheels of the cart sunk deep into a deep morass. Forced to struggle on by foot, he walked for a mile in the direction of Fly Flat then fell badly, fracturing his knee. A search party battling against the elements found his frozen body. Shep was weak but still vigilant by his master's side.

Ben's body was carried through a blizzard to a private house newly erected by George Whitaker. It is known today as the Wagon and Horses Inn, Dyke Nook, Oxenhope. Jumper and Shep silently followed their master's body. The corpse had to remain here for three days until the fierce winter storm subsided. Jumper lived for many years afterwards. Shep outlived his master by fourteen years and went blind towards the end. Ben Foster's headstone, which stood at Denholme Wesleyan Chapel grounds, read,

> To the memory of Benjamin, son of Matthew and Hannah Foster, of Denholme, who lost his life on Cockhill, through the inclemency of the weather, February 4th 1831, aged 22 years.

> Say, sprightly youth, dost thou on life presume,
> Observe the date, and tremble at this tomb,
> To health, nor strength, nor youthful vigour trust,
> Behold! here, death hath laid them in the dust.

Following the tragedy 185 lime-painted stone stoops were driven into the roadside in the hope of thwarting the claims of the weather upon ill-prepared travellers. Today the original stoops have been replaced in part by reflector posts.

In 1869, there were two very good pictures of Shep at Denholme. They were painted in oils shortly after Ben Foster's death. Where are these paintings today?

Ben Foster's corpse lay here for three days until the winter storms subsided
(picture: Mrs Betty Humphries)

Skull Burnt to a Cinder

One Sunday morning in the winter of 1849, a watchman found the gruesome remains of James Dufton's body inside a burning flint kiln at Leeds Pottery (owned by Messrs. Warburton & Co). Dufton's head had completely burnt away. His skull was reduced to cinder ash. The right side of his body was badly burned up to the arm socket. Only his legs remained intact. It was supposed the tramp had crept into the kiln for warmth and had suffocated. He had been a regular inmate of Hunslet Workhouse, Leeds.

Lad o' Crow Hill

Further on over Stanbury Moor from Top Withins lies a solitary pointed rock resembling a small haystack 1½ metres high. In the past a stonemason has carved into it, 'LAD ORSCARR ON CROW HILL.' According to local lore the inscription commemorates the place where a young orphan boy perished after losing his way over the moors in atrocious weather.

Neither Yorkshire nor Lancashire would accept his recovered body for burial, each claiming that he had died over the other's border. Finally, Trawden buried the boy where he lay. By this act the stone became a boundary marker, pushing the borders of Lancashire further into Yorkshire. Heptonstall's parish register may hold a possible clue to the unknown wanderer for in the index page for principle items we read, 'Page 124, 20 April 1659: A man found dead in Walshaw Dean, in Wadsworth and buried there.' The actual entry on page 124 says the man's name was 'Richard Hudson, otherwise Pighills, found dead in Walshaw Dean, in Wadsworth and there

buried 20/-(£1).' Keighley-born poet Gordon Bottomley immortalised the story in
For a Grave on the Moor, near Stanbury, Yorkshire.

'Calmly I lie in the heat and the cold,
In the new year, in the old,
Ashes to ashes, dust to dust;
Here I live, I have no lust:
Body, rest in upland bleak:
Forth I go, old friends to seek.'

Less romantic locals believe the inscription to be a guide and the word Ladd an ancient
word for a boundary stone.

Children Lost on Haworth Moor

Two reports separated by almost half a century record the deaths of children bearing
the same surname in almost identical circumstances. The first report by Miss M.
Heaton appeared in the pages of the *Keighley News*. It revealed that on a bitter February day in 1801 Joseph, two-year-old son of Thomas Helliwell of Enfieldside Farm,
followed his father outside. Helliwell took the road to Pecket Well near Hebden
Bridge by way of the old Haworth Road – 't' stairs'. The child was unable to catch up
with him and was soon lost on the moor. He was found frozen to death the following
morning on moorland above the area known as Harbour Lodge. The dead boy was returned to his distraught family for burial. In 1837 Emily Brontë wrote of the tragedy in
Redbreast in the Morning.

'What woke it then? A little child
Strayed from its father's cottage door,
And in an hour of moonlight wild
Laid lonely on the desert moor.'

The following report appears in the pages of *Mayhall's Annals Vol. 1* dated Saturday, 27 January 1849. 'Joseph Halliwell aged four years lost for three days on the
moor. He was the son of farmer William Halliwell (of Far Intake Farm). Body discovered on a Wednesday morning three miles from his home.'

Inspired by the tragedy, James Hey, the blind Harbour Lodge gamekeeper, known
also as 'Jim o' Bleucher's', composed a poem entitled *To a Lost Child*. Local Baptist
and mill-worker John Kitson also wrote of the affair. An unknown poet composed the
following poem, *The Dead Boy.*

'He is dead and gone – a flower
Born and withered in an hour,
Coldly lies the death frost now
On his little rounded brow;
And the seal of darkness lies
Ever on his shrouded eyes.
He will never feel again
Touch of human joy or pain;
Never will his once bright eyes
Open with glad surprise;
Nor the death-frost leave his brow –
All is over with him now.' *I.J.*

Taken two years after the tragedy, the Haworth census of 1851 confirms that William Helliwell, a farmer, wife Anne, son John aged twelve and twin sons, Edward and Henry aged ten and a child of two years were living at Far Intake. The tiny body of Joseph Helliwell lies united with his family in Haworth's old cemetery, close to the parsonage. His epitaph reads,

> In Memory of Joseph,
> Son of William Helliwell of Far Intake,
> who died Jany. 28th 1849
> in the 4th year of his Age.

Through the medium of *The Bradfordian* William Heaton published a tale in 1862 entitled *Lost Child of the Moorlands, a Tale founded on Facts*. Using the tragic Helliwell case as background to his story, he transforms the tale into a cautionary lesson for children.

Branwell's Death

In 1879 Branwell Brontë's friend Francis H. Grundy gave an account in his book *Pictures of the Past* of his final meeting with Branwell at the Black Bull, Haworth. 'Presently the door opened cautiously and a head appeared. It was a mass of red, unkempt, uncut hair, wildly floating round in a great gaunt forehead; the cheeks yellow and hollow, the mouth fallen, the thin white lips not trembling but shaking, the sunken eyes, once small, now glaring with the light of madness, – all told the sad tale but too surely … he glanced at me a moment, and muttered something of leaving a warm bed to come

The Black Bull, Haworth, was the last place Branwell visited before his death.

out into the cold night...our last interview was pleasant, though grave... He described himself as anxious for death – indeed, longing for it.

When at last I was compelled to leave, he quietly drew from his sleeve a carving-knife, placed it on the table and holding me by the hands, said he had given up all thoughts of ever seeing me again, he imagined when my message came that it was a call from Satan. Dressing himself, he took the knife, which he long secreted, and came to the inn...I left him standing bare headed in the road, with bowed form and dropping tears.' A few days after this visit to the Black Bull, Branwell was dead. The young man died on his feet with a pocket stuffed full of letters from a lady he loved.

Double Suicide

In the spring of 1847 two teenage lovers from Lincolnfield Place, Newtown, Leeds deliberately jumped into the icy River Aire and drowned themselves. The pair had previously said their goodbyes to all their closest friends, telling them they were going to look for work in the town of Harrogate. In truth, Maria Wilson and Joseph Bolland were both so depressed at being out of work that they deliberately tied their bodies together with cotton handkerchiefs before committing themselves to the swollen, muddy waters of the Aire.

Remains on Show

William Dyson and his son John were executed together at York for the murder of John Dyson senior in April 1828. John junior's body was delivered to Leeds for dissection. On 3 April the gruesome remains were on view to the general public. Large numbers turned out to see them.

In 1832 the Leeds Workhouse Board agreed to supply Leeds Hospital with the corpses of paupers to be used freely for dissection purposes.

Blacksmith Shoots Wife

On 16 March 1850 John Jessop, a Clayton blacksmith, bought two pistols. He endeavoured to shoot his wife dead but his aim was poor and he only managed to graze her left breast. He promptly turned the second gun on himself and blew his brains out.

Hussar Suicide

Richard Norton, paymaster's clerk of the 10th Hussars, wilfully took his own life in a bedchamber at the Horse and Trumpet Inn, Briggate, Leeds in 1831. His military friends carried him to Quarry Hill graveyard on the following Sunday for interment but Revd Mr Wardle steadfastly refused to read the burial service over a suicide death. Mourners and sightseers created a great scene but Wardle continued to refuse burial rights. As a consequence, Norton's corpse was abandoned inside the church. The next day Revd Wardle had a number of other funerals to attend to and was shocked to find several thousand people including men from the 3rd Dragoons on his doorstep demanding a Christian burial for Norton. The reverend gentleman agreed to read the burial service over Richard Norton's coffin. Satisfied spectators left without incident.

Perpetual Will

Presbyterian Jacob Hudson, an eccentric character, was buried alongside his wife Grace in the yard of the dead at Chapel Lane, Bradford. Jacob's perpetual will of 1772 left property, which he stipulated must be kept in the family forever! Subsequently, an application was presented to Parliament, paid for by his numerous relatives, for the first private estate bill, freeing the land and property for sale. The Hudson Estate Act was passed in 1848. Two streets in the area today perpetuate the name of Jacob Hudson.

Bradford Man Savaged

The Cordingley family occupied one of Hudson's buildings known as The Skinhouse prior to 1801. James Cordingley, a tanner, stumbled home late one night after frequenting several alehouses in the vicinity. He collapsed outside his home and his two pet dogs set upon him. His arm was almost severed from his body and his throat and windpipe were ripped out. Cordingley died of his horrific injuries on 24 October 1827.

A later occupant of the same premises, John Blamires, was found dead with his head lolling over the mouth of the well. The Skinhouse was eventually sold off in 1850 to Mr Thomas Dewhirst.

Sad Plight of Pauper Family

'Rattle his bones over the stones;
He's only a pauper, who nobody knows.' 1839

The pitiful story of a child's death and subsequent funeral unfolds from the pages of a Bradford newspaper dated October 1887.

'In connection with the burial of the body of a pauper in Bradford yesterday afternoon there were circumstances which call for the most searching inquiry by the Poor-law authorities of the town. It will be remembered that on Tuesday night last a girl named Mary Ann Sleaford, aged nine years, who had been tramping with her father and mother and two other children from Halifax to Bradford, was suddenly taken ill with a fit in George Street, and died shortly afterwards in her mother's arms. The body was taken to the mortuary in Aldermanbury, and was afterwards measured by somebody who had been entrusted by the Workhouse officials with the task of making the coffin. Yesterday was fixed as the day of the funeral, and about noon the coffin was brought to the mortuary by the undertaker. The father and mother of the deceased child were at the mortuary, and as the undertaker was putting the body into the coffin they protested that it was too small in every respect. The man at once admitted that it was too small, and that he had made a mistake, and asked the father of the child to go up to his house, and fetch some 'ribs' to attach to the sides of the coffin, so as to deepen it. The father objected to do this on the ground that he did not know his way about the town, and could not find the house. It then occurred to the undertaker that some wood could be obtained from a neighbouring joiner's shop, and he went out and invested a few coppers in some strips of rough wood, to be used for that purpose. Prior to this the body had been forced into the coffin in spite of the protests of the grief-stricken father, and the appearance which it presented is stated by all the witnesses to have been shocking in the extreme. The head and feet were tightly jammed against the walls of the coffin, the shoulders were forced forward as a result of the narrowness of the receptacle, and the arms had to be crossed over the body, which protruded so much that it was impossible to get the lid to meet the sides within an inch or so. The body was not removed whilst the strips of wood were attached to the sides; but whilst it was lying in that condition the undertaker went to work with hammer and sprigbit to patch the wretched apology for a coffin to such an extent as to allow of the screwing down of the lid. The barbarity of this performance was accentuated by the heartrending sobs of the parents, whose unavailing distress excited a deep compassion on the few spectators. The undertaker was about to screw the coffin lid on at once, but Sleaford begged him to leave it open until the hearse arrived, and himself undertook the responsibility of seeing the matter attended to. When the hearse came the father obtained a couple of screws from somebody at the fire station, and, with the assistance of the driver of the conveyance, fastened the lid down. But, even then, the coffin was not deep enough, and when the lid was put on one of the strips of wood split, and it is believed that some portion of the body – at any rate, the hands – were crushed by the cover. It should be mentioned that the head was prevented from contact with the bare wood only by means of the father's handkerchief, which he tenderly wrapped round it; and some shavings which were put into the coffin by Sleaford relieved the bare appearance of the sides to some degree. In this fashion was the body prepared for burial; and notwithstanding the exquisite cruelty of the incident, the funeral was proceeded with. There was nobody in authority to see that the arrangements were consistent with common decency, and nobody to authorise such an act of mere justice and ordinary humanity as the delaying of the funeral for a day in order that the mistake might be put right.

'The coffin was conveyed into the hearse, which formed the whole of the funeral procession, and the father, mother, daughter, and baby in arms were all mounted on the box seat, along with the driver. They were perched up, uncomfortably enough, as may be imagined from the number of them and the accommodation with which they had to be content; and the curious spectacle attracted the glances of passers-by as the vehicle proceeded to the cemetery. On arrival there the hearse stopped at the end of the carriage road which leads through the main entrance to the mortuary chapels, and the coffin was deposited on trestles. No other funeral was taking place, and the cemetery had a singularly deserted and desolate appearance, the only persons in attendance being the priest (the Revd Father Slattery) and two labourers who were at the grave which they had dug for the child. As the coffin lay on the trestles, its hasty and patched-up construction was obvious, it consisted of the roughest materials, put together in the roughest and readiest manner. The boards were of deal fastened together with common sprigs. No attempt had been made to plane the wood, and its surface was rough as that of a packing case, and smeared with lampblack in lieu of paint. Even this slight pretence of decency was omitted, however, with regard to the rib which was added to deepen the coffin, and which did not appear to have been dressed in any manner. In fact, the coffin appeared to have been so slightly and defectively constructed that little violence would have been required to break it to pieces. Whilst it lay on the trestles one of our representatives roughly took the dimensions of this strange receptacle. It was about 4ft. 4in. in length, 9in. deep (including the extra 1½in. added after the body had been placed in the coffin), and about 9in. wide across the foot. The lid bore a thin plate having the following inscription: – "Mary Ann Sleaford died September 28th 1887, aged 9 years". This plate was the only evidence of any attempt to observe the usual forms of decency which the coffin showed. The priest read the Burial Service in Latin over the body in a low voice, the father, with his little girl beside him, and his wife, with her baby in her arms, making up the whole of the mourners – as piteous a group as one could look upon. Although it did not rain, the ground was wet and the air was raw, and their thin and tattered garments fluttered in a damp and cheerless wind, which whistled among the trees in the cemetery, and whisked the decayed leaves about unpleasantly. At the conclusion of the burial service a delay occurred. There was no one to carry the coffin to the grave, and there was no alternative but for the father to carry it thither himself. The poor fellow did not seem to realise this until his attention was called to it by the priest, when, in a half-dazed manner, he took up the coffin from the trestles and carried it under his arm in the direction of the grave, which lay underneath the wall at the Bradford end of the cemetery. One or two labourers who had been digging the grave, and who came up during the service, offered to help him with his load, and took hold of one end of the coffin, and in this manner they proceeded to the graveside, preceded by the priest speaking prayers for the soul of the deceased, and forlornly followed by the little girl and her mother, with the baby of three months in her arms. The little girl, who is only four years old, seemed scarcely sensible of the occasion of her parent's mourning, but the father and mother were both in great distress at the violence which had been done to the remains of their daughter and at the unfeeling negligence which had been displayed in the arrangements for the burial. The very lampblack which had been smeared on to the coffin came off in the hands of the bearers as they carried the corpse to the grave. On arrival at the graveside the coffin was lowered into its last receptacle by the two labourers, and further prayers were repeated by the priest for the soul of the deceased. He stood at the foot of the grave, and at the opposite end were the father, mother, and children, with their heads uncovered. The father tenderly placed his arm around round the neck of his little girl, who was standing by his side, and fairly broke down crying. After the prayers were concluded the priest took his departure. The hearse had already started back, and the poverty-stricken mourners, who had been brought two miles out of the town, were left to get back as best they could. They were last seen by our representatives as the latter were leaving the cemetery, at which time they were wandering – the father, the mother, with her infant, and the little girl of four – aimlessly and disconsolately through the wet and dirt towards the entrance to the high road.'

Only a Pauper

"They were only tramps; these people to suffering hard inured,
The slings and the darts of Fortune they passively had endured;
The waifs of the children crying and starving for rest and food
Oft fell on the ears of the parents, so powerless to give them good.
'Twas but a pauper's child that died and closed a life of pain;
'Twas but a pauper's child, and so a rough-hewn box to gain
Were good enough for her no doubt, *she* wouldn't mind it much,
Nor heed the harsh, irreverent, unsympathetic touch.
'Twas but a pauper mother, sobbing as her heart would break,
'Twas but a pauper father, fastened fast for torture's sake,

'Twas but two wide-eyed children, gazing in a wondering way,
The while the noble ritual was murmured o'er clay.
Yes, paupers must be buried, and of course in such a case
Such things as paupers' feelings are extremely out of place;
A wooden box, besmeared with pitch, a foot or two of ground,
Were quite enough – for paupers, as we know, too much ground.
Ay! Let them go their weary tramp, with sore hearts seamed and scared,
What matters if what such like feel unto the gently reared?
What comfort can these outcasts clam, accustomed to their sights?
They should feel happy that at last they can claim holy rites.
What's that you say? "'*Tis not enough*" Why sir, I stand aghast!
What! "Paupers still are human beings, and feel the cruel blast
Of winter storms; the summer heat; and have a *right* to feel,
To love and hate, to laugh and cry?" – that theory pray repeal.
"That decency of treatment too, is due to folk like those;
That some consideration is the title of their woes;
That those whose callous conduct. And whose wanton, wild neglect,
Has caused such heart-rung agony should forcibly be checked."
You say "The lash of scorn should be with strongest arm applied!"
Go to! – I think your sympathy is somehow rather wide;
What does it matter how they deal with paupers, quick or dead,
Who haven't got a decent suit, a home, or e'en a bed?'

Occupational Hazards

At Low Moor Iron Works, Bradford in 1880 a stoker fell into one of the furnaces. Although his work companions rushed to cut off the draught nothing at all was found of the man except a trouser button, which had fallen on to the floor. A huge explosion occurred in August 1916 at a chemical plant next to the iron works. A memorial to the 39 people killed was erected at Scholemoor Cemetery.

Samuel Tomlinson aged 14, a cloth dresser of Jolly Tar Yard, Marsh Lane, Leeds was killed by overlooker Joseph Radcliffe at Mark Walker's flax factory, Mabgate, Leeds. Six hundred factory waifs attended the boy's funeral. However, factory children's lives came cheap for bully Radcliffe only received a one-year prison sentence for his wicked deed.

Mysterious Death

June 1856 found a Mrs McKnight at the Ben Rhydding Hydropathic Establishment near Ilkley, taking the curative waters at a cost of around £1 11s 6d plus board and lodgings at £1 1s. 0d. Shortly after her arrival she took a constitutional walk to Ilkley, leaving about 10am. She was seen leaving Ilkley about two hours later heading towards Ben Rhydding along the Cow-pastures. This was to be the last sighting of her alive.

A couple out walking found her body between four and five that afternoon. It was lying at the bottom of a deep ravine. 'She was lying upon her side, with her arms on her chest and stomach, quite dead. Her dress was not at all disordered or soiled, and her body exhibited but slight marks of external injury. It was strongly suggested that she met her death by some gypsies, who were seen in the neighbourhood about that time, and this suspicion had an air of probability, from the fact that her purse and pocket handkerchief were gone. From superficial marks on the neck, it was strongly suspected that she had been murdered by strangulation. The affair however remains a mystery.'

The Hydropathic Establishment where Mrs McKnight spent her last night was to be demolished this century after serving the community for 110 years. It was placed below the Cow and Calf Rocks on Ilkley Moor and leased out to private tenants until requisitioned by the British Government in 1939. Afterwards its 100 bedrooms echoed only to ghostly footsteps until it became the Craiglands Hotel.

Gunpowder Explosion

A fearful explosion was heard coming from a firework manufacturer's establishment at Blackburn's Yard, Holbeck Lane, Leeds in 1835. Five persons were buried beneath the ruins of three cottages. The violence of the explosion was so great it shook windows and doors in almost every part of Leeds. Gas lamps were blown out, hundreds of panes of glass were smashed and tall buildings visibly shook, causing great consternation. The congregation at their devotions in St Paul's Church was convinced Armageddon had arrived. The cause of this calamity was Susannah Dockray, an employee at the factory. She was about her work in the gunpowder room when, attempting to snuff out a candle, she accidentally ignited gunpowder. 'At first only a hissing noise accompanied by repeated cracking occurred, and Dockray came running downstairs with her clothes on fire, screaming out "Oh Hannah," and rushed out of the house. Mary Wilkinson, Mary Wildman, and a little girl of Wood's, apprehending danger, followed her example. Not so Mrs Wood, who notwithstanding the entreaties of Wilkinson to the contrary, ran up the stairs with the intention of throwing the squibs and crackers out of the window. She had just attained the threshold of the room, and the parties below had only got a few metres from the door, when a barrel and a half of gunpowder exploded with a noise as of the discharge of a park of artillery; the house rose into the air, and the next instant, together with the houses adjoining, sunk to the earth, a mass of blazing ruins.

The death of Mrs Wood, Mrs Stephenson and her child was instantaneous, they being in the very centre of the explosion. On the opposite side of the lane was the house of James Walker, at a distance of about 12yds. Walker and another man named Windsor were weaving in an upper room. The slates of the roof were completely blown off, the wall burst in, and the ruins descended into the room in which they were working. Walker was buried in the rubbish that fell about him; but being partly shielded by the rafters, was extricated without having sustained any material injury. Windsor had placed himself under the loom, and by that means was protected from injury. Walker's wife was buried in the ruins. A child of hers about three years of age had a miraculous escape. It was found near the body of its mother in a state of insensibility, but afterwards recovered. An old man named Stead, upwards of 70 years of age, who had been confined to his bed for twelve months was dreadfully scorched, and subsequently died. His wife was very much scorched but afterwards recovered. The event caused

the deepest sensation in the town, and a fund was soon raised for the benefit of the sur-
vivors. Four alms houses were erected on Holbeck Moor in 1838 with the surplus of
money...' *Mayhalls Annals Vol. 1.*

Artist's Death

One of the best-known watercolour artists in the country, A. Reginald Smith of
Grassington, fell victim to the Strid on 14 September 1934. The services of a water diviner were employed to find his body. The *Telegraph & Argus* wrote of the affair,

Strid Mystery Solved

'The body was recovered from a deep crevice which last week was indicated by a
water diviner, Mr R. Brotton, of Richmond, as the point where a body would be
found. Mr Smith's disappearance was a mystery, and caused a big stir in the Dales.
He left home to do some sketching at the Strid...A search was made and on a boulder in the middle of the Strid at a point where it can be jumped, were found the
missing artist's easel and sketching bag and in the latter were a number of
sketches of scenes in the vicinity...Two days after Mr Smith first disappeared a
tweed cap, identified as belonging to him, was found lower down the river than the
Strid...Mr Brotton, who offered his services, visited the scene.' He was able to locate the whereabouts of the missing artist by means of hazel twigs.

Young Hampshire honeymooners married for less than 48 hours became victims
of The Strid in August 1998. The alarm was raised when a man's body was seen floating in the river and a woman's jacket was discovered lying on the riverbank nearby.
The pockets contained the keys to a holiday cottage at Appletreewick. The woman's
body was plucked from the water at Addingham almost a week later. The man's body

The Strid at Bolton Abbey, where many have met their deaths. *(The Yorkshireman)*

was also recovered and their funeral was at the church in which they had so recently been married.

Christmas Mystery

The wedding of Thomas Longbottom to the daughter of Frank Armitage, a farmer, took place on Christmas Day 1853. A few days after the marriage the couple retired to bed an hour before midnight. It was still dark when a stranger rapped loudly on the front door and called out that the new daughter-in-law, dressed only in her nightdress, was lying on a stone landing outside raving and babbling. It transpired that she had fallen from the upper bedroom window. Her husband Thomas was missing. A search party was sent to find him. His body was found floating in the cold waters of the River Aire at Hunslet, Leeds. The wife recovered but was never able to recall what happened. Thomas Longbottom's father afterwards killed himself by flinging himself down the shaft of his own pit on Sunday, 30 May 1859 in an apparent fit of severe depression.

Mixed Blessing

Mary Blessing, an Irish immigrant living in Gay Lane, Otley, callously attacked and killed her husband's 84-year-old uncle, Francis Blessing. Taking a hammer she repeatedly struck the unfortunate man about the head until he died. In 1855 she was sentenced at York to transportation for life.

A Dark Deed

'On a dark winter's night, I found myself seated alongside the driver of the little country coach plying between Skipton and Kettlewell.' At each stop – Rylstone, Cracoe and Grassington – one or two travellers alighted until only two passengers and the driver remained. One of those passengers, James Burnley, takes up the story. 'By this time the darkness had been intensified, and made more cheerless by a steady relentless rain, which had evidently set in for the night, and was urged upon us all the more forcibly by the fitful wind.' A storm rose in earnest, the wind driving icy rain hard against the men's faces. It had grown darker now and only the flicker of a single candlelight could be glimpsed at a lonely cottage window and the sound of a farmer's dog howling could be heard somewhere in the blackness of the night. On entering Grass Wood the driver obligingly pointed out places where sad individuals had ended their lives or had been murdered. Burnley continues his narrative, '...the trees shook, and the wind whistled in such a weird and ghastly way as he delivered himself of these legends...we came upon a corner of the wood, to which the driver pointed with his whip... "That's t' place where Tom Lee murdered Dr Petty, and I've heard folks say ..." but his travelling companions could hear no more for the horse suddenly shied. "Ho, my lass! whoa! steady! I've heard 'em say 'at his ghost comes..." But the wind carried off the rest of the driver's words. Just then the horse bolted forward causing the driver to concentrate upon his work.

The journey ended for the night at a hostelry named The Race Horses. After a hot meal Burnley and his Arncliffe companion set off to visit their Bradfordian friend on foot. At his friend's home James Burnley idly picked up a book entitled *Rambles in Upper Wharfedale* by Bailey Harker. Whilst flicking through the pages he chanced upon the story of the Grass Wood murder, but he was at that moment drawn into the conversation and manners dictated he abandon the book and its contents. It was after midnight when the pair returned to their night's lodgings. James Burnley went directly to his room but on hearing the rain's constant tapping against the windowpane he writes, 'I lit a candle, locked the door, and walking quietly back, seated myself on a chair near the light. Involuntarily I put my hand upon the table; then, after looking yawningly around, I was just on the point of rising to undress, when I perceived that my hand was resting upon a little book in a dingy red binding, I took it up, and opened it, and the first words that met my eyes were "Tom Lee!" I was startled. The awful shadow of Grass Wood rose before me once more; once again I felt the thrill of fear which had possessed me when the horse took fright: and, under these influences, I set myself there and then to read for the first time the story of the murder of Dr Petty. I shall never forget that night.'

Tom Lee, the village blacksmith and innkeeper of the Blue Anchor Inn, Grassington, was a bully and thief. One day in 1765 he lay in wait, in good highwayman tradition, to rob the local mining agent. The robbery backfired, leaving Lee badly injured and forcing him to seek out the help of a local doctor, Tom Petty, on the quiet. A few months after the incident the good doctor called at the Angler's Inn, Kilnsey, entering just as Lee was about to thrash Dick Linton who had accused him of burglary. The doctor nodded at Lee to warn him he would be for the gallows if he didn't leave Linton alone.

Dame Truelove handed Dr Petty a stirrup cup filled with whisky-punch. When he had drunk the golden liquid the empty glass slipped from his grasp, falling to the ground with a crash. Doctor and landlady looked down in horror as they perceived the glass lying unbroken – in Dale lore this portends certain death. The landlady begged Petty to take special care on his journey home that evening.

Meanwhile Tom Lee, brooding upon the doctor's interference, left the inn and hid himself near a path frequented by the physician – a dark haunted place in Grass Wood below Ghastrill's Strid. Lee had not long to wait before seizing Petty from his horse. The men faced each other for a moment before Lee dealt a heavy blow to the other's head and stabbed him. Temporarily hiding the battered body, he fled homeward. He told his wife what he had done and ordered his apprentice, John Bowness, to return to the wood with him to dispose of the corpse. Shocked to find Petty still breathing, Lee forced Bowness to finish off the dying man. The corpse was then bundled into a sack and dragged to a rocky pile high above the wooded grove.

Search parties failed to find the missing doctor and rumours were rife. Lee and Petty's names were linked but nothing could be proved. During this time the murderer again moved the remains – to a boggy part of the moor at Dib Scar Glen. Not content with this, he and his wife returned and pulled the rotting body from the bog and carted it over the moors to Burnsall. Their gruesome burden was weighted down with stones and rolled into the river. The following Sunday a party of churchgoers discovered the

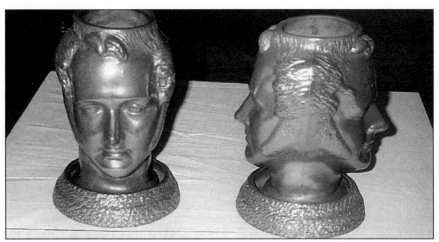

Janus heads reputed to have belonged to the ill-fated Dr Petty *(The Craven Museum)*

bloated remains of the doctor floating on top of the water. It was fished out and taken to the Red Lion Inn at Burnsall.

Tom Lee was tried for the murder but was acquitted due to lack of evidence. He was re-arrested and remanded for seven days then acquitted a second time. Three years later John Bowness, unable to live with his guilt, turned King's evidence, naming Lee as the killer. On 25 July 1768 Tom Lee was measured for gibbet irons before being taken to Knavesmire, York and hanged. His corpse was carried to Grass Wood and gibbeted on rocks above the exact spot where the murder took place. Here his body dangled for four years until the bones fell apart. Gypsies came and stole the buckles from his shoes and some of the bones for making charms. A long time afterwards the gibbet irons were found in the riverbed at Ghaistrills and thrown into the River Wharfe. There they lay for some time before being found by young boys out playing. They were buried beneath the eastern side of Grassington Bridge until a farm labourer employed in digging a grave for a cow found the irons and carried them off. The location of the gibbet irons today is not known. The stirrup cup was carefully preserved by the landlady of the Angler's Inn and was eventually taken to America when its owner emigrated. Two glasses in The Craven Museum are presented as claiming to be the stirrup glass Dr Petty dropped that fateful day.

Chapter 9

Forms of Punishment

'Justice brings sorrow to all concerned.' *M.C.*

Wooden Prison

A Statute of Labourers enacted in 1349 states, 'Servants refusing to take the oath or perform what they had sworn to (that is, to carry out their contract) shall be put in the stocks or sent to the next gaol, and there remain until they will justify themselves; and in order to enforce the same, that stocks, be made in every town for such an occasion betwixt this and the Feast of Pentecost.'

By the year 1405, an Act of Parliament decreed every town 'shall provide a pair of stocks.' For the convenience of the churchwarden and constable the stocks were to be situated near to the parish church. A hundred-shilling fine (£5) was levied on towns that refused to comply. In the reign of Good Queen Bess agricultural labourers were set in the stocks for two days and one night if they refused to work the harvest. Lawbreakers in Henry VII's time had fared little better. Those who abandoned babies were placed in the stocks for it was a most serious crime to leave the parish to pay for the rearing of a child. Sabbath breakers were also treated to time in the stocks if found gaming or bullbaiting on a Sunday. A beggar could expect to spend three days in the stocks with only plain bread and water to sustain him or her. In 1535 those caught begging could suffer the cutting off of a right ear lobe. Thankfully, transportation to other climes took the place of detaching the ear lobe in 1713. By 1745 profane cursing was punishable by a stint in the stocks if a fine could not be paid. The fine for swearing began at 1s. (5p) if the culprit was a sailor or labourer, rising to 2s. (10p) if the offender was a gentleman. Those of an even higher rank paid 5s. (25p).

Keighley Stocks

Keighley stocks were erected at Church Green, between St Andrew's Church and Ye Olde Red Lion (Lord Rodney Inn). Repositioned at least twice during their long history, arguments once raged as to which way the lawbreakers should face in the contraption. A Victorian gaslamp nicknamed 'Old Paul' conveniently illuminated the stocks and surrounding area after nightfall. Police Constable 'Pie' Leach wrote of an incident taking place in the summer of 1850. At, 'One Clock on Wednesday morning John Gledson the new Church Sexton was drunk and some person or persons had set him fast in the stocks.' By 1864 the stocks had a full and eventful history. Part of the wood was worn away from overuse, but the stocks still fascinated townsfolk and outlying villagers. Characters like Old Codger mesmerised his audience with fascinating tales of Wakefield Prison and it's even less salubrious inmates, providing the crowd with endless hours of free entertainment. In adverse weather conditions the offender would be taken into the Lord Rodney, where he was at liberty to warm his hands and feet in front of a log fire for a few minutes before being returned to complete his sentence. The stocks played host to many drunken sots who might have profited from the following ancient verse.

Degradation and Drunkenness

'There is no sin which doth more
deface God's image than drunkenness
it disguiseth a person and doth even
unman him.
Drunkenness makes him have
the throat of a fish,
the belly of a swine
and the head of an ass.
Drunkenness is the shame of nature,
the extinguisher of reason,
the shipwreck of chastity
and the murderer of conscience.
Drunkenness is hurtful to the body,
the cup kills more than the cannon,
it causes dropsies, catarrhs, apoplexies
it fills the eye with fire and legs with
water and turns the body into a hospital.' Anon.

Within the walls of the Temperance Movement headquarters, zealous plans were underway to position a new water drinking fountain in enemy territory—that is to say on Church Green, where no fewer than six or seven alehouses sold the Devil's broth. Miss Sarah Hannah Butterfield of Cliffe Hall (where Cliffe Castle now stands) provided money for the fountain. This new attraction was to replace the well-worn stocks. In a successful application to the Sessions House in 1864 requesting permission to implement their improvements to Church Green the movement stated that the water fountain would, 'be of greater value to the public at large than the stocks'.

Jemmy Doodle, Tommy Broadley (alias Keighley Tommy who murdered a workmate just for teasing him) and others, having personal experience of the stocks' hospitality, threw a wild and riotous party in celebration of their abolition. Arrested for being drunk and disorderly, they were hauled before the Bench the following morning and sentenced to seven days at Wakefield Prison or payment of a fine of 5s (25p). In 1868 an unknown signing herself only as 'Henrietta' related the following tale to the *Keighley News*. 'Got some interesting information concerning the lamp-post and the stocks which used to be directly under the light. "Well mum, you know, Bob Guzzles, what got drunkken as often as he cud, and wer sent to Wakefield so often that t'heead Governor went mad wi't seet on him, wor put in for six hours. When he wor let aat he wor way drunkken than ivver a'cos his mates browt him some tea which wor fand to be nowt else but rum afterwards. Policeman i' charge gat sacked for misconduct; stocks wer riven up becos they were no good..."'

Bingley Stocks, thought to have been the last used in England.

After the stocks were dismantled to make way for the new fountain they were stored at Keighley Corporation's stone-yard at Lawkholme. The stone was eventually broken up and used for street repairs.

Before she died aged eighty in 1900 Dolly Jackson of Bingley reminisced about 'the good old days'. In 1855 her cousin Henry Dixon, a nailer by trade, was fastened in the stocks just above the Bingley bullring for gambling. Dolly took him a cup of tea but this was refused in favour of a pint of beer courtesy of Mr Slicer the landlord of the Queen's Head opposite. In 1818 the Bingley stocks were renovated and new stone posts were purchased at a cost of 5s (25p). The last victim was released from Bingley Stocks in the 1870s. It is thought that these stocks were the last to be used in Yorkshire.

Shipley stocks stood on the higher part of the market place at Stocks Hill, which was then a popular mustering place for villagers.

Waterlogged Stocks

The Flappit Inn is on the road from Keighley to Halifax and takes its name from the area on which it stands. This was known to locals of a bygone age as the Flay Pit. Animal hides were brought from around the district to undergo a tanning process here. A set of very soggy wooden stocks was recovered from a blocked well situated by the gable end of the old inn in 1990.

Bramley Stocks

Bramley stocks were placed upon Stocks Hill in the centre of the village, next to the water pump where there was always plenty of activity going on. Here too stood a lone stone pillar known as the market cross that had been erected during the time of the Leeds plague for trading purposes. At the top end of the grassy slope stood St Margaret's Church. The stocks were relocated next to the church steps when the pump was removed in 1827. Here 'the natives sat with their ankles in the stocks during service hours on Sunday to atone for the sin of Sabbath-breaking'. This contraption was put to other uses such as straightening out handloom weavers' cloth pieces while the owners discussed business matters over a pint of beer or two at a nearby local inn.

Will Perigo, the man who almost perished at the hands of the infamous Leeds witch Mary Bateman after eating her mercury 'charm' pudding, took up the post of Bramley duty constable and thus became master of the stocks. One day he stocked a village man for loutish drunken behaviour. The offender's wife went and fetched a jug of strong home-made ale. After taking a gulp of the brown liquid the delinquent offered Will Perigo a swig saying, 'Here, Will, tak 'od an' sup, man? Ther's no mercury i' this 'ere.' A remark that no doubt earned him double time in the stocks!

The Pillory

Named the pillory by Anglo-Saxons, the hole in a horizontal plank was separately referred to as heal-fang or neck grasper. A particularly vicious medieval version was *stretch neck,* so named because the unfortunate delinquent dangled by his neck. Later, more humane models incorporating wrist holes and a narrow platform were invented, 'for the better exposure of notorious cheats, impostors, libellers, immoral people, and political offenders, to open shame, derision and practical abuse, in the form of filth and foul things being hurled at them.'

'Mad Quaker-Christ'

Born in 1616, James Naylor, a native of East Ardsley near Wakefield, was converted to Quakerism by George Fox. He had previously served under General Lambert as a quartermaster during the Civil War.

In 1656, claiming to be the Messiah, he raised a woman named Dorcas Erbury from the dead at Exeter prison. Parliament found him guilty of, 'horrid blasphemy... a grand impostor and seducer of the people and that he should be set on the pillory, in the Palace Yard, Westminster during the space of two hours, on Thursday next, and be whipped by the hangman through the streets, from Westminster to the Old Exchange, London; and there, likewise, he should be set on the on the pillory, for the space of two hours, between the hours of eleven and one, on Saturday next, in each place wearing a paper containing an inscription of his crimes; and that, at the Old Exchange, his tongue should be bored through with a hot iron, and that he should be there also stigmatised in the forehead with the letter B (for blasphemy); and that he should afterwards be sent to Bristol, to be conveyed into and through the city on horseback, with his face backwards, and there also should be whipped the next market-day after he came thither; and that he should be committed to prison in Bridewell, London, and there restrained from society of all people, and there to labour hard till he should be released by Parliament; and during that time he should be debarred the use of pen, ink, and paper, and he should have no relief but what he earned by daily labour.' Naylor was released from his prison cell on 8 September 1659. The Quaker Society forgave him after he publicly made a full confession, reducing those present to tears. He died in 1660 on the road to Wakefield as he returned home to his family.

Bradford Pillory

Bradford's pillory stood alongside the Bull's Head Inn at Westgate. This contraption was last tenanted for one hour by a couple from Thornton in 1813. The pair had stolen a piece of bacon from an employer.

In 1677 James Ollerton of Bowling, Bradford was ordered to stand in the pillories at Bradford, Leeds and Halifax between the hours of 11am and 2pm on market day. He was to wear a paper on his head proclaiming 'James Ollerton, a common barrachter.' Two centuries later the law was softer in the case of William Davis, a Bradford plasterer, and James Watson of Gisburn who failed to pay their fines of 5s 6d (27½p). The two were locked in stocks in front of the Courthouse at Hall-ings; Bradford but were released early as it had started to rain. The last person in Bradford's stocks was Idleite John Dodgson who received a sentence of six hours in July 1860 for being drunk.

Whipping of Vagabonds

Anglo-Saxons flogged lawbreakers with a whiplash of three cords, each knotted at the end to ensure maximum effect. Many servants were whipped to death for petty crimes. A magistrate was forced by law to make searches four times a year to flush out vagabonds. Any person taking pity on or found harbouring such a felon would be fined the considerable sum of 10s. (50p). In 1572 the Vagrants Act was passed. Under the new law any able-bodied vagrant beggars could expect to be publicly flogged while half-naked on their first arrest, punished as a felon on the second and hung if apprehended a third time. Before this time beggars were dragged to the nearest market place. There the 1530 Whipping Act decreed that they be 'tied to the end of a cart naked, and beaten with whips throughout the market town, or other place, till the body shall be bloody by reason of such whipping.' It was about this time that whipping posts were substituted for travelling carts.

At Skipton a Beadle was employed to keep out all 'foreign' persons. Records of banished vagrants who suffered whipping in Skipton are to be found in Kildwick Parish Registers. On 7 October 1600 Elizabeth Rawling and her two children suffered punishment and were sent to Brigham in Cumberland. In 1601, on 'September 4th, sent Jane Walker to Bradforde and 2 children.' Dated 8 February 1699, an entry made at Skipton Sessions reads, 'Charged in haveing sev'rall hedge breakers before Mr Ferrand att Kighley. Some ...were ffyn'd and oth'rs whip'd 6s.(30p).' Public whipping of vagrants became less common and it was noted that, '...the towne and p'ishe of Skipton is greevously pestered with rogues and vagabond persons that swarme in those parts more then in form'r tymes, because they now escape punishment.'

Sir John Lister Kaye of Bradford dealt harshly with those who dared break the law – for example, the penalty for stealing a hen or old iron pieces was often a severe public whipping. A shop in Wood Street, Leeds in 1885 did a brisk trade in birch rods for the punishment of naughty children.

Public Humiliation

George Clapham of Keighley was charged with fathering an illegitimate 'male/man child' and the mother, Mary Watters of Keighley, made a claim for damages against him on 27 June 1701. Although it was Watters herself who instigated the charges she was, 'subsequently ordered to be punished by being stripped naked from the waist upwards, tied to a cart and then drawn to Stone Brigg and back to the churchyard, and on the way backwards and forwards between these two places be whipped until her "body be bloody".'

Bingley Inns of Court

Courts leet, medieval manorial courts, were periodically held at the King's Head, Bingley. Magistrates also sat in judgement of wayward wrongdoers in the oak room of the White Horse Inn. The vaulted cellar below may have served as a prison at one time. The Old Elm Tree, named after a tree in its grounds, and a large room in the Brown Cow played host many times to the Bingley Petty Sessions.

Brought to Book

'In 1761, May 30, at the Quarter Sessions, held yesterday, at Moot Hall, in this town (Leeds), Mary Hardman, alias Moll Fagg, for stealing a candlestick from Mr Nichols, the Red Bear, in this town, was ordered to be publickly whip't.' On 17 August 1764 Lydia Longbottom of Bingley was whipped as she was drawn through the streets of Wakefield Town. Her crime? 'Reeling false and short yarn.' It was customary in Bingley to tie felons to the backboards of carts. As they were dragged slowly along the main thoroughfare bare-backed prisoners had their flesh cut by whips. In the last century Thomas Longbottom recorded that in 1834 a man caught stealing fruit from Mr Hulbert's orchard at the back of the vicarage 'was ordered to be flogged until his body was bloody'. An overseer was sent from Wakefield to watch as the town officials implemented the sentence. The thief was dragged from Market Street to the topside of Main Street to receive his punishment.

Boxer Bullied

The crumbling diaries of Moses Heap (1824-1913) record Sunday contests between naked street fighters at Keighley. One such entry refers to an old woman encouraging her son to brawl in this fashion. The old woman boasted to potential opponents that she would 'rather carry his bones home in her apron than see him beaten'.

Ignorance No Defence

Mr Justice Wills heard a case from Haworth at Leeds Summer Assizes in 1885. Two incompetent witnesses caused the judge to ask where the village of Haworth was. He said, 'I've never heard of it before today, but if this is a sample of its intelligence and common sense I should like to know where Haworth is.' A whisper immediately circulated around the courtroom and the name of Charlotte Brontë, the Haworth novelist who had been dead for a number of years, was on everyone's lips. Upon hearing the name the judge instructed the tipstaff to call Charlotte Brontë to the witness box!

A Haworth Gang

Isaac, Joseph and John Farrer were known members of the notorious 'Haworth Gang'. They were tried and convicted for breaking into the house of James Heap of Warley Cold Edge on 14 May 1818. The gang had appeared before the justices the previous year on an identical charge but had escaped the death sentence. This time they were less fortunate but the verdict was later changed to transportation to foreign lands.

Head Branks

An ancient brank belonging to Morley's late historian was presented to Leeds Philosophical Museum. The brank was a mode of punishment for women who refused to hold their tongues. It was an iron structure like a cage and was set upon the victim's head. A length of sharpened iron covered with spikes was forced inside the mouth so that it was impossible for the scold to move her tongue without causing herself an injury. A chain hung down from the cage. This was used to drag the unfortunate victim through the streets. Sometimes women were chained to the town stocks and left there for a time. Only two other branks have been found in Yorkshire.

Ducking Stools

'I'll speed me to the pond, when the high stool on the long plank hangs o'er the muddy pool. That stool, the dread of ever scolding quean.' Gay's Pastorals, iii.

'Quean' is an old English word meaning 'a woman of worthless character'.

The advent of the ducking stool was warmly welcomed in many places in West Yorkshire. Women were by no means the only victims of the water punishment: in 1269 brewers and bakers committing frauds or passing a bad article were sentenced to be ducked in stinking water. A ducking stool in the village of Morley, Leeds (near where the pinfold was afterwards built) was used to punish brawling women. The contraption was moved to Morley Hole and then on to Flush Pond, close to Ratton Row, Leeds.

'At the court of quarter sessions, at Leeds it was ordered that Anne, the wife of Phillip Sands, a person of lewd behaviour, be ducked, for daily making strife and discord amongst her neighbours. The like order was made against Jane Milner and Elizabeth Wooler.' The last two went straight from the sessions to the pillory and stocks that stood in front of the ancient public building Moot Hall.

In about 1723 a ducking stool was added to the pillory and stocks in Skipton and claimed shrews and 'unquiet women' as victims. The first written references to ducking stools in the old township of Skipton are to be found in the accounts.

1730. Pd Jno. South for 2 staples for ye cucking-stool   £0. 0. 4d

1731. Thos Moorhouse for mending ye ducking-stool   £0. 1. 0d

1737. John Ellot, for ye ducking-stool and sheep-fold door   £0. 14. 0d

1768. Paid John Brown for new ducking-stool   £1. 0. 11½.d

The last time this instrument was used in Skipton was around 1770. The ducking stool in Haworth was situated at the village pond, not far from Emmott Old Hall. A 1673 tombstone in Bramley churchyard announces, 'Houses and riches are the inheritance of fathers, but a prudent wife is from the Lord.' It seems there were few prudent wives in Bramley for the ducking stool had to be repaired many times.

Man Traps

Man traps were used in Leeds to trap poachers. They were likened to great rat traps with spiked steel jaws. The traps and the use of spring guns were banned in the middle of the 1800s.

Shadow of the Gallows

'Steal not this Jug my honest friend
For fear the gallows will be your end
And when you die the Lord will say
Where is the Jug you stole away.'

(Motto on a Leeds pottery jug made for Sarah Hainsworth of Bingley in 1780.)

An Inquisition taken in 1277 tells us that the right to raise a gallows was extended to the Lord of the Manor of Bradford, and the Wapentake of Morley. These structures were usually constructed in a prominent position such as the top of a hill or some popular mustering place. It was a jealously guarded privilege: 'Henry de Lacie hath many liberties in the town of Bradeford; to wit, a gallows, assize of bread and beer, a market-place and a free court from ancient times.'

There were at least ninety-four gallows in Yorkshire at this time according to the Hundred Rolls. Bradford's gallows stood in Gallows Close, later renamed as Cinders Hill. This land was purchased by butcher Thomas Pullan in 1777 and was situated near to what was to become Bowling Iron Foundry Works. At the time of writing, Fowler Street Industrial Estate fills the site.

A century later William Cudworth describes for us the scene at Gallows Close, which was positioned between Bowling Back Lane and Wakefield Road – the land had by then acquired the name of Cinder Hills on account of the red-hot cinders spilling out from the iron works. He writes, 'at night, when live scoria and ashes glow...and the lake is lighted up by vivid and fitful gleams emitted from the blast furnaces, the scene is strange and weird-like...one might almost fancy himself in immediate proximity to an active volcano. Puffs of white vapour rise incessantly from the sides and summit of the cinder hill, over which hangs a dense canopy of smoke.'

Official Executioner

On 13 March 1884, a former West Riding policeman, James Berry, successfully obtained his first hanging commission. His home at 1 Bilton Place, Bradford (demolished and replaced by Bilton Place Medical Centre) became known as The Executioner's Office. Here, in the family's best room, he proudly displayed family portraits amongst portraits of those he had executed.

Towards the end of his career, Berry took the view that capital punishment was both barbarous and ineffectual and so the hangman quit his chosen profession. For two full evenings in May 1898 he addressed a large gathering from the platform of the Keighley Temperance Hall. Delivering his speech 'Death by Hanging' he advocated

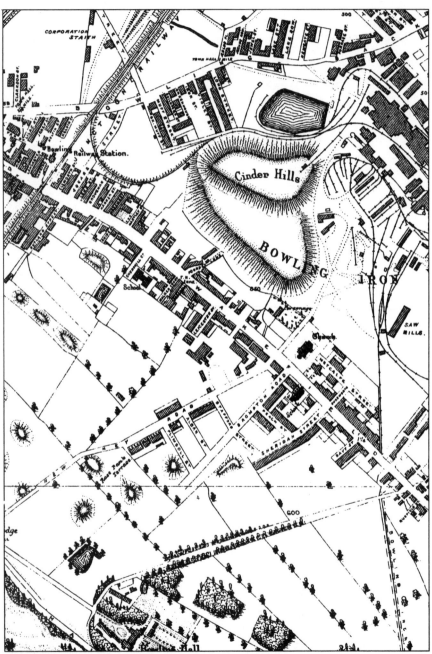

Cinder Hill, site of Bradford's gallows (Wm. Byles Plan of the Town of Bradford prepared for the Post Office Directory 1887-8)

BERRY, AHOY!

James Berry as a cartoon character
(The Yorkshireman)

the abolition of hanging and prophesied the time would come when the awaited reform would become fact. *The Yorkshireman* had this to say on the subject:

Berry's A Better Man Free From The Noose

'Berry had a little game,
He'd run a one-horse show,
But everywhere that Berry went
The crowds weren't sure to go.
Sing a song of hangman,
Who's bid his rope good-bye,
And now would hang all hang-men,
And let all hanging die...'

Ignoble End

'1748. March. Thos. Grave was most barbarously murdered in his own house by a domineering villainous lord of the manor, Josiah Fearne, 24th Feb., 1748, with four wounds to his body of which he died 2nd Mar. Fearne was taken and committed to York Castle, and tried before Sir Thomas Burnett, was committed and hanged 25th March, 1749. Soon after Fearne was condemned, he sent an attorney to Mrs Grave to offer her twenty pounds a year for her life, or for twenty years to come, at her own option, in case she wou'd sign a petition to the judge in his favour, (which Fearne said, was a sufficient recompense for the injury he had done to her and her eight children) but she prudently declin'd the offer, well knowing there is no satisfaction to be made for the blood of a murderer. This probably is the first lord of the manor of Leeds that made his exit on the gallows, and God grant that he may be the last. Fearne's temper was extremely rigid to the poor and his dependants, that he was dreaded by all, and beloved by none. He was buried at Clifton, near York, 31st March.'

First Hanging at Armly

Mrs Lofthouse, a resident of the district, witnessed the first public execution at Armley on 10th September 1864. Apparently she made a habit of watching executions and even had the good fortune to watch the double hanging in Liverpool of a sea captain and a bricklayer. She said of the captain, 'I saw him on the scaffold and ay, but he was good to look at. He had beautiful black curly hair...he was a bad 'un, and I never saw a man hanged with so much pleasure...' The plucky little bricklayer apparently took off his cap and threw it into the air towards the waiting crowd, causing a fight to break out amongst those who craved the hat as a memento.

Bilton Place, Bradford – the former home of James Berry, the public hangman

Historic Place of Death

Above Otley cemetery is Gallows Hill, once a feared place of execution. Close to the gallows is the place where in 1267-8 robber Ralph Brun was beheaded. There was also a quagmire used as a drowning pit. Here Anglo-Saxon women caught stealing were submerged. Horsfall Turner claimed the area was still recognisable at the turn of the century.

Man Hangs Son

A starving boy was hanged by his own father for stealing a morsel of bread at their hovel near Wakefield Road. The boy's younger brother cried out, 'Father, you'll not hang me, I took no bread.' The man was imprisoned at Wakefield for the murder in May 1674.

Haworth Gibbet?

J. Horsfall Turner in his *Annals of Wakefield House of Correction* 1904 says that a stone with mortice holes into which a gibbet-frame was fixed was preserved in Haworth churchyard. An added footnote taken from a manuscript belonging to Dr Johnson describes the apparatus as being, 'Two stones; namely, one East and one West, and the other at the head North and South with three mortices.' Today there is no sign of the missing gibbet stone in the churchyard – perhaps it was buried beneath the foundations of Haworth Church during the Revd Wade's alterations in the late 1870s.

Coiners' End

Nestled in a secluded green hollow off the old packhorse route alongside Harden Beck, Bingley, this inn has prospered since 1636. Built to serve as a farmhouse it has led an eventful life as a coaching inn, manor courthouse and prison. Several coiners were imprisoned here before being taken to the moors and executed on rudely cobbled gallows.

Two pairs of clipping shears made in 1864 by goldsmith Arthur Maugey of Briggate, Leeds to make the Leeds mace are linked to a curious tale. This goldsmith had in his employ a man by the name of Norcross who exposed his employer as a clipper and coiner of false mint. Maugey strongly refuted the accusations but was adjudged guilty and hanged at York in 1696. When his house was being demolished in 1832 two small pairs of clipping shears and an Elizabethan shilling still waiting to be clipped were found hidden within a secret chamber in the roof.

Stubborn to the End

John Defreni aged 83, once a respected Leeds merchant, was found dead in 1856 at the Infirmary of the Queen's Bench Prison. Defreni had spent *forty-three years* confined to a Leeds prison because he refused to answer questions regarding a commission of bankruptcy taken out against him!

Old Dungeon

The Dungeon was a small building constructed from sturdy stone which stood in solitary isolation in the White Hill area of Oakworth. It is believed to have housed Oakworth poachers.

A Parish Constable's Lot

The old parish constable nominated by churchwardens was made redundant by the County Police Act implemented in 1839. Part of the new constable's duty was to inform the justice of the peace of all unlawful acts known to him within the parish. The law stated that, 'If a felon resists or flies and cannot otherwise be taken, the constable or any person assisting him, and who saw the felony committed, is justified in killing him...Constables are to compel persons inflicted with the plague to keep to their houses...Constables are, under the magistrate's warrant, to levy the penalty of 3s. 4d (16p) on all persons who exercise unlawful games and pastimes on the Lord's day.'

Special Parish Constable accounts written between 1815 and 1817 for the township of Keighley show that night rounds cost from 1s. 6d (7½p) to 3s (15p). On fair days and festivals this sum rose to 6s. 4d (31p). Constables collected subscriptions for Waterloo and made careful lists of names for the militia, delivering the completed list to Deputy Lieutenants in Craven. The Vagrancy Act kept the constable busy ensuring paupers were removed and escorted back to their place of origin. Numerous entries in the account book show vagrants, beggars, tramps and the like being removed. They were issued with a vagrant or court pass. One such beggar removed by cart from the parish of Keighley was blind Mary Johnson. An entry for 26 May 1815 reveals, 'Relieved a black Man (sick), 2.0; Easter Bland for her trouble, 10. Pd, (paid) Doctor Robinson for examining black man before I removed him. 5.0. Paid for his Carriage to Denholme, 1.0. Constables expenses herein, 1.0.' Making a grand total of 19 shillings (95p).

Early Victorian handcuffs *(The Craven Museum)*

Lock-ups

The old lock-up in Keighley was situated in High Street, not far from the market cross. Used during the 1700s, traces of holding chains in a cellar were said to be still visible in the middle of this century. An old constable's account book records a total of £4. 12s. 11d (£4 67½p) was spent on materials such as wood and lead for the prison. A rent totalling £4 14s.6d (£4 72½p) was paid to the landlord of the prison, a Mr John Carrodus, between 1815 and 1817. It was often the case in the early days of policing that felons were restrained by the use of chains and handcuffs in private houses. For example, one Harry Fortune was paid a handsome sum for 'keeping care of a suspicious person...'

Prisoner's Account

Benjamin (Codger) Laycock lived in a thatched cottage at Myrtle Place, Bingley, close to the old parish lock-up. He wrote a booklet in April 1856 entitled *Life and Sufferings, Persecution & Punishments* in which he describes his own experience of Keighley jail and how he came to be there. 'A wretch named Isaac Turner attempted to entrap me by selling me a scrap of lead. Accordingly, on 21st May, (1855) between seven and eight o'clock in the morning this fellow came to our house, and enquired of my mother if a young man named Benjamin Laycock, a broker, pot-hawker, &c., did not live thereabouts. My mother called me downstairs, when he informed me that his master had a quantity of old lead to sell, and that if I would only go to Keighley on the Thursday, and call at his house, which was the second door through a throughway in East Row, I should find him. I did not go, but on Thursday night, about nine o'clock, he attended again with a small bundle, and enquired of me again. I happened to be out, and my mother wanted to know if she would not do. "No," was the reply, nobody but me would do; but as he had a little business to do in town he would call again. He attended again about half-past nine with the bundle containing the small quantity of lead, for which he agreed to take a shilling, and I bought it at that price. Within about three minutes after, the three (Keighley constables) came into the house, enquiring if I had been buying lead. I said at once that I had, and that if they would give me a bit of time. I could overtake the man who sold it to me. Of course they would not allow this, and seemed so overjoyed with their success that they immediately commenced hurrying me out of the house. I had been out all day with my horse and cart and, being hungry and tired, begged for a few minutes to get something to eat, but was denied even this humble request on the plea that it was train time and they wanted to be back at Keighley.'

For his part in entrapping Laycock, Isaac Turner received a meal of ale, bread and cheese at the Brown Cow Inn, Bingley (the original Brown Cow dated back to the time of Cromwell, had acted as Bingley Assizes and even became the headquarters of Bingley Chartist Movement!) 'I was thereupon dragged out of the house like a dog, hurried to Bingley Station, and conveyed to Keighley with as much joy as if they had caught some enormous criminal, or taken a whole Russian army prisoners. On arriving at Keighley the whole body of night-watchmen were waiting to see me brought in, and joined in a general horse-laugh, shouting out "Ben, lad, what's up now?" they made a kind of idle rogue's march, and escorted me to their lock-up, where I was thrust into the darkest cell, the whole body of idlers singing in chorus:

'Here we go where all sorts go;
Fal de rol de rido.'

I was carefully searched, and my knife taken from me, which was kept by them, left without a bite to eat, and nearly suffocated for want of air. Next day I was examined before two magistrates, one of them is a very cunning man. I wanted them to allow me to bring my witnesses, but they said they could not waste their time in allowing this, and I was committed on the evidence of Cheesey and Curseschaw to take my trial at Skipton sessions. I remained in Wakefield thirty-nine days awaiting my trial. At Skipton sessions I told my tale honestly, and how I had been entrapped, and that I had three witnesses in the house at the time I had bought the lead who could prove what I had said. My opponents were brought separately against me, and Cheesey swore that when they found the lead there was no person in the house. Curseschaw on the contrary swore there were three young men in the house, which contradiction broke down their evidence and caused my acquittal.'

Laycock had endured eight trials between 14 October 1854 and 24 May 1855, and was even committed to walk the treadmill at Wakefield prison. He had suffered the stocks in Keighley churchyard five times. Innocent of all charges, Laycock said of his mother that she, 'almost lost her sight by crying and fretting while I have been in prison.' It took a Bradford policeman, Mr John Shuttleworth, to bring Isaac Turner (alias Judas) to justice for his part in Ben Laycock's false arrest. Amongst other jobs Ben hawked oranges and fish and 'many a joke was cracked as to whether his herrings were mummies from Egypt or the genuine articles'. Poor Ben did indeed suffer trials and tribulations in his blighted lifetime. Fresh out of Wakefield jail he saw his poor horse sprawled out on Druids' Altar Road. The animal had been stoned by some vindictive person and died. Once again Ben found himself before the magistrate who wrongly charged him with beating the horse to death, thus ensuring a further month in prison.

Bingley's Prison Cells

Joe Green, pinder and bellman of Illingworth Yard, Bingley was also the village constable. Until 1857 he had a large iron ring attached to the mantelpiece in his cosy parlour where he shackled degenerates until they could be removed to Bingley lock-up (incorporated into the local workhouse during 1821). Mrs Green, a kindly soul, would listen to many tales of woe and often fed the criminal with her tasty cakes and pies.

A new courthouse was erected in Myrtle Place in 1860 after the old whitewashed workhouse—known in 1726 as the Tavern—with its dank prison holes was razed to the ground. The new courthouse was used until 1927.

Haworth Jail and Stocks

Drunks, petty criminals and murderers were taken to 29 North Street, Haworth and led though an arched doorway at the side of a stone building. The small jail lodged the felon until he or she could be conveyed elsewhere. A Haworth map of 1853 marks the exact site of the little prison. Later the lock-up was used as a fire station. Haworth Council sold the building in 1932, after which it was converted into a shop. The old stocks can today be found set in time-honoured fashion between the Black Bull Inn and the church steps.

Old Bradford Prisons

Throughout the reign of Henry VII, the Abbot of Kirkstall presided over affairs at the Hall of Pleas. Access to the court was by way of the Strait in Kirkgate. It was set above Old Chatterton's Shop at the bottom end of Westgate and the downstairs portion was in constant use as a tollbooth and prison. During the process of re-roofing it was noted that the tiles were held in place with sheepshanks. Rogues and vagabonds did not have far to travel if judged guilty by the Abbot. The prison lay under the tollbooth and was divided into two cells, each no more than 3 metres wide. On one side lodged male prisoners; the other side contained female felons. A further dungeon below this level teemed with vermin. Preacher John Nelson, the last person to tenant this disgusting hole, said about his incarceration here in 1744, 'it stank worse than a hog sty'.

In September 1985 the long-defunct courthouse became an inn, oddly christened the Ram's Revenge. The old dungeons and cellars beneath are intact and it is said that secret tunnels run from here to various parts of the city. The building had previously been The Grosvenor and then a Berni Inn. One of the previous tenants opened the dungeons and made the area into a cellar bar with the added attraction of a real prison cell. However, this novel scheme was abandoned when several customers complained of an uneasy atmosphere in the place. One customer patiently waited to be served by a phantom barman. Another described seeing a man dressed in tight-fitting grey trousers, long black boots, a white frilled shirt and a grey cloak hovering close to the bar before vanishing before her eyes! The inn at Upper Millergate is now the pub known as the Fates & Firkin.

The new town prison was at Sun-bridge (formally Ive-Bridge) and was described in 1868 as 'a low two-storied erection, placed there apparently after that in Ivegate had been disused; and somewhere here, it may be remarked, there existed formerly the Chapel of St Syth (Sitha)'.

It was dark, cold and filthy. A prisoner's misery was completed by water running down the walls because the building backed onto the beck. Public licensee Johnny Gibson was made deputy constable and as such he was in charge of the prison. His two assistants were his sons, Jimmy and Robbie Gibson. One morning a fight broke out in the White Lion Yard. Jim's wife dashed out holding her husband's staff aloft and yelled to the troublemakers, 'I charge ye all i' ahr Jim's name, for he's drunken in bed!'

Bradford debtors' jail was nicknamed Will Lee Hoil after Constable William Lee. Debtors were taken before the Hell-fire Court to receive their sentence. When they were admitted to the four-roomed prison a ditty was recited to encourage them to stump up 2s.6d (12½p) as garnish brass. This was used to buy alcohol for the inmates.

'Welcome, welcome, brother debtor,
To this poor but merry place,
Where no "bailiff", "bum", or "sotter"
Dares to show his frightful face.
But, kind sir, as you're a stranger,
Down your garnish you must lay,
Or your coat will be in danger.
You must either strip or pay.

Will Lee Hoil was closed in 1844 and the inmates set free.

Shipley Lock-up

Built in 1593, the oldest house – Shipley Hall or Low Hall – in Shipley had a stone in the yard inscribed with the words, 'The site of this lock-up was given by William, Lord Oxmantown, Lord of the Manor of Shipley, &c. in 1839.' The prison cell was in Chapel Lane but was demolished to make way for street improvements during the erection of the West Riding Police Office.

Leeds Highwaymen

Three highwaymen were tried at York for attempted robbery on the highway at Leeds on 17 November 1819. The victim was James Nicholson. James Grey, Ben Taylor and Will Shiers all pleaded not guilty to the charge. Mr Nicholson offered the following account to the court.

'I had been dining with Mr Pullan, of Leeds, on Wednesday...and set off for my return to Chapeltown, where I reside, about eight o'clock in the evening: I was about half a mile from Sheepscar turnpike, when I met three men, one of them on foot, and the other two mounted on one horse. The man on foot wished me "good night"; I returned his salutation and went on. I had proceeded about thirty metres when I heard a footstep: I turned, and saw a man close to me: it was dark, and I saw but distinctly; he said something, concluding with "I will blow your brains out." I struck him immediately with a stick, which Mr Pullan had lent me. I struck the man down. Another came up and said, "let him go," but I still held the man who had first attacked me. The second man then went to the roadside and took up a large stone and threw it at me; he subsequently threw another, a smaller one. I continued to hold the first man. The second man then produced a pistol and fired at me, but it flashed in the pan. He then rushed in, but I held the first man with one hand, and struck at the second with my stick. The man whom I held called out "Bill, why dost not thou come on." A third man appeared (Shiers), and joined in the attack. I fought as long as I could, but they got me down and rifled my pockets. They took my watch and some patterns of scarlet cloth. I cried out "Murder," and one of them put his hand over my mouth. When they had got my watch, they gave me two or three blows on the head with a stick, and then left me. I felt very weak, but got up, and seeing a cottage near, I was going towards it, when a man came up and said someone was coming with a light. I had lost my hat and stick Mr Pullan had lent me in the scuffle: I found my hat and proceeded towards the turnpike, where I found the prisoner Taylor in custody. I went to Leeds in a coach, which passed soon after. I was very ill and confined to my bed for five weeks, and to my house for six weeks afterwards.' The culprits remained silent as the judge delivered a sentence of death on each of them. Shiers' and Taylor's sentences were reduced to transportation for life; Grey's to a long term of imprisonment.

Halifax Gibbet

'I couldn't advise the notorious Whitechapel 'Jack' to pay Halifax a visit.'
The Yorkshireman, 1889

Bentley provides this description of a gibbet and its operation. 'A guillotine worked by means of an engine called a gibbet which was raised upon a platform four feet high, and thirteen feet square, faced on every side with stone, and ascended by a flight of steps. In the middle of this platform were placed two upright pieces of timber, fifteen feet high, joined at the top by a traverse beam.

Within these were a square block of wood, four and a half feet long, which moved up and down by means of grooves made for that purpose; to the lower part of this sliding block was fastened an iron axe...The (hasty) axe was drawn up to the top by a cord and pulley. At the end of the cord was a pin, which, being fixed to the block, kept it suspended till the moment of execution...'

Town bailiffs escorted the condemned prisoner to the scaffold. As the victim awaited his end a minister of his own choosing prayed for his soul while a musician piped the Fourth Psalm ('I will lay me down in peace and sleep') until the blade fell.

Prototype

The gibbet is thought to be the prototype of the French guillotine. Earl Morton, when passing through the town, saw an execution in progress. Impressed by the contraption the Earl ordered an exact copy to be made for Scotland. The Scots fondly named her *The Maiden*. Ironically, Morton fell foul of the maid's charms and was himself beheaded on 3 June 1581. Naples and Germany also had their own versions of the gibbet.

Off With His Head!

'At Halifax the law so sharp doth deale,
That whose more than thirteenpence doth steale,
They have a jyn that wondrous quick and well
Sends thieves all headless into heaven and hell.'
Taylor, The Water Poet

A countrywoman on her way to the market place passed by the gibbet just as a thief was about to be executed. 'The axe chopped his neck through with such force that the head jumped into one of her hampers.' Another version of this tale says the teeth seized her apron 'and there stuck for some time'.

Hope of Freedom

If a felon could escape his captors before the axe fell he was declared a free man. The law stated that 'if he escaped out of the liberty, even after condemnation, he could not be brought back to be executed; but if ever he returned into it again, and was taken, he was sure to suffer; as was the case with one John Lacy, who, after his escape, lived seven years out of the liberty, but, returning, was beheaded on his former verdict, 1625AD. This man was not so wise as Dennis or Dinnis, who, having been condemned to die, escaped out of the liberty on the day destined for his execution (which might be done by running five hundred yards) and never returned again.'

Turncoats

Two Parliamentary soldiers were hanged at night on 4 January 1644 on roughly made gallows hastily erected near the gibbet by Sir Francis Mackworth's men. They had joined the king's army at Heptonstall – the Royalists' last stand.

Final Victims

Dr Samuel Midgley wrote *Halifax and its Gibbet Law placed in a True Light* in 1708. It was an account of the last executions. He writes that on the last day of April 1650 a jury condemned Abraham Wilkinson and Anthony Mitchell to suffer death at the Halifax gibbet.

Gibbet Hill

An early deed of 1613 refers to the Halifax gibbet standing at a place commonly known as The Green, Halifax, on the west side of the town. It was to the right of Gibbet Lane where a replica of the gibbet can be seen today. The *Halifax Guardian* of the 15 June 1839 revealed its later history. 'The remains of the Gibbet on land lately belonging to a Mr Bates was unearthed when workmen employed removing the rubbish from Gibbet Hill, have this week succeeded in uncovering the remains of an ancient gibbet. When the usage of the gibbet had ceased, the ground upon which it had stood appears to have served as a receptacle for the refuse of the town for the space of at least a hundred years, and the heap of rubbish thus formed became so large as to acquire the name of Gibbet Hill. The very existence of the platform of the gibbet was nearly forgotten, and the received opinion was that it stood *upon* a hill, when in reality it stood under it, on level with the present road.'

When it was revealed the gibbet attracted many curious sightseers. Two headless male skeletons were unearthed at the site. Two heads later discovered under Bates's warehouse were thought to have been the remains of Wilkinson and Mitchell.

The hasty axe can been seen at the Calderdale Industrial Museum, Halifax.

The Thieves' Litany

'There is a Proverbe, and a Prayer withall,
That we may not to three strange places fall;
From Hull, from Halifax, from Hell, 'tis thus,
From all these three, Good Lord, deliver us.
This praying Proverbe'e meaning to set downe,
Men doe not wish deliverance from the Towne;
The Towne's named Kingston, Hull's the furious river;
And from Hull's dangers I say, Lord deliver.
At Halifax, the law soe sharpe doth deale,
That whoso more than thirteen pence doth steale;
They have a Tyn that wondrous quick, and well,
Sends thieves all headless unto Heav'n or Hell.
From Hell, each man says Lord deliver me,
Because from Hell can noe Redemption be.
Man may escape from Hull and Halifax,
But sure in Hell there is a heavier taxe:
Let each one for themselves in this agree,
And pray – from Hell, Good Lord, deliver me.

Chapter 10

A Medley of Curiosities

''Tis well to walk with cheerful heart, Wherever our fortunes call.'
J. Foster

Wolves in Craven

The last wolf was brought down in Craven during 1306. A hunt organised by the Duke of Lancaster felled the animal at a place named John o' Gaunt, where a public house of the same name was erected at a later date. The ground where the wolf was killed lay three miles outside Leeds on the Pontefract road.

Wall Inscription

The Golden Fleece, situated at the corner of Cook-lane and Low Street, Keighley, was erected by Robert Parker, a curio collector who occupied Marley Hall. Lord George Cavendish, the proprietor of the Devonshire Arms, Church Green, purchased the inn from the Parker family. An inscription on one of the walls bore the date 1697 and the initials R.P. A further inscription read 'Olim. Parkinson, Hodie Parker, Nuper, Slater and Cras, nescio'. Translated this means 'Parkinson formerly, and Slater lately, lived here; Parker lives here today, but who will live here tomorrow I know not'. Another tablet set in an upper portion of a wall bore the legend 'C.G. 151 33, 34, 1450'. A sun-dial dated 1782 led some to believe its date corresponded with that of the erection of the inn. A Marks and Spencer shop now stands on the site.

Heave-ho!

Isabella Cryer, a native of Leeds, died suddenly in 1775, aged forty-one years. She weighed forty stones and measured three metres around her middle. It took the efforts of ten men to carry her coffin to the grave.

Sinking Feeling

When sinking a new pit in Bradford in January 1827 workmen were surprised to discover a human skeleton buried 20 metres down. Why or how the skeleton came to be there remains a mystery.

Grave Shortage

Medical students were expected to have attended more than two dissections before their examinations. Legal channels of obtaining corpses were either by execution of wills or by execution of murderers. Although these cadavers were gratefully received there were problems. Firstly, corpses were in short supply; secondly, those that were available were often damaged in some way or in an advanced state of decay causing some limitation to the student's exploration of anatomy. News of the shortage soon reached the ears of those out to make easy money. Offering their own bodies for cash in advance of their deaths, safe in the knowledge that relatives were under no obligation to hand over the corpse, was the most innocent occupation of the resurrectionists.

Snatching!

Early expansion of the body-snatching business prompted the following observation from anatomist Sir Asley Cooper regarding Yorkshire and other counties prior to the 1800s. Resurrectionists were to secretly supply the hospitals with human bodies for dissection. 'All sorts of expedients were adopted to obtain bodies, which were sold a price of 16 guineas each; but a check was in some measure put to the trade by a startling disclosure this year, (1828) which showed that a regular system of murder had been going on for some time, in order to supply subjects for the dissecting rooms.' Should the snatcher be arrested, fines and or compensation for loss of liberty were usually paid surreptitiously by the surgeons who ordered the bodies. One man caught stealing cadavers from a churchyard in 1784 was whipped through the streets for his pains. The diary of Sir Asley Cooper reveals he himself paid for, 'Four subjects, two male and two female (by Murphy) twelve guineas each, £50 8s 0d. January 29th, 1828. Paid Mr -, to Mr – half the expenses for bailing Vaughan, and going down, £14 7s 0d. May 6th. Paid Vaughan's wife 6s. May 29th. Paid Vaughan for 26 weeks confinement, at 10s. per week.'

Unofficial Exhumations

Corpses were retrieved by means of a specially made contraption which prised the coffin lid upwards, allowing snatchers to easily remove the corpse from a freshly dug grave. This created jealous competition amongst resurrectionists. Burke and Hare were the most infamous– 'Burkers' admitted to committing fifteen murders. The devilish pair would generally lure their prey with alcohol and then suffocate them.

Corpses Reprieved

Thomas Daniel was buried at St John's churchyard in Leeds on New Year's Day 1826 after being killed by a blast from a shotgun. As resurrectionist activity was rife in the area Daniel's son dug down to check the contents of the coffin a few days after interment. He found only the grave clothes so called for the police. The body was intercepted at Newcastle. It was labelled '*For the attention of Mr Simpson, Surgeon's Square, Edinburgh*'. Daniel identified the body of his father by 'various well-known marks imprinted upon it with gunpowder'. The corpse had had an uneventful journey and was restored intact to its grave. A Leeds boxmaker proved to be the culprit and received a six-month prison sentence at York.

On New Year's Eve 1828 grieving parents Mr and Mrs Heeson visited the grave of their young child in Whitkirk. They were devastated to find the small shroud and coffin discarded in a lane close to the graveyard. The remains of their infant were never recovered. Bodysnatcher George Cox was arrested and convicted for this crime despite claiming that a stranger of the Jewish faith had commissioned him to make a large box and deliver it to a Leeds coach office. He was imprisoned at York Castle for the term of six months. Fifteen-year-old Martha Oddy was taken from her grave in Armley churchyard Leeds in 1826 and travelled as far as Edinburgh before her body was intercepted. Her parents had been keeping a vigil at the graveside and had pursued the resurrectionists. Of the three men originally charged, only Michael Armstrong received a six-month sentence at Leeds Sessions.

A gruesome discovery of a stolen corpse was made on the Courier coach that stopped at the Rose and Crown Inn, Leeds on its journey northwards. The body was found to be that of Robert Hudson who committed suicide at East Ardsley in 1831. At the trial a thief by the name of Teale turned King's evidence against his fellow robbers: John Craig Hodgson, John Crabtree Pickering, William Henry Bradley, William Germain and James Norman, all of Leeds. The men were charged with 'unlawfully digging up and disinterring from out of a grave in a church yard at East Ardsley, the body of Robert Hudson.' Only Pickering walked away a free man.

The Duke of Leeds coach delivered a long wooden box from Manchester to the Bull and Mouth Hotel, Leeds. Inside were the corpses of a female and a child. It was addressed '*To the Revd Geneste, Hull'*, and carried the instruction 'to be left until called for. Glass, and keep this side up, Nov.11th'.

In 1830 Sarah Gomersal's stiffened body was slid from its coffin on a dark winter's night in Calverley churchyard. This time the snatchers were caught in the act.

Dyed Twice

Thomas Rothery died accidentally after falling into a boiling dye pan on premises belonging to Messrs. Scarth & Sons, Leeds. His interment took place at the Episcopal Chapel at Wortley on Sunday, 5 June 1831. He remained in his coffin at the chapel for only a few days for the following Thursday his body was taken by bodysnatchers. John Hodgson, clerk to Mr Gaunt a Leeds solicitor and a gentleman of some respectability was arrested for the theft of Rothery's easily identifiable corpse after it was found hidden at his employer's offices. On 4 July, after four hours' deliberation, Hodgson was sentenced at Leeds. He admitted to being, 'connected with a medical man in the taking of the body, and it was for the purpose of mutually dissecting it.' He steadfastly refused to give the name of the doctor for fear of ruining his career. He received a six-week prison sentence. A fine of £100 was levied and he was ordered to keep the peace for two years.

Charlotte Brontë was clearly aware of the work of the resurrectionists when she wrote of the artful snatcher troubling her imaginary Glasstown Township. In 1830 she penned a vivid account of body snatching when she wrote of resurrectionists caught in the act of digging up bodies ordered by an anatomical group. The gang intended to substitute library books for the corpses.

Unlucky Ben Heaton

Ben Heaton died at his home at Delph Hill, Baildon from a sudden mysterious illness. Villagers thought he had fallen victim to a local witch living at Ellison Fold. Misfortunes suffered by locals were always accredited to the old woman. Having odd eyes, 'one yoller and t'other green,' her physical appearance did much to enhance her reputation. Poachers meeting her as they set out would return home, believing she had 'drained their luck'. Villagers shunned her for her links with the Devil.

The night of Ben Heaton's funeral, two Baildon resurrectionists worked quickly and quietly in the graveyard. The loose earth of Heaton's newly dug grave yielded easily to their spades and the pair grasped Heaton's corpse and departed. On nearing Kefflicks they were annoyed to see a lantern swinging back and forth to the beat of an unsuspecting villager's footfall. Discerning the owner of the lantern to be the midwife abroad on call, they kicked out the poor woman's light to avoid detection then hid themselves and their ghastly burden in the old woolcombers' wash place adjacent to the Primitive Methodist Chapel. In the scuffle Heaton's knitted mortuary cap accidentally fell to the ground. On reaching their destination – a house at the east of Towngate – they met with their sponsor's agent, a local schoolmaster. He took the body and gave it to two Bradford surgeons who were waiting to dissect the corpse in another room. The anatomical exploration over, the grave robbers hastily bundled the badly mutilated corpse into a sheet and carried it back to the churchyard where it was re-buried. In their haste they forgot Ben Heaton's head. The next day the mortuary cap was discovered by its creator. She returned to the village and shared her fears that Ben Heaton had escaped his grave by devilish means.

Towards evening, above the jolly festivities of the village games in progress at the rear of the Angel Inn, a loud piercing scream reached the ears of village folk. Ben Heaton's head, which had been 'hidden inside a cupboard near the fireplace of the old house', was held aloft by its finder. In the last century the dissection room of the old Towngate house was named 'Ben Heaton's 'oil' by the owners.

Protection Beyond the Grave

Grave Clubs were brought into existence to protect the dead from the living. Vigilantes and the parish beadles took up posts in wooden watcher shelters erected next to newly dug graves. Foundries produced iron coffins with steel locks in which to lay the privileged. Thwarting most of the bereaved's efforts, the resurrection men continued to harvest their gruesome crop. Grave Clubs continued to collect subscriptions until Parliament passed the Anatomy Act in 1832. This Act provided new channels with which to supply the surgeon's knife.

Signed in Blood

A piece of tattered paper was picked out of a small crevice of a defunct stone quarry at Armley, Leeds owned by Benjamin Gott. On it were written the words,

'Rambling in pleasure
Beauty will decay,
Life will not last forever
So I'll go my own way.
The first opportunity will the above be put into execution. Witness my hand, this 16th day of September 1833, in my own blood. Signed ABRAHAM HUTCHINSON.'

It is not recorded whether Hutchinson kept his promise or not.

Hark!

Bell ringers at Wakefield in 1891 were having such a good time they *forgot* to ring out the old and ring in the new year. Picture if you will the consternation of those waiting for the bells to toll the midnight hour that never came.

Full Moon

Cowling folk once tried to rake the full moon out of a dam!

'I like to see thy quaint owd face
Lewk softly daan on me,
E'en though I ne'er could find thy rise
Nor catch thy watchful e'e'

Joseph Eccles, Halifax.

Cannon Balls

Workmen taking down the old building next to the Union Inn, Ivegate found a cannon ball wedged under the roof. Historians believed the cannon ball to have been used by the Earl of Newcastle's men during the Siege of Bradford in 1642.

In 1853 about sixty 17th-century cannon balls were picked from ground near Adwalton Common near Bradford by workers who were preparing a new road for Messrs. Terry and Harrison.

Petrified Relicts

A bole of a tree 4 metres long was found during the winter of 1793. It was lodged beneath solid rock at a quarry in Coulton near Leeds. A number of fossil trees embedded

Fossilised tree dug from beneath St John's Market and now in the grounds of Cartwright Hall, Bradford

in a solid block of stone came to light when workmen at Morley Quarry dug 8 metres below the surface in 1824. They also picked up eight or so fossilised acorn nuts.

Mayhall's Annals Vol 2 records that in June 1836, '...workmen employed by Coppy Quarry, (where St John's Market now stands) situated almost in the centre of the town of Bradford, belonging to Messrs. Cousin and Thackray, struck on a fossil tree. It was embedded in sandstone about thirty feet below the earth. One side of it had been laid bare, and was visible from the top of the pit. The upper part of the stem and branches were wanting, but the trunk and roots were in a very perfect state: there was also what seemed to be one of the loose branches. The diameter of the trunk was about four feet; the roots ran out to a great length, and were of proportionate thickness. The appearance to the eye was of wood – a knotted tree with rough bark; but touch destroyed the illusion. It was as heavy as stone, and although when scraped it presented still the grain of wood, it showed by its hardness, grittiness, and sparkling crystals, the metamorphosis it had undergone. Part of the surface was covered with a black substance, which appeared to be of the nature of coal, and to have been formed by the decomposition of the bark.' The fossilised tree from Coppy Quarry can be seen in the grounds of Cartright Hall, Lister Park, Bradford.

At Fall Top, Clayton, not far from Thornton Vale, contractors Messrs. Murgatroyd found a fossilised tree embedded below the coal measures in a soft, sandy shale known as 'yellow loam'. Angus Holden offered the firm £600 for the petrified relict. A conifer was found at Ilkley in a quarry near to the Cow and Calf Rocks. When the conifer tree was first discovered its bark was intact but relic hunters chipped it away.

Bonfire Battle

A huge felled tree donated by Colonel Tempest to the boys of Tong, Bradford for the Guy Fawkes celebrations was stolen by the 'wicked boys of Westgate Hill. The Tong lads hearing of the theft sallied out in great force. A terrible fight ensued at Westgate Hill, between the parties, in which great injury was done to divers heads.' The victorious Tong side carried their tree back to their bonfire and a peal of church bells from Tong Church hailed the conquering heroes.

Cow Eats Plans

The *Keighley News* reported a very curious affair in the 1860s. 'A strange incident has occurred at Haworth Railway, now in the course of construction between Keighley and Haworth. It appears that last week the engineers in connection with the above line were doing their necessary business with their plans and levels, which they left two hundred yards behind them on the ground. The level 'stood very bold on three legs, and in their absence a cow, the property of Messrs. Sugden, manufacturers, went up to it, and, thrusting her horns amongst the legs of the level, tossed it up above her head, and smashed it into pieces. Not content with this, the animal ate or swallowed the whole of the plans belonging to the line-a thing which she ought not to have done, for the Haworthites have been planning for this railway for fifteen years.' The first sod was ceremoniously cut on Shrove Tuesday 1864.

Contaminated Water

The *Keighley News* of 26 April 1899 reported on, 'A dispute about bad smells at Council meeting.' Haworth's Main Street then had many open drains. A resident living next door to a milk kitchen complained that her guests often commented on 'a funny deathly smell!' Another told of a visitor overcome by the putrid stench from the slop stone drains and asked, 'If someone had died about there for the smell was like death.'

Worried that rotting corpses might contaminate the water supply drawn from close to the churchyard, residents drew their Council's attention to the deadly outbreaks of typhoid fever that had claimed many lives in neighbouring Kildwick.

Klondike Gold

Thomas Wright, born at Shelf, Halifax in 1846, emigrated to Klondike, Canada in his middle years. He was the owner of a general store in Dawson City in 1902 and made a living supplying prospectors with basic provisions. Writing to his sister Emma, back home in Bradford, he gave no clue of his intention to sell up and move on to Alaska. He promised her some trinkets and souvenirs by the next post and assured her all was well with him. Taking leave of Dawson City, Wright was not seen alive again; he was found dead at the roadside before he reached Alaska. Some concluded that he had perished in adverse weather conditions whilst others argued that Wright had been murdered for his money.

Thomas Wright's mother, (née Thomas of Haworth) had been a great childhood friend of the Brontë girls. She had been given an autograph book containing verses written by the Brontës, thought to have still been in her possession at her death.

Wedding Hoax

This story appeared in *Mayhall's Annals Vol. 1* on 14 September 1852. 'A most successful matrimonial hoax was played off at the Bull and Mouth Hotel, Leeds, upon a Mr Winter, who had shortly before advertised for a wife in the London papers. One or two wags thinking to have a joke at the expense of the advertiser forwarded to his published address a delicate and perfumed *billet doux,* purporting to have been written by a Miss Bailey. Mr Winter in the simplicity of his heart replied, Miss Bailey answered, and thus a correspondence satisfactory to both parties resulted eventually in a meeting on the 14th of September, at the hotel above mentioned, when Miss Bailey would explain her worldly affairs more fully, and introduce Mr Winter to her relatives. A fair young gentleman whose face was not encumbered with hirsute superfluities was dressed for the occasion, and acted the part of Miss Bailey with admirable tact. Mr Winter was true to his appointment, and was ushered into the room to Miss Bailey. After a while, and when matters had in some measure being satisfactorily arranged, Miss Bailey had her relatives introduced; first came her affectionate brother, then followed in rapid succession her uncles, cousins, and all her other male relatives. With the first half dozen the lover shook hands with vigorous cordiality; but when they poured upon him in one unbroken tide, he found that he was hoaxed to his heart's content. His only means of escape from Miss Bailey's very many relatives was to treat them to wine, &c., which he did with right good nature, after which he was suffered to escape.'

Lions' Tales

Wallace, the Untameable Lion

Wombwell's travelling menagerie had stopped in Leeds when Jonathan Wilson made the fatal mistake of putting his arm through the bars of Wallace the lion's cage. The lion clawed at the man's arm, pulling it with all his kingly might. The badly mauled man was taken to Leeds Infirmary where he died of mortification eight days later. A monologue written by Marriot Edger and made famous by Stanley Holloway has young Albert Ramsbottom swallowed whole by a lion called Wallace.

Man Mauled by Lion

East Parade, Keighley played host to Chipperfield's French Menagerie Circus in 1897. Crowds flocked to the brightly coloured tents to welcome thirty-two-year-old American Franco Montano, a fearless lion tamer. Tumbling clowns, dancing horses and daring trapeze artists entertained the crowd until Montano entered the lion cage. Enthralled, the crowd fell deathly silent as he tackled the notorious lioness that had already attacked two male lions and killed two lion tamers. Montano, who had already been injured by the animal thirteen times, bravely entered the cage with his arm in caught up in a sling. Brought from Hamburg, Germany, the lioness had been judged worthless. Her unpredictable temperament and fearsome reputation had caused Montano's eight predecessors to retreat in fear. The lioness watched Montano circle her cage twice before pouncing. A hot iron was employed to rescue the injured lion tamer. Franco Montano told the *Keighley News* that his first job had been a cabin boy. His father, a trapper, had taken up lion and tiger taming and so had his uncle. Tigers had killed his father and a Derbyshire lion had slaughtered a cousin. Brave Montano signed up as a lion tamer with Barnham in America and finally came to England with Bostock Menagerie.

Dog Attacks Lion

A Yorkshireman once owned a tame lion. One Christmas the lion broke his chain and escaped. He wandered around the town until he met a butcher's bulldog that immediately pounced on him. The howling of the dog and roaring of the lion quickly alerted a motley crew of inhabitants who regarded this as an extra bit of festive fun. They actively encouraged the animals to attack each other! The dog triumphed when he tossed the lion into the air and grasped him by the throat as he landed on his back. At this point someone from the crowd rescued the lion from certain death.

Secret Passage

Keighley's old corn mill was known as King's Mill. The first record of the mill says it predates 1130. Rector Miles Gale's book *Magna Britannia*, printed in 1721, records some of the ancient mill's distribution of revenue. The Rishworth brothers of Ingrow — Henry, Israel and Clapham ran the mill between 1853 and 1898.

An underground passage beginning at the foot of an ancient stairwell ran from under the oldest part of the building. Snaking beneath Bridge Street to the opposite side of Halifax Road, it opened out on Old Bridge Street, Damside. From the arched cellar here the mill's extension could be accessed from under Halifax Road.

Once run by an eccentric Victorian landlord, Mr Harry Tap, the Royal Oak (previously named the Black Bull) situated at the rear of the mill was discovered to have a secret double cellar beneath the beer cellar. The reason for the double cellar remains an unsolved mystery. The Royal Oak closed its doors in 1869.

Anyone for Turtle Soup?

The first mayoral ball in Keighley was held in March 1883. A new coat-of-arms and crest were embossed on invitation cards. A grand banquet for 'the elite of Keighley' was held at the end of the council's financial year at the Devonshire Hotel on Church Green. A large turtle was sent live from London by train to be included in the soup. This was a rare delicacy by the standards of London and no local butcher could be found familiar with the art of turtle slaughtering. The poor thing was finally killed and made into soup but many of the elite found they could not stomach the dainty. The soup was distributed amongst the poor of the parish and lent an exotic flavour to their menu. The turtle shell was painted with the arms of the Cavendish family and those of the proprietor of the Devonshire Hotel, Mr Tom Ecroyd. It hung on a wall at the Devonshire for some time but was eventually donated to Keighley Museum.

Devil visits Wilsden

Interest in unclaimed sums of money set aside by the parish for 'boggart catching' was revived when the *Wilsden Almanac* of 1890 announced a visit by his 'Satanic Majesty'. He was seen in the midst of a blue fire on Wilsden Hill, causing frightened inhabitants to run for their lives. On further investigation by the would-be bounty hunters this proved to nothing more than a practical joke! Parish cash was set aside at Yeadon for anyone brave enough to catch a boggart.

Leeds Invasion

Towards the end of September 1855 residents between Leeds and Headingley suffered a furious attack of thousands of black-winged aphids. Those unfortunate enough to have been outside at the time of the invasion found their mouths and noses crammed with insects – finally covering them so completely that no part of their clothing could be discerned.

Hypnotic Performance

In 1927 James Elston, a farm labourer, attended hypnotist Professor Morritt's Monday evening performance at Keighley's Municipal Hall. Volunteering to be hypnotised on stage he was soon in a deep trance. Exhibited in this state as 'the living dead', he was transferred to a coffin. Left that night in the casket at the Municipal Hall, Elston's 'body was retrieved for the following nights performance.' As the audience thrilled to the antics of the *living corpse* a notice was served on Morritt by Keighley's

Education Committee. Morritt was ordered to remove Elston from the premises overnight or the Council would close the show. The *Keighley News* reported, 'James Elston, looking like death, was laid in a casket covered with flimsy draperies, and that at one time he was in danger of being put outside in the street in what was said to be a totally helpless condition.' Morritt rented a garage near the hall for a few nights and installed his assistant and the entranced Elston. The assistant welcomed incredulous visitors to the garage during most of Wednesday. On Thursday night James Elston, still mesmerised, was immersed in a tank of water then wheeled before a cheering audience. After this Elston underwent preparation for the grand finale. In full view of more than one thousand cheering people on Friday night, Elston was at last awoken from his trance. Thinking it was still Monday he stepped down from the stage and took his seat in the audience.

Bogus Marriage

As the leaves changed their livery to welcome the first days of autumn 1863 a Cullingworth couple – a widow aged forty-three and her fiancé aged sixty-nine – set off in good time to tie the knot. 'The old gentleman appeared at the bride's residence dressed in his best bib and tucker and was glad to find his true love in the same mind as he had left her the previous night. After taking breakfast together they proceeded to the Registry Officer at Keighley, where the marriage knot was tied for better or worse. They then returned home where a party of young men readily received them with three hearty cheers. The bridegroom exclaimed at the top of voice that he had made the best bargain that morning "'at he'd iver made i' all his life" adding, "An' I'me noan baan to dee i't shell yet; here's five shillings for ye lads an' go to Harries at Tap an' drink it."

In fact, having arranged the marriage in the wrong parish the couple had returned as they left – unwed. Swearing the witnesses to secrecy, the wedding party celebrated the non-event with their unsuspecting guests at the reception.

Three weeks later someone tipped off the Keighley News. 'When t' couple went t't registering office at Keighley at time at 'at I tell on, Charley 'at weds 'em for Bingley parish hed goan aat at t' office. When they gat thear, Spencer 'at weds 'em for Keighley were int' office, but he said he couldn't wed 'em becos they com aat o' Bingley parish. He said they mud sit 'em daan a bit; Charley wad happan be comin' in in a bit; yo see old Jim hadn't teld 'at they wer gaing that morning to t' office to be wed, soa, they stopt wae 12 o' clock, but Charley didn't mack his appearance. Spencer said they mud as weel goa, for it ed sttrucken 12'o clock and they couldn't be wed that day. When they hed geeten aat o' t 'door Jim said to his intended "Tha's noa cashan to be uneasy. I'll niver turn mi back o' thee; I'll goa daun to Bingley a Monday an' tell Charley to cum up at Tuesday in t'office en weel be wed. When we get to Hainerth I'll give 'em five shillings to drink. Tha'll niver know but we geten wed." So Charley cum up to office to Keighley at Tuesday, but Jim en his spouse nivver made their appearance soa Charley letten cat aat o' barrel an teld 'at they warent wed. I thout I wad write ye another bit to let ye know 'at it wasn't my fault; it wer old Jim's; he sudant a' said they wer wed when they warant, so I think when public gets to see this they wilant blame me.'

Double-Dealing

During the closing months of 1899 the *Keighley News* published a warning from the Chairman of Keighley Corporation's Finance Committee. He wished to draw 'attention in the public's interest, to the fact that a professional money lender, whose real name was Schaffer, is sending out circulars from an address in Hanover Street, Keighley offering loans in the name of Alfred Lister. As this happens to be the name of our able bodied Borough Treasurer – the keeper of the town's purse – it was feared that some unsuspecting persons might be led into believing that this money lending office had some connection with Mr Lister. Of course, such is not the case, but it is well that the fact should be known, so that no innocent person may be led astray.'

Hog Holes

Once the only route to the South from Keighley was via Hog Holes Lane. This descriptive name was from ancient times and locally shortened to *Og oiles*. On taking up residence there in about 1870 a newcomer thought the name to be vulgar. He was successful in his application to change the name to Glen Lee and a christening party was organised. A few years later Mrs Fred Walker told a reporter from the *Evening Post*, 'It was my father David Fowlds, who really organised the affair...At that time Hog Holes consisted of only two or three cottages and a farm, and it got its name because of the piggeries in the neighbourhood. When my father became the owner of property there the piggeries were done away with, and as he did not like the name Hog Holes he took steps to bring about a change. The old signpost was pulled down and burned, and a new signboard with the name Glen Lee was fixed to a house wall by the bridge over the beck. A Miss Dixon did the "christening". After she had uncovered the new sign she broke against it a bottle of "whisky" – cold tea it really was – then a band from a neighbouring hamlet played a sort of "requiem". People came from all over the district for the ceremony and there was a public tea and dancing.' In reply an old inhabitant had this to say, 'I suppose t' younger end wanted a fine name, and that's why they changed it...Og 'oiles suits me reight so long as they keep out of my pocket. I don't see why they wanted to alter t' ancient name.'

Sundial Cottages

One of three stone cottages standing at Glen Lane and possibly built by the Newton family has a sundial built into the gable end. Roman numerals relate sun time in reverse to a normal timepiece. The name J. Smith and the date 1841 are inscribed upon the face together with a text warning the observer, 'Be ye also ready; for in such an hour as ye think not the Son of Man cometh.' Sundials have been in use since Saxon days. Villagers without clocks thought nothing of popping along to the nearest church to check what time of day it was. Dial House in Laycock, Keighley was recorded in 1906 as having a sundial plate made by Thomas Crow standing on a fine two-step pillar in the garden.

Child's mortuary slab masquerading as a paving stone
outside Haworth's Tourist Information Centre

Haworth's Mortuary?

Beneath the modern interior of Haworth's small but busy Tourist Information Centre is a low-vaulted, whitewashed cellar that is now used to store Christmas decorations and cleaning materials. In earlier days corpses were borne from their deathbeds to the dissecting tables here, carried through a low, side door entrance at Changegate. Just off the mortuary room, to the left-hand side of the building, is a very low, dark passage which leads to a deep well that once provided villagers with drinking water. Outside the tourist centre on Main Street, underneath a 'No Parking Sign', a curious paving stone can be seen. This was once a child's mortuary slab. You can see where a groove has been hollowed out around it, apparently to allow the blood to drain away from the corpse.

Cellar beneath Haworth Tourist Information Centre, thought to have been used as a mortuary.

Quaint Ideas

A pocket watch and fob chain were found lying by the roadside in Haworth. The villagers had never seen a watch before and, hearing it tick, thought it was a dangerous wild animal. After much agitation and consultation they 'killed' it by jumping on it! At Schloes, near Cleakheaton villagers once stoned a watch to death. At Low Moor, Bradford 'Wise Willie' was sent for when a lost watch was discovered ticking. After turning the second hand a few times the soothsayer decreed the timepiece to be 'some mak ora toad!' After further consideration, Willie decided the safe course of action would be to bury it.

They say Haworth folk once 'mucked' the roots of the church steeple hoping to make it grow. When this method failed they applied German yeast.

Brontë Clock Mystery

I am indebted to Mrs Sandy Pimm (née Skerrit) for supplying the following story. 'It was about 1952 that, together with my parents and younger brother Nigel, I moved from Ilkley to live in Guernsey in the Channel Islands. My father found suitable premises and opened a dental practice in St Sampson's; a small harbour port filled with cargo and local fishermen's boats. The premises were quite spacious and for a short time we also lived "above the surgery" until my parents found the house we eventually moved to.

Is this the face of the missing Brontë clock?

'My father, "the Major", was a very popular man and mixed well with the local people. One of these locals was a clock/watch repairer whose shop was close to the new surgery. One day, knowing that we had come to the island from Yorkshire, he said to my father that he had 'an old long case clock that purportedly had originally been in the 'Brontë Parsonage in Yorkshire.' This did not really mean much to the shopkeeper, but he felt my father would like it because he also came from Yorkshire. Of course, my father could never resist anything old and historic so when he saw the name '*Barraclough*' painted on the dial he immediately settled on a purchase price and excitedly waited for the clock to be delivered to the surgery waiting roo, where it proudly stood, ticking the hours away for the whole time that we lived there.

'Finally, when my father's health seriously deteriorated we had to leave the island to get the treatment he needed and, of course, along with everything else the old 'Brontë clock' returned to England. After some years I purchased the clock from my parents due to their lack of space and my 'inherited' love of old furniture. I always took it for granted that it was the clock from the original Brontë home but never really thought of any value to it, either monetary or historic interest. When, sadly, my marriage ended in divorce I left the old clock in the home of my ex-husband on the understanding that I could purchase it back anytime in the future for the sum of £25. Of course, no one ever realises what the future may hold and it is only since I came to live in Yorkshire again that I have now thought how foolish I may have been.

'I have, of course, now visited the Parsonage and note that there is a long case clock by *Barraclough of Haworth* on the stairs. Now, of course, I am very puzzled to know which clock *really* was the one that was in the parsonage when the Brontë family resided there. My old clock, as the photograph shows, was, in my opinion, the correct style and quality and I really will *always* believe that it was the clock that would have heard all the secrets of Brontë family life all those years ago.

'Without searching I do not now even know where my ex-husband is or if he still has my old clock, but I will always feel privileged to have once owned something that used to belong to the Brontës. How did it ever get taken to the Channel Islands – who knows, but as my family proved, items of furniture do travel long distances over the years. There is no reason why the person that purchased the clock from the sale of parsonage contents may not have moved anywhere in the country, finally settling in Guernsey many moons ago.'

Cannibalism

In June of 1867, whilst drinking at the Royal Oak Inn, Keighley, James Burke attacked George Blakey of Blind Lane. Sergeant McDonald discovered the assailant hiding at the old Barracks and took him into custody. Burke appeared before the Bench at Leeds Assizes. At his trial PC Nicholls produced a portion of nose which had been recovered from a pool of sticky blood at the scene of the crime. When he was arrested Burke's lips and face were covered with congealed blood. It transpired that after striking his victim to the ground Burke had attempted to bite his nose off. Failing in this endeavour he had hooked the torn flesh in his nails and ripped it from Blake's nose.

Return of the Dead?

Thomas Butterfield of Barley Cote, Keighley, A soldier in the Royal Horse Guards at the battle of Waterloo, had been reported killed in action. Some time after the dead soldier was seen in full uniform making his way by the old road across fields at Morton Bank towards his home at Barley Cote. Believing Butterfield to have 'returned from the dead' villagers were both relieved and overjoyed to discover he wasn't a ghost. Local hero Butterfield was presented with a medal for his bravery at the Battle of Waterloo. The medal is now in Cliffe Castle.

Joseph of Arimathea and the Glastonbury thorn (Thomas Gent, 1733)

Holy Thorn

A tiny branch of white Glastonbury Thorn planted at Birstal in 1767 budded on Old Christmas Day 1781. Folklore maintained the original thorn wood was used as a pilgrim staff by Joseph of Arimathea (the patron saint of undertakers) as he preached to a mass of people about the birth of Our Saviour at Glastonbury one Christmas Day. He struck the earth with the rod, which began to blossom like Aaron's Rod. Thousands of pilgrims have travelled to witness 'the budding of the thorn on Christmas Day in the morning, blossoming at Noon, and fading at Night.' The Birstal thorn blossomed for several years on Christmas Day. On Christmas Day 1781 it 'put forth green leaves and blossomed as usual, which continued for a few hours, and then disappeared.' Great numbers of people gathered here each year to witness this great curiosity.

Deadly Dream

Just before daybreak one day, Jane Shepherd aged seventeen rose from her bed above Issott's grocer's shop at Briggate, Leeds whilst in a dreaming state. She dressed herself then opened her fourth-floor bedroom window and flung herself out. Luckily, her dress caught on one of the spikes adorning an iron railing and saved her.

Rough Passage

An accident occurring in Bingley in 1710 caused John Skirrow to hand over £3 (the equivalent of four years' highway repair money) to Dr Swain for amputating a leg belonging to Christopher Colton and curing it.

Dog's Suicide

A black Newfoundland dog committed suicide by drowning itself in the river at the rear of the home of its solicitor owner, Mr Floyd of Holmfrith, Huddersfield, in 1815. The animal was seen repeatedly flinging itself into the icy waters, endeavouring to sink itself. Rescuers pulled the exhausted pet from the water many times and tied it up but as soon as it was set free it ran to the river and again hurled itself in. This action was repeated many times until, keeping his head underwater for several minutes, his goal was attained.

Mann's Artificial Legs

Recording the demolition of Springfield House, Manningham Lane, Bradford to build the Royal Arcade, local writer Charles Federer tells us that John Mann erected the house in 1816 and lived there until his death in April 1846. His brother Thomas built Mannville near Randal Well Close, Great Horton Road. This house was built inside and out with dressed Yorkshire stone!

John and Thomas Mann were the first worsted stuff merchants to set up business in Bradford. They ran a warehouse and shop selling woollen articles at Kirkgate in the early 19th century. The brothers had a yard, Mann's Court, close to their drapery business.

The business pioneered the introduction of cork legs and was known as 'Mann's Legs'. Although Thomas Mann insisted that *he* was the inventor of the cork leg, some thought he bought the idea from David Haigh of Silbridge Lane, Bradford. John Brunton, a Southcottian and 'cripple-mender', traded as a leather breeches maker. He was employed by the company to bind the cork legs in leather.

'With half their limbs in battle lopp'd away,
Beg bitter bread through realms their valour sav'd.'

After the Battle of Waterloo in 1815 (where 52,650 men lost their lives) legions of limbless strangers descended upon the town from far and wide – all enquiring as to the whereabouts of Mann's Legs.

During 1794, Admiral Paisley arrived in Bradford to order a new leg to replace the one he had lost in time of war – most likely at the storming of Hindostan. John James in his *History of Bradford* relates the tale of the 1st Marquis of Anglesey (Lord Uxbridge) on a visit to the Mann brothers from Staffordshire whilst waiting to be fitted with a replacement cork right leg after the battle of Waterloo. 'The noble officer was received with many marks of respect, and conducted through the Piece-hall, which nearly adjoined Messrs Mann's premises. Legend has it that when Anglesey lost his leg he shouted to Wellington, 'By, God, sir, I've lost my leg.' Wellington replied, 'So you have.' The leg was buried in a coffin under a weeping willow tree. Beneath the inscription someone added the words, 'Here lies the Marquis of Anglesey's limb; The Devil will have the remainder of him.' Colonel Kutusoff, a Russian officer who had faced Napoleon and 'the cause of more bloodshed than any man that ever disgraced this earth' in the bloody field of Borodino, was under Mr Mann's care at the time. The two maimed gentlemen had dinner together. Mr Swithenbank eventually bought out Mann's Legs. He carried on the artificial limb business from Toad Lane, Bradford.

Advertisement, Leeds Intelligencer

THOMAS MANN

Linen and Woollen-Draper, Mercer, Haberdasher, Hatter, and Hosier, Bradford.

TAKES This Opportunity gratefully to acknowledge his Obligations to his Friends and the Public in general, for part Favours, and to folicit a Continuance thereof; at the same Time begs Leave to aquaint them, that he has returned from London, Manchester, and other principle Markets, where he has purchased a large fashionable Assortment of excellent GOODS, in the above branches of Businesses, remarkably low, particularly printed Linens, Calicoes and Muslin's; plain, (prigg'd, check'd Modes, Armozeens and Persians; black and white Lace, &c, &c.- The best Wiltshire Superfine Cloths; Huddersfield and Saddleworth Plains; great Variety of Fancy Waistcoats, Breeches Stuffs, &c. &c. &c.

The very lowest Prices fixed.

He also wishes to inform the Public, that he has a very handsome New PALL, and other FUNERAL APPENDAGES, &c. also a complete Assortment of BLACK GOODS. – COACH and HEARSE procured on the Lowest Terms.

The Patent Artificial Leg,

A perfect imitation of the Natural one, and exercising all the necessary Functions. – The said T. MANN is the Inventor and Patentee, and may be consulted by such mutiláted Persons as wish to avail themselves of this very convenient Instrument.
Dated May 28th 1792.

Crow Hill Bog

Patrick Brontë reported the eruption of the Crow Hill bog in 1824. A particularly heavy rainstorm had occurred after a very dry season. A yellow-coloured liquid spilled out over the Worth Valley with such a force it carried away with it almost everything in its path, causing problems as far away as Leeds. Brontë used the incident in a sermon warning sinners to beware the wrath of Jehovah.

Inscribed on a Halifax Bell, 1691

'All you that hear my mournful sound,
Repent before you lye in ground.'

Chapter 11

Eccentric Oddities

'However blind a man may be, Another's faults he's sure to see.'
Anon

Cottingley Eccentric

Jack Lob alias John Robinson was born at Coppy Coppice but moved to the old hall at the top end of the village of Cottingley near Bradford. Jack's parents were honest, hard-working individuals; their son was a completely different kettle of fish. An account written by John Smith of Cottingley gives an insight into the life and times of Jack Lobb.

'The life of Jack Lobb was a continued struggle for existence; want of instruction, deprived of his parents when young, and isolated from working classes by his own indolence, and partial insanity, he wandered from one place to another wherever he could pick up a penny or a crust of bread. In the cold nights of winter, in frost and in snow, he crept into old barns, stables, mistals, pig sties, under haystacks, and into hedge bottoms, with an empty stomach and scanty clothing. The privations and suffering to which he was exposed would have killed half-a-dozen ordinary men. It is well known that he did not sleep in a comfortable bed for thirty years, and even an old horse-sheet and "long feathers" (straw) to rest upon, were a luxury to him. He was rather *short*, his physiognomy exhibiting a want of intelligence, having the appearance of an Ourang Outang or a wild man of the woods; he was furnished like other half-maniacs, with the instinct of self-preservation and a knowledge of the use of money as a means to procure something to eat.

Some of his best friends repeatedly advised him to clean himself and appear more respectable and seek for some sort of labour that would be most agreeable to his capacity and abilities; and under persuasion that it would be better for him, he commenced working at various coal pits, where he could find employment as a drawer of coals, but his long habits of vagrancy and mendicity led him to fall back again to his old course of begging, for he said he liked liberty with all its privations better than labour. He was once confined as he called it, in the Bastille, or Thackley Workhouse, where his wants were amply supplied. But with the comforts and accommodations of the house he was dissatisfied, and one night, while the inmates were engaged at their devotions, he contrived to slip through the closet seat and so escaped from the house. Some endeavours were made to find him and bring him back, but he contrived to evade the vigilance of the parish officers; and after concealing himself for some days and nights, covered with straw in an old shed, he crept forth again into his own wilderness of want and desolation, where he enjoyed the liberty and chances of begging. He was particularly fond of visiting the town of Bingley where he never went without meat.

Jack was not over nice in his moral notions of honesty, for in his begging excursions he sometimes called at houses where the inmates were out, and whenever he had a chance of purloining cake or potatoes, he seldom lost an opportunity of adding to his stock of provisions, by serving himself without leave. He entered into a house one day, at Harden where the mistress of the house had only stepped out for a few moments, and in returning she met him, and charged him will stealing her cake – he said to the woman "advice to thee ould lass, is, whene'er you go out, lock the door, and put the key in your pocket."

At one time when he was employed in drawing coals out of a pit; and a collier who had teased him respecting his insanity, said, "now Jack, let me down with a wallop!" Jack left off the rope, the man slapped down to the bottom and fractured his leg; when complaint was made to Jack about his duty, Jack said, "he wanted to go down with a wallop, so I let him go as fast as he wanted, full speed oud lad, full speed.'"

According to a sketch entitled the *Life and Vagaries of Jack Lobb* (published by Thomas Harrison, Queen Street, Bingley) Jack once 'found' a plum pudding. The mistress of the house spoke to him sharply bidding him to leave the pudding alone for she had a family to feed when they came home from the mill at Baildon. Jack carefully picked off fleas from his infested attire and dropping them into the plum pudding he said they should be "having some fresh gravy today". The unfortunate woman threw the contents of the bowl at him whereupon Jack ate it fleas and all.

Visiting Cullingworth one day he was encouraged to remove his clothing for a small payment from a group of high-spirited young men. They then painted his whole body black. Looking like some demented devil delivered from the bowels of hell's flames he wandered into the house of a woman who had just given birth. The woman was alone in the house at the time and upon seeing Jack Lobb went into shock, believing his 'Satanic Majesty' had come to fetch her. She died of sheer fright, leaving her newborn child motherless.

'Mr Hartley, who attended Jack on his death bed, says, his sufferings were neither extended nor severe, but he died without pain.' Mr W. Ferrand of St Ives Estate, Bingley kindly paid for the pauper's medical expenses.

Rogue by Name and Nature

Joseph Holmes, born in 1720 at Rigton near Otley, was better known as Joe Rogue, a labouring man and moneylender. He gained a reputation far and wide as a begging miser. Never in his long, mean life did he buy a morsel of food or clothing for himself. A few days prior to his death Joe Rogue was heard to say 'that he had never himself been at one penny expense, in either meat, wearing apparel or anything else, during his lifetime'. In fact, Joe parted with nothing unless he made a return on it. One day a robber, attempting to fleece him of his precious money, almost had his thumb bitten off by the miser. The robber was afterwards sent to York Prison for highway robbery.

After Joe's death on 5 February 1790 money was found hidden about his clothes in many little packets. Borrowers owed him upwards of £500. He was buried on Tuesday, 9 February at Kirkbyoverblow – having reached his allotted threescore and ten.

South Sea Bubble Beggar

Poor Thomas Hudson of Leeds lost his whole fortune when he invested his inheritance in the South Sea Scheme of 1767. He left his ancestral home after the death of his wife and wandered the county as 'a lunatic mendicant'. On reaching London he was often to be seen 'perambulating the fields about Chelsea, bare-footed, wrapped in a rug, and supported by a crutch, under the name of Tom of ten thousand'.

Patter Poet Laureate

Reuben Holder (alias Holdsworth) endeavoured daily to sell his so-called 'stupid Teetotal doggerel' on the streets of Bradford.

> 'E cowd, nasty wether like we been havvin
> a drop o brothe jinrally reckend just t'reight
> sooart o stuff ta keept cowd aht.
> Pooar fowks hes hed a fearful lot a broth latly
> ans grummalid a deeal abaht it. Bud then ye see its
>   snaw-broth.'

When Holder died, Stephen Fawcett, the Bradford poet, wrote two mocking poems: *The Ghost of Reuben Holder Apostrophised* (which follows) and *Rest in Peace Great Reuben Holder.*

> 'Rest in peace, great shade of Reuben Holder,
> Why still obsess, our Bradford poet brood,
> We only laugh'd and often deem'd thee bolder
> Than most men – climbing with thy cumb'rous load
> Of fusty wit Parnassus' mountain. Colder
> To thee, poor fellow, than the world allow'd.
> Is it, dear ghost, for past or present crimes,
> That even yet thou pourest out thy rhymes...
> Peace Reuben – for we would not now be cynical –
> Could not the Faculty invent a good brain-wash
> For persons unaware that thy pen was trash.
> Yet, Reuben thou wert harmless, Thou did'st prattle
> Of things that rang'd within thy comprehension...
> Good Tennyson, hold fast thy laureate crown,
> O Reuben's ghost may seize it as his own.'

Reuben, an ungainly, unkempt figure, was born at Hunslet in 1797 and christened Samuel Holdsworth. At five he drove a gin-horse at the pit top, at eight he worked down the pit. By trade he was a bricklayer and was once voted MP for Wapping but he found writing doggerels preferable to working. As a joke he arranged to be baptised as Reuben at Rothwell Church when he was twenty.

Reuben Holder hawking his poetry
about the streets of Bradford
(*The Yorkshireman*)

Carrying before him an empty beer barrel or placard on the end of a long pole, he took to loitering outside the mill gates of Wood & Walker's or Marshall's Mill in Manchester Road on weekdays, just as the workforce were ending the day's shift. To them he would recount in a rasping voice the horror of the new Poor Law Bill and other topics of the day, selling his penny pamphlets as he spoke.

John Nicholson, the Airedale poet, wrote this of Reuben when he saw him sitting in Bradford's Market Place one day,

'Here sits Reuben Holder
At his old scheming tricks,
Too idle to get clay,
And too lazy to make bricks.'

Reuben lived at Cannon or Dunkirk Street, Bradford and hawked fish from a stall at the bottom end of a yard in Kirkgate to supplement his existence. One of his first printed poetical efforts was about a girl who drowned in Bradford Beck on her way to Ackroyd's Field Head Mills, Thornton Road where she was employed. 'Reuben flourished only when before the public gaze, and in the end went out like a farthing rushlight with very little splutter.'

Merchant Prince

Situated high up on Harden hillside, Hill-End (or according to E. Parsons 1834 Arthing Hall) is Samuel Sunderland's substantial farm building. It has passed almost unharmed through centuries of harsh Yorkshire weather. Once reached by way of an-

Hill End Farm, Harden home of old miser Samuel Sunderland.

cient Dolphin Lane where a weather-worn stoop informed the weary wayfarer 'To Kighley, 2m.' (3 miles in reality owing to the old 'long mile'). Dolphin Lane was possibly named after old Dolphin, the son of Gospatric, Lord of the Manor prior to the Conquest. The farmstead stands empty and forlorn and in need of loving care and attention although its little garden is well tilled.

Samuel Sunderland's initials and the date 1650 are carved over the mistal door. Sunderland was known locally as the Merchant Prince for he possessed wealth most men could only dream of. A habitual miser, they said Sunderland's money 'rusted for want of use'. He hoarded his own gold and that belonging to his brother Peter in moneybags. Two shelves on which the bags rested in his private quarters were rumoured to groan under the weight of their burden and were often the topic of conversation in pot houses as far north as Wetherby.

Deep into the night of the 11 May 1674, when snow lay thick upon the ground, nine robbers arrived at Hill-End. They were mounted on horses purposely shod back to front by a Collingham blacksmith to confuse the law. Leaving the inhabitants bound and gagged in their beds, the thieves disappeared into the darkness of the night having scooped their prize of £2500. Weighed down by the gold, on reaching Blackmore, they were forced to abandon some of their booty by the wayside.

Emerging from darkness into a dimly lit inn at Collingham, the gang quietly filed into an upstairs chamber. Climbing the rickety narrow stairwell they closeted themselves in a small, low-roofed room lit only by a single candle. Their suspicious host, having crept upstairs behind them, put his ear to the door. Peeping through the keyhole he saw the glistening gold. Entering unannounced, the landlord demanded a share or he would summon the law. The robbers paid off the greedy landlord and prepared to flee once more into the night.

Just then another band of visitors to the inn arrived to the complete surprise of the robbers. Samuel Sunderland and his neighbours had discovered locked in the house a small dog parted from its owner – one of the thieves. Breaking the animal's leg lest it should outrun the horses, the dog was set free. The injured animal soon sought out its guilty master. Sunderland and his men took ten prisoners that night and retrieved most of the stolen gold. The landlord was sentenced to death together with the luckless robbers – thereby receiving his cut! On the day of the execution the hangman could not be found so the gruesome job fell to the thieves' young apprentice who, although innocent of the crime, incriminated himself and was hung alongside his friends on the gallows at York Castle. Mrs Mary Midgley of Moortown, Leeds, Sunderland's niece, was accustomed in her old age to tell the tale of how the very day after the robbery her uncle Samuel took her to see the empty shelf.

One bitter, late January morning, Sunderland, who had retired from his duties as rector of Bingley Church, felt unwell. He went to his bedroom and ordered his servants to fetch his beloved treasure chest. His money was kept safely locked inside an oaken chest that had a key the size of a house key. Gazing upon his gold for the last time and knowing shrouds have no pockets he bid a solemn farewell to his riches. Sunderland, aged seventy-four, was buried on the chill day of 4 February 1676.

Skinny John Booth

In 1802 Skinny John Booth lived to the north side of Horton Green, next to the Old Hall, Great Horton, Bradford. Skinny, once a rustic farmer, became the tenant of Mr James Swain Booth (the two were unrelated). Skinny's greatest love was to carry a table into his garden each Sunday. There he would proceed to arrange his gold coins to discover just how much more his treasure would cover. They say that after the miser's death room upon room in his large mansion contained nothing but broken junk. Some of the rooms were found locked and, having been unused for many a long year, had become home to hundreds of spiders and insects. Skinny used the whitewashed walls in other rooms to tot up sums and write down the names of his various debtors, making remarks upon 'the sin of not paying twenty shillings in the pound!'

Bradford Miser

When he arrived in Bradford from his birthplace in Ripon John Turner, of wealthy yeoman stock, took up an appointment with Mr Sayer as a linen-draper's assistant. His work was divided between two shops: one next to the old Bowling Green Hotel near the Sun Inn, and the other over in Keighley. Turner soon became well known in both places. Decorated in bobby dazzler gold jewellery and dapper clothing Turner was a 'swell'.

Turner bought Sayer's linen business in Bradford after borrowing £1000 from his expected inheritance. He employed two apprentices whom he drove hard. He disposed of all his finery and jewellery except his gold watch and chain (although he never wore them again) and began building his empire in earnest. He opened his shop just before dawn and closed when all hope of a last customer had faded. The coaching inn next door provided Turner with many good customers night and day. When horses were being exchanged for fresh ones, coach parties stretched their legs and purses in his fine drapery store. Often sleeping at the shop on piles of material, the miser saw little of his home and housekeeper. Turner's business sometimes required him to visit Manchester. On these occasions he would do his best to cadge a free lift in a carrier's wagon, failing this he would set to and walk.

As he waited at the side of main thoroughfares Turner was often fortunate in his attempts to purchase from 'hand-loomers' that had failed to sell all their wares. In relieving packhorses and loomers' backs of their burdens Turner succeeded in saving carriers' wages and avoided paying the full market price for his stock. Two years later, having acquired enough money to buy a public house in Kirkgate, Bradford outright, he entered into the property market with much enthusiasm. Soon he had properties returning him healthy rents – always collected by him at the exact time and day they were due. His health was affected by his mean ways and Turner became incapable of managing the linen business. He sold it after nine years for £16,000.

Leaving Bradford behind, Turner established himself at Beech Grove House, close to the North Eastern railway at Starbeck, Harrogate. Here he set up a thriving moneylending business charging 5 per cent return on all transactions made. He once took possession of a grindstone from a defaulter, wheeling it all the way from Ripon to

Starbeck! He was often seen roving the streets with a wheelbarrow and his constant companion – a dark blue moreen bag – in search of anything he could find to sell. Townsfolk were not surprised to discover that he had been seen walking barefoot on Rombalds Moor in order to save on shoe leather.

Surprisingly, Turner married and had a son. Carrying on the tradition of penny pinching he insisted his domestic bills did not exceed £20 per annum. He only allowed his long-suffering wife to light the fire to cook the family's meagre meals. He owned two suits: one he wore to conduct business, the other, multicoloured and made up of hundreds of patches, he wore at home.

On learning the builder of the property next to his home had gone bankrupt Turner bought it outright. He moved into the incomplete building and lived there until his death at the age of eighty-one. In 1895 Turner died. He left his home and grounds full of other people's cast-offs and about £100,000 in cash and property.

Pyrotechnic Prophet

A play entitled *The Fire Raiser, or the Prophet of Low Moor* once ran at the Theatre Royal, Bradford for a few nights only. The show's creator, Charles Rice, changed the name of the area to fit wherever the play was being staged. In this instance it paid off because curious Bradfordians packed the house each night. It was not until making enquires that Mr Rice discovered that there really *had* been a fire prophet in Low Moor – Jonathon Pyrah, who had visions of death and despair. This man was able to foretell the fall of the houses of Bourbon, Austria and the battle of Fontenoy with great accuracy. Returning from overseas after active service in the army he again settled at Low Moor in 1745. The aristocracy heard of his wondrous powers, sent for him and questioned him closely about his uncanny second sight. Eventually, after predicting many future events, Pyrah went insane and ended his days shackled by chains to a tiny hut outside Holroyd Hill Workhouse in Wibsey. The fire prophet once stood at Hill Top and said, 'I see something like hell in Black Syke.' Twenty years afterwards the blazing furnaces of Low Moor Iron Works belched over the once empty marshy ground.

Wild Man

Coming from a respectable background, Edward John Raynes had chosen the profession of schoolmaster and taught at Wesley Place on Halifax Road. He then removed to Derbyshire where he earned the nickname of the Wild Man of Bakewell. Escaping from Cheddleton Asylum at Leek, Staffordshire in the early 1900s, Raynes made his way back to Keighley. 'Sowing seed by the wayside' in Mornington Terrace, he was arrested by Police Sergeant Beaton. He advised the Sergeant to do the same to reap a good harvest. He was taken directly to the workhouse and from there returned to the asylum.

Little David

When Highfield House, a low-slung farm building in Keighley was completed the local townsfolk made up this odd rhyming ditty which was still remembered in 1912:

'There's little David,
Stretching like a louse.
He led the stone fra Paget Delph
To build the Highfield House.'

But who was little David and why was he compared to a louse? Highfield House was eventually turned into several shops facing towards Rook and Mornington Streets but was demolished this century to make way for modern buildings.

Merrybegot Hermit

In his later years the pilgrim of the wild moor could often be found hobbling through Morton, Bingley, Shipley and Otley singing for coppers. Old Job Senior's unkempt locks and dishevelled appearance were a familiar sight. He often passed a night in the back barn at the sign of the Old White Horse Inn, Bingley after spending pennies given to him by Bingley Grammar School boys who poked fun at him. This wandering minstrel's talent was the supposed ability to sing four different pitches: alto, tenor, treble and bass. Job sometimes exercised his powerful voice at the Leeds Theatre, Woolsorter's Gardens, Bradford and at several other open-air events. His repertoire included *While Shepherds Watched, Old Hundredth, My God, the Springs of all my Joys* and the rousing *Christians Awake.* He maintained he had been trained to sing at Leeds Parish Church.

Job – a 'merrybegot' – was the result of an illicit love affair conducted in the 1780s between his mother, Ann Senior who lived near Beckfoot, and a wealthy, married Ilkley landowner by the name of Haworth or Hawksworth. Job, born at Middleton near Ilkley, was left money in his father's will.

Job fell in love with a girl from Whitkirk who bore him a son. She repeatedly rejected his offer of marriage. Heartsick, he drank away his inheritance and some say lost his mind into the bargain.

He was often sacked from his work as a woolcomber and drystone builder for excessive drinking in Leeds and Skipton. He had gained quite a reputation for his walling, often working deep into the night by the light of a candle although some claimed he was work shy. Job finally married an eighty-year-old dame, Mary Barrett. She owned a little thatched cottage at Coldstone Beck, Burley Wood Head on the edge of Rombalds Moor. The couple wed at Otley Church around 1830. Six years later she took ill and Job did his best to care for the old dame. One night she complained of the cold saying, 'I's coud, Job, I's coud e this bed, an th' fire

Job the Merrybegot in his later years (S. Cryer)

doesn't reik me.' Job replied, 'Tha sal be warm...Tha sal be warm an comfortable. I'll bring tha nearer th' fire.' As soon as he could he took up two of the stone flags thinking, 'I'll mak a hole just deep enough for th' fire to shine on her, poor thing, sho'll noan be long here' and laid her inside the hole. His failing wife again asked a favour of old Job saying, 'O Job, I wish – I wish.' 'What does ta wish na,' replied her husband. 'I wish I'd sumat goed an nice afore I dee.' 'Tha sal ha sumat goed ey an nice an all.' Job promptly begged a pound of bacon from his neighbours and roasted it over the open peat fire. Taking the hot fat on a spoon he told his wife to 'tak this, it'll nurish tha within, and may be, recover tha awhile.' But instead of the hoped for recovery after complaining about the hot fat she fell back and died. She left Job her cottage, a potato garden and a field of about half an acre. A nephew of hers lay claim to the property and caused a good deal of trouble for old Job. Upon his return from Otley market one day soon after the funeral Job found the cottage destroyed and his money box stolen by the dead woman's jealous relatives. Job later described as 'savage as wolves....they com and termin'd ta drive ma off – be day an bi neet – be promises and threatnins – be law an be counsel – why an I tell yer, they left noan means untried, fair or foul, reit or rang which they thought ad get me off.'

The Revd Robert Collyer knew the hermit well and described his life. 'I knew Job, as far back as 1838...He was then in the habit of dropping into Birch's smithy, in Ilkley, very often, especially in winter, to warm his frosty nose at the fire, gossip with the farmers' men who came in on their errands, and get his chance at any stray "sup o' drink" which happened to be in the great brown jug. He was rather a simple old fellow at that time, not at all fond of work, but very fond of beer and tobacco, of which one of the towngate roughs told him one day he had chewed as much in his life-time as would "theik a lathe", and to see him at the loathsome work, would compel you to think there was more truth than poetry in the remark.

He used to mix hemp with his tobacco, to make it go further, as he said, but I have wondered since then whether this might not be one of the last remnants of a habit reaching back to a period long anterior to the introduction of tobacco into England. At that time Job did a stroke of work at the coarser kinds of woolcombing now and then, and at building the old-fashioned stone drains; and Widow Barrett was getting on to eighty and to her dotage. She had a small thatched cottage, a bit of land, and as rumour went, about twenty pounds in money. All this Job, who was then under sixty, secured by marrying the widow; and while the money lasted he lived in clover. But the old woman lasted longer than the money, while Job lost what little taste he ever had for work, and so they fell on evil days, and were very poor indeed – so poor that when the silly old woman was on her death-bed they had to depend on neighbours, who were kind and generous, as the Yorkshire folk always are in such a case. Job was her nurse, and was feeding her, as he told us afterwards, "with a soft haver-breead an' baacon when shoo deed." There was a rumour that this hastened her end; perhaps it did, but we never thought it was Job's intention to get his wife in that way out of the world; he always believed that if she could have eaten the food she might have lived. After her death, her people wanted the house and land, but Job had no idea of giving it up. They pulled the place down in his absence, but this did not answer, for he then built a sort of flue, into which he could worm himself head first, and there he slept when the weather would permit, with the dim idea that by this means he would hold onto the estate. The flue "drew" as managers would say.

Visitors to Ilkley, with nothing in the world to do, would ride over on donkeys to see Job come out of his hole feet first. He always had a turn for singing when he was in his cups; this he turned to account by-and-by in a marvellous composition he called "t' Weddin' Anthem, I' two voices"; one was a groan, the other a yell. This he would give you leaning on his staff, and then you gave him pennies, and in the course of time the two voices grew to four. In a year or two after his wife died he was out of linen, and made up his mind to make his own to suit him. So he procured some material some-how, lay down on the floor of a barn, chalked his outline, allowing a margin cut his cloth to the line, sewed the pieces together with twine, and got his shirts. He also made his own shoes in some such fashion; tagged his old rags together "wi' leather wangs", put a belt round his waist to keep all snug, mounted a hat over the whole, equally comi-cal, and there he was, as picturesque and as dirty a hermit as was ever seen between the four seas. And Job had just sense enough to see that this was the way to such a living as he wanted. Indeed, he added little touches now and then in a way that was almost clever. He had settled down to the cell business (Job's home) before I left England; but he only attended to this business when visitors were in Ilkley; the rest of the year he wandered round singing his "Weddin' Anthem", and picking up pence and sups o' drink.

He often came to cook his supper in those latter days at our smithy's fire. The way he did this was to warm some water, mix oatmeal with it into heavy balls, and bolt them. This last picture of Job I have in my mind is seeing him stand eating those oat-meal balls. The simple truth is, that the man drifted gradually from the condition of a human being of a poor type, to that of a beast. There was no romance about him at all. No echo or intimation of a gift of song like that which would touch you now and then to tears, in Billy Matthews, of Addingham. No stumbling into the heart of things like that famous Pudsey Joe had forty years ago and more, as when once he met one of the Lords of Harewood in his park, and getting sixpence from him, said in great glee, "Thank tha, lad." Whereat a footman coming behind him gently scandalised and whis-pered, "Joe, don't you know that's the Lord?" "Is that the Lord?" "Aye Joe." "Can he mak yan o' them?" pulling a blue-bell from the sward. "No, Joe he can't make a blue-bell." "Then he isn't the Lord, thah fooil." Job had no gift of broken melody or human wit or wisdom, only that facility of getting pennies and pints of ale, and living like beasts that perish.' (Note: Harry Speight believed it was not Pudsey Joe but Job who met Lord Harewood.)

Job liked visitors to call on him and would sing or gossip to them. Some of his more romantically inclined guests believed him to be a visionary and weather prophet. It was considered a lucky omen if Job agreed to sing *t' Weddin' Anthem* at a wedding feast. The *Old Hundredth,* the song he liked best to 'blast', was often used as a charm to ward off witches when out walking alone on dark nights in lonely places. Witches could not abide hearing the words and the louder it was rendered the more effective the charm. Sometimes Job would tell tall tales in the village tap-room of his family history and sing his songs for the amusement of the company there gathered – for a free ale or two, of course.

After drinking beer in a Silsden inn seventy-seven-year-old Job was taken ill with a sudden attack of dysentery. Some whispered he'd been poisoned but it was more likely to have been an attack of English cholera. Stumbling and clawing his way back to Ilkley he was discovered dying in a barn adjoining the Wheat Sheaf by the landlord. He was removed to Charlton Workhouse where he died on 6 August 1853 'unpitied and unmourned'. His body lies buried in an unmarked grave somewhere in Burley-in-Wharfedale's graveyard. The Hermit Inn (once known as the Woolpack) on the way to Burley Wood Head was so named in his honour and kept his gnarled holly walking stick as a memento. Job saved the money he earned from his singing. The old man advised those all those who would listen, '...whenever yer can get a penny, keep it, put it by, tell nobody on it – never len ony body ought, not a penny, for yer know they never gets it back yer see. Get all th' brass yer can.' Whatever became of the old man's hidden hoard of gold remains a mystery.

This song-like poem dedicated to Job gives a detailed description of his outlandish appearance.

'Old Job is dead that droll old man,
We ne'er shall see him more;
He used to wear an old drab coat,
With buttons and bands before.
A low crowned hat with brim much torn,
To keep his cold head warm;
His clogs were made of blocks of wood,
His stockings straw and yarn.
His breeches hung below his knees,
No straps to keep them up;
His sullied shirt bob'd out before
Just as his breeches top.
His coat was of old fashioned shape
Braved many a pelting storm,
With scores of patches he'd stitched on
With hemp and stocking yarn.
Long was the waist, the back was broad,
One button on each hip,
Two old oak staves he two did wear
For fear his feet should slip,
A handkerchief tied round his chin
For fear he'd get a cough;
Another too, tied fast his hat,
For fear it should blow off.
Drab woollen mittens he did wear,
To keep the frost wind out,
A bag he carried on his back
To put in what he got.

An hempen belt went round his waist,
To keep his rags to 'th skin;
A waistcoat pocket very large,
To put his clay pipes in.

From *The Life of Old Job Senior, The Rombalds Moor Hermit, with an account of his Eccentricities and Remarkable Life,* by S. Cryer

T' Packhorse Doctor

Bonesetter Fawthrop Fryth

Fawthrop Fyrth was born in Cottingley in 1815 and moved with his parents to Thornton, near Bradford, at about the same time as Patrick Brontë and his family. His father, a respected horse and cattle healer, taught his doctoring skills to his musically talented son. After the death of his father in 1842 Fawthrop took over the family business at Thornton. A lintel above the doorway announced, 'T. FAWTHROP, Doctor and Farrier, 1815'. He also took over a second surgery -a rickety room at the rear of the Old Packhorse Inn, Bradford (where he never once paid any rent). He was famed for his skills as a bone-setter and often travelled as afar afield as Skipton. Fawthrop was never still for one moment and would hare from one place to another followed by his faithful brown retriever, also named 'The Doctor'. In later years Fawthrop was described by *The Yorkshireman* as having a, 'fair large front, so sparsely clothed with hair, it is generally hid from view by a top hat of wonderful proportions and colour. If the old bone-setter be marked by no other characteristic he may at any time be distinguished from ordinary mortals by his hats...Beginning life as respectable white beavers, they weather the storm...' before finally appearing to have died from

Fawthrop held his Bradford surgery in a rickety room at the rear of the Old Packhorse Inn

some terrible disease! Fawthrop was a kindly soul and never charged more than his client could pay in cash. His medical bag contained a hotchpotch of medicines made up in recycled pop and Yorkshire Relish bottles. Fawthrop once paraded the streets of Keighley during election time decked out in blue ribbons. He is said to have received a 'warm reception' from the locals. Before his death, the famous Bradford artist W.O. Geller painted his portrait in oils. Mr Abraham Holroyd wrote a mock epitaph for Dr Fawthrop Fyrth, which he recited at the Fox and Hounds at Shipley in the presence of the good-natured doctor.

> 'Poor Fawthrop Fyrth is dead and gone,
> And a worthy man was he,
> As ever looked into a well,
> Or up into a tree.
> …Great was his skill, and small his pay;
> In courage strong, he knew no fear;
> In doing good he spent each day;
> Thus worked away from year to year.
> Then let us this small tribute pay,
> And to his memory shed a tear.'

Old Three Laps

William Sharp senior was a fairly wealthy man and a manufacturer of worsted goods. One day he took some material to the tailor and ordered a new coat to be cut from the length. The tailor complained that the cloth was too narrow to make four laps but Sharp told him to make it with three laps rather than provide a larger piece. Thereafter he became known as Old Three Laps. With his small fortune he purchased two farm-steads in Keighley: Sheep Hoes near Two Laws and Whorles Farm, facing the Aire Valley.

Old man Sharp once rewarded a small boy with a penny for running an errand. The boy in return said, 'Thank you Mr Laps!' To his surprise he received a hefty clout to the side of his head before being told, 'I'll have thee to know that my name's Sharp, not Laps.' The boy walked away in tears. Old Three Laps, feeling sorry for the lad, called him back and tossed him another penny for smacking him! Another time, when Sharp found all his hay had floated off into the river after a heavy bout of rain, he was heard to solemnly remark, 'The Lord gave and the Lord hath taken away, and wherever that hay may go to they'll want the rakes, I dare say.' With that he threw the rakes into the water to follow the departing hay.

Son of Three Laps

William Sharp, the son of Old Three Laps and Mary Sharp, was born in 1777 and later lived in a gloomy farmhouse at Laycock, a grim-looking place named Whorles. A neighbouring farmer's daughter, Mary Smith of Bottoms Farm, Newsholme Dene, left Bill Sharp standing at the altar in 1807. She had already borne him a son but Bill's greedy father Old Three Laps refused to give his son a decent allowance after the wedding so Mary's father called off the marriage. Broken-hearted, Bill went to bed (although it was said he retired to bed because his father took three guineas from him and asked for three more so Bill vowed he'd never work again). Anyway, whatever the reason, Bill took himself and his injured pride off to bed for the rest of his life! His self-imposed prison cell was 3 metres square, damp and held a bed devoid of hangings. A tiny wooden table stood by the bedside and in the corner was a fireplace that could only be lit when the wind blew in the right direction. A battered oak clock that had given up telling the time adorned the otherwise bare walls. Winter and summer came and went and the world turned on but Bill Sharp, who according to the *Preston Chronicle* had 'the most enormous teeth', refused to budge from his bed or even have the window opened in his outhouse bedroom. He was fed four times a day and turned out of bed once a month for the changing of sheets. As the years passed his bulk grew until his fleshy body weighed 240lbs (110kgs). His hair and beard grew thick and wiry. Eventually death released him from his voluntary prison at 4am on Monday, 3 March 1856. Four days later hordes came to watch the funeral proceedings at St Andrew's Parish Church, Keighley. The oak box was said to resemble a square chest (being 70cms deep) rather than a coffin and was carried to the graveside by no less than eight strong men. The Revd R. Richardson read the burial service.

Bradford Scientist

Abraham Sharp was acknowledged to be the foremost scholar of mathematics in the 1700s. His father, John (who died in 1704), was a Presbyterian who fought under the banner of General Fairfax at the siege of Bradford.

Abraham studied navigation and advanced mathematics. During the course of his studies he met Flamsteed the Astronomer Royal who employed him for some years as his assistant at the Royal Observatory, Greenwich, London. Flamsteed died whilst preparing *Historia Coelestis*. Sharp, acknowledged as 'one of the most accurate computers ever known', worked with Flamsteed's successor, Joseph Crosthwaite, to finish the ephemeris using his own calculations, maps and charts. His contribution was never acknowledged or recognised, Crosthwaite gave himself full credit for the finished volume. Abraham Sharp left London and returned to his Bradford home in 1694 and spent many years attempting to 'square' a circle.

A handsome portrait of Abraham Sharp (J.H. Turner)

The arched entrance to Abraham's ancestral seat boasted the family's crest above the central keystone. In 1694 he added a square tower to use as an observatory. A small chamber up above the wash place was utilised as his workshop and was fitted with astronomical instruments fashioned by his own hands. Sharp was now living as a virtual recluse and allowed only two gentlemen to visit him in his study – Dr Swaine of Hall Ings, an eminent apothecary, and Mr Dawson. Both men had to rub a stone against the wall of his workshop as a signal of their arrival – sometimes they were admitted; sometimes they were not. Amongst eminent scientists who sought out Sharp's advice was the celestial cartographer Dr Halley. Abraham Sharp rarely ever left the comfort of his home, but was once so desperate to solve a difficult mathematical problem that he ventured to Scotland. He set out his problem to a learned Scot and after much careful deliberation his answer came, 'There is but one man that can help you...Abraham Sharp of Little Horton, near Bradford!'

In the years towards to the close of his life the mathematician would each Sunday walk the mile from his home at Horton Hall at Little Horton to the Presbyterian Chapel. This he did with the aid of a walking stick fitted with telescopic glasses. His pockets full of coins, he would fill one hand with halfpennies and hold it behind his back, allowing the poor to share it as he passed along the way. It is known he kept an account book of every halfpenny he spent during his long lifetime. His ancestral home housed a great number of relics including suits of armour and a fine collection of family oils including those of Abraham and Archdeacon Sharp. There was also a picture painted by Hogarth, antique needlework and a good selection of heavy Jacobean oak furniture. Many very valuable books and several collections of papers, including a very old manuscript 'in Gothic characters rescued from monastic archives on the continent', were housed in his extensive library. Oliver Cromwell was supposed to have slept in the large, ornate oak bed here.

A fearsome spectral dog, the Horton Guytrash, appeared at the gates of the hall to foretell bachelor Sharp's death on a July evening in 1742. He was 91. Sadly, ignorant servants used a good deal of Abraham's life work to light the hall's fires. Abraham Sharp's fine memorial stone can be viewed at St Peter's Church, Bradford. His epitaph is written in Latin. It translates,

'Here is buried what could die of Abraham Sharp. He was born of an ancient family and linked by blood ties to the Archbishop of York of that name. He was rightly counted among the most accomplished mathematicians of his day. He enjoyed constant friendship with very famous men of the same repute, notably Flamsteed and the outstanding Newton. He very accurately drew up the description of the heavens, made by the former of these, in (astronomical) tables...as a bachelor, had carried on undisturbed and useful life in these studies, being noted for his reverence towards God, his kindness to the poor, and his goodwill towards everybody, only then at last, in the 91st year of his life did he, having had his fill of worldly affairs, pass on into Heaven on July 18, 1742.'

Haworth Water Wolf

The *Keighley Herald* dated the 10 December 1909 tells a strange tale of a woman possessed by a water wolf. It looked 'like a frog, grey, rough and hard about as big as a knob on her oven door and three inches long.' Maria Judson had drunk water from the spring at Leeshaw for a number of years and it was here that she claimed that the wolf entered into her body.

She lived at 7 Prospect Street, Haworth. It was there that she prepared to dine one evening on onion mashed with salt and butter. The wolf climbed out as she opened her mouth, tempted by the subtle aroma of the delicacy she was preparing to devour. Remembering a tale of a woman at Crossroads who had not closed her mouth when her water wolf had jumped out so allowing it to return, Maria firmly snapped her jaws shut. After throwing her food out into the street she saw to it that the parasitic wolf died a slow, painful death on her coals.

Pyrrhic Victory

Cockle Tom, alias Thomas Wood, once took up a wager made by Ben Laycock to run a mile-long race on horseback. The stake amounted to £2 10s (£2 50p) or half this amount a-side. 'Pie Dough', a Bingley character, was to act as judge and jury. The race began in the afternoon on Rombald Moor above Bingley. Both men dressed for the occasion. Ben wore a flashy huntsman's suit of bright red and had his top lip blacked. Tom borrowed a blind horse for the race. A large crowd gathered and a cart selling sandwiches arrived so it was some time before the pistol fired to signal the start of the race. Soon the nags were off—the crowd whooping and running behind. Unfortunately for 'Pie Dough' his own horse's leg was broken during the hullabaloo—so he claimed the winnings as damages!

Bradford Hermit

Known to many only as J.J., John Jackson a native of Bradford wrote many penny pamphlets on politics and other subjects that he felt strongly about. One such pamphlet *The Demagogue Done Up* was directed against Chartist leader Feargus O'Connor. For upwards of fifty years Jackson resided in a cottage at Legrams, but for some unaccountable reason he left his comfortable home to live in a tiny hut in his garden. Refusing all attempts to move him back to the cottage, he continued lived as a hermit in the hut until his death in March 1875.

Keighley Busker

Before the days of retirement pensions an elderly fellow used to walk the streets of Keighley singing songs in exchange for housewives' coppers. His favourite hymn was *I am but a stranger here, Heaven's me home!* One day, just as he finished rendering the song, a lady stepped from her doorway to offer him a slice of dry bread. The old man looked at the woman with disdain and said, 'Nay, Missus, I'll sing Heaven's me home till Hell taks mi afore Ah will ate that!'

Tombstone Aggie

Miss Agnes Bailey of Utley, Keighley, a relative of the late Sir Abe Bailey, the foremost founder of Keighley's Laycock Institute, took over the family business in 1948 when her brother Tom was killed in a Swiss road accident. Aggie, one of the few woman to work as a monumental stonemason, was a gifted sculptress, accomplished violinist and played the piano skilfully. She also played cello and saxophone. She lived at a convent in Italy for almost six months as resident organist. Aggie's family motto was 'Courage is my Fortress'. The sculptress better known as 'Tombstone Aggie' lost no time in building up the business and searched the death columns diligently. She would drum up business by calling personally on the bereaved family soon after a death occurred – dressed in men's clothing. She was often to be found drinking Guinness at the Commercial Inn in Keighley.

Rich Beggar

A bag lady presented herself at an almshouse, begging shelter from the outside world. The caretaker was puzzled for her actions and speech belied her appearance. She spoke in an educated way and her manners were impeccable though she wore shoddy, patched clothes and shoes that had seen better days. Refusing outright charity the old dear always insisted on paying her own way. As time passed she spoke of notable families in the district with authority and knew a lot about a family living at Roundhay on the outskirts of Leeds into which Lord Moynihan had wed.

After being unwell for a short period of time and refusing all attempts to send her to a doctor or hospital, she passed away in her sleep. When her room was being cleared dirty pieces of newspaper were discovered hidden inside her slippers and other hiding places which contained a total of £500 in cash. Her true identity and family connections were never discovered and she went to her grave alone.

'Pie' Leach

'Then arose that man Leach, who had been baptised James, a vendor of greens, and who spake as the oracle of the people.' *The Chronicles of Wakefield*, 1869

James, alias 'Pie', Leach, was a great Victorian character. He somehow wangled Keighley Burial Board's permission to erect his own memorial stone in Utley Cemetery prior to his death. This lengthy tribute to himself begins with the words, 'We the undersigned have pleasure in certifying...' I expect that during Pie's lifetime certain citizens wished he was certified – to a lunatic asylum!

Born at Harewood Hill, Oakworth in 1815 he was the eldest of five siblings. Pie certainly was not modest when it came to writing his own epitaph for he wrote of himself in glowing terms. He described his many earthly achievements in minute detail, including the testimonial he received after leaving the police force. He would have been satisfied to read his obituary, which stated that he could sell or swap any item 'from an oven tin to a steam boiler or from a hedgehog to an elephant'. Pie lived in a building he named Balmoral House (now Mogul's Curry Restaurant) at Skipton Road with his second wife. He had the local carpenter measure him for a coffin, which he kept behind the kitchen door in readiness. A stone plaque is still in situ on the front wall extolling his wife's good business sense! In true Leach tradition, it reads, 'GO YE AND DO LIKEWISE. These buildings were erected by James Leach, Esq., greengrocer, and Sarah his wife, of 31 Low Street, Keighley, 1869. Also our Sarah told me, James Leach, that she paid 480 pounds, for a house and shop, 31, Low Street, Keighley, in 1840. She died August 19ᵗʰ 1889. The premises were sold in October, 1889, for 1950 pounds, and was very cheap I think indeed.'

After his wife died, old 'Pie' hired the Temperance Hall and delivered *Two Funeral Sermons* in honour of his deceased wives. Two years later, in 1892, he placed this advert in the *Keighley News,*

WANTED, a SERVANT or Housekeeper from 35 to 50 years of age. Apply 86, Skipton Road, Keighley, for particulars of wages etc. Character required; no washing, only her own clothes; wages good to a suitable person; nothing to do much but make meals. Last servant I had stopped betwixt a year and two and went away last Thursday.

From the moment 'Pie' set eyes on thirty-five-year-old Miss Margaret Bowes—a lady little more than half his age—he was smitten with cupid's arrow. Within days the couple were wed at Skipton Road Register Office by special licence. Hundreds of well-wishers turned out to watch the proceedings. Bill o' th' Hoylus End stood at 'Pie's' side throughout the marriage ceremony. Afterwards Bill recited one of his creations *Come, nivver dee I' thi shell, old lad.* Journalist Joseph Rhodes (the first person to introduce Esperanto into Britain) acted as the couple's witness. Outside the Register Office crowds split their sides as Bill o' th' Hoylus End recited at full belt the words of *The Joyful Widower* by Burns in local dialect.

Pie had his 'bumps' read by a phrenologist when holidaying at Morecambe in 1884. The bump reader listed Pie's pluses and minuses thus, 'Mental Temperament: *only fair,* Love: *strong.* Combativeness: *always ready to resist.* Acquisitiveness: *full* Secretiveness: *deficient.* Cautiousness: *moderate.* Approbativeness: *deficient.* Self-esteem: *large.* Image: *large, can be stubborn.* Veneration: *small.* Wit: *large.* Agreeableness: *average.* You are excitable; you at times forget yourself and say very disagreeable things, for which you would soon be sorry.'

'Pie' Leach died after a long and colourful innings on 13 October 1893. This poetical epitaph signed J.L appeared in a September edition of the *Keighley News.*

'Reader beneath this monument there lies
The dust of him who once sold pies
Let others write the story of his youth;
In manhood's prime – if I must tell the truth –
Aside he laid the games once his delight,
A constable because he walked the night.
Drink he forswore, lived frugally, and sold
His fruit and vegetables to young and old;
Grew well-to-do (assisted by his spouse),
Studied the town's affairs, till in the house
Where local Parliament in session sat
He found a place, and 'long hung up his hat.'

Who Was Old Moore?

Le Figaro's front page once proclaimed, *'Old Moore s'arreto là. Il n'announce la fin du monde'* – 'Old Moore stops there; he does not announce the end of the world.' If you have browsed through an *Old Moore's Almanack*, have you ever wondered just who Old Francis Moore was? Apparently, he was a London physician deeply interested in astrology. In late Victorian times the publication became the responsibility of Mr Albert Walker of Otley. Albert's father, William, owned a printing shop in the busy market town and owned several newspapers including *The Wharfedale and Airedale Observer, The Shipley Times and Express* and *The Ilkley Free Press* and *Gazette*. Albert wrote a number of books during his lifetime and was known by those who paid to see him perform as *The Whistling Commercial*. He entertained folk with his joyful tunes, recitations and monologues. Following in the footsteps of Old Moore, the 'infallible storehouse of prophecy', Albert oversaw most of the work that went into the Almanac. One day an employee asked him what should he write down for the weather the following summer. Albert sarcastically advised him to 'put snow'.

Albert Walker lived at Ashfield Place, Otley, with his wife Jane until his death. He was buried in Otley Cemetery in 1923. W. Foulsham & Co. Ltd of Berks now publish the almanac.

Innkeepers' Lot

Nicholas Green, landlord of the Goose Eye Inn, Laycock, Keighley died aged 39 in February 1879. He had been a tall, athletic man until he suddenly began to pile on weight. He weighed 24 stone and died of dropsy and a severe heart condition. His coffin measured 2 metres long.

Another hefty innkeeper is buried in St John's graveyard, Leeds. His epitaph proclaims his claim to fame.

'Sure the Fattest man
That Yorkshire stingo man,
He was a lover of his can,
A clothier by his trade.
His waist did measure three yards round,
He weighed almost 300lb.
His flesh, I say he had no bone.
At least 'tis said he had none.'

In Pannel graveyard lies the body of innkeeper Joseph Thackerey who expired on 26 November 1791. His epitaph is succinct.

'In the year of our Lord 1740
I came to 'The Crown'
In 1791 they laid me down.'

Chapter 12

Homeward Bound

'The curse on the hearth wound's deepest.' *Anon*

Bolling Hall Lodge, Bradford

'It was my mother, Mrs Doris Emsley, who first noticed that the big house was up for sale. After making enquires she found that it had been on the market for a very long time. The agents put forward an offer of £500 on our behalf and this was accepted 'for a quick sale'.

My mother was quite excited about this as she enjoyed dabbling in buying and selling property and considered that this was a real 'snip'. She encouraged me to view the house, pointing out its potential – the large rooms and the fact that open fields where the children would be able to safely play surrounded it. But at the same time it was close to all amenities such as the school, transport and, of course, the beautiful park and the famous Bolling Hall. At the hall the Earl of Newcastle is reputed to have been visited by a nocturnal female ghost dressed in white entreating him to, "Pity poor Bradford."

The house was at the end of the coach road to the famous Bolling Hall and had at one time belonged to the property. To say that the house was 'basic' was definitely no under statement – it was old, old, old! When my husband looked over it he thought that I had completely lost my senses. He said it would take hundreds of pounds to bring it up to our standards. But I insisted that we should obtain a good price for our house and would have plenty left to do the improvements.

To cut a long story short, we sold our house easily – just as I predicted – and we proceeded with purchasing "the big house". We arranged for workmen to start installing a damp course, new windows and frames, new wooden flooring and a hot water system. Electricity was to be installed and the roof overhauled.

Without warning the foreman came to us one day and said that the workforce was pulling out. He would not give any explanation apart from flicking his thumb towards our new lounge and saying, "We can't work in there." We were naturally very annoyed and disappointed but he did recommend someone else who finished the work by installing a luxury bathroom, two beautiful fireplaces and a lovely modern kitchen. As my husband was in the trade, all the fittings were of top quality and standard.

While the workmen were busy we were scraping walls ready for decorating. What a job that was – seven varnished papers on the downstairs walls and we even found a paper pattern for a crinoline dress wedged into a door frame. Upstairs there was no wallpaper, just whitewash – with a touch of dolly blue I suspect. When the workmen had finished we paid them off and the decorators moved in. They did an excellent job, but one day they asked if we would stop the children playing with the pasting table and their tools. I said that they had not even been in the house and the decorator replied, "Well, someone has and a right mess they have made as well." We couldn't fathom out what the problem was. After they finished their work, we had all new internal doors fitted and two impressive external doors. I was absolutely thrilled with the result and happily told them so, but the decorator replied, "It might look lovely now but rather you than me lived here." I asked him what he meant. He grimaced and said "Maybe you'll see or maybe it's me who needs a holiday!"

We proceeded to buy new carpets and extra furniture. As I had served a year or two of an apprenticeship in the soft furnishing department of Christopher Platts I had great pleasure in making up new curtains to hang at our lovely new leaded light windows. Eventually we moved into the house. What a wonderful transformation with the new light fittings sparkling away. I was so thrilled and even my husband had to admit that it was really magnificent. We then decided to arrange a house-warming party for all our family and friends.

The day of the party arrived. My mother and I prepared a meal and set the dining room out in all its splendour. With half an hour to spare before our guests arrived we decided to sit down and relax in the lounge for a few minutes. What horror! As we entered we could see the walls were soaking wet, just as though someone had poured water over them. The strange thing was that the carpets and curtains were quite dry and the windows were not even steamed up. We immediately rushed upstairs to check and found everything was as it should be. Obviously we could not possibly have our visitors go into the lounge to see the mess on the walls but as soon as the guests left we looked into the lounge again and found that the walls were bone dry and miraculously everything was back to its former splendour. *This really puzzled us.*

After my husband had left for work and the children had gone to school one day I was working in the kitchen. Knowing I was alone and that there was no one else anywhere in the house I was petrified when I distinctly heard a woman crying. Our dog suddenly shot out of the kitchen and sat trembling at the end of the garden. When my husband Joe came home and I told him about my fright he passed comical remarks like "take more water with it" and "we will have to have earlier nights". Later I started to hear very heavy sighing and crying. The dog flatly refused to go upstairs or anywhere near the cellar area. I began to suspect I was going mad.

Sometime later we decided to invite more visitors and the soaking walls appeared again. We had the roof, damp course and pointing checked. Taking builders' advice, we had the gable cement rendered and a diagonal fall pipe fitted. But whatever we did, every time we had guests the walls got soaking wet again although at all other times they were normal.

Our daughter Margaret's bedroom was over the lounge and many times we would hear her call, "Daddy, there's a man in my room." She told us that he had a great big hat with feathers in it (a Royalist?) but we never saw anything. However, one evening as we were watching television we heard heavy footsteps marching from one side of the house to the other. The time must have been about 10pm. We raced upstairs only to find both our children were fast asleep and there was nothing untoward to be seen.

Another inexplicable occurrence was that most mornings when we came downstairs we would find our wedding photograph face down in the centre of the sideboard although it had been securely placed on one of the pedestals before we went to bed. The cushions from the sofa would be piled up in the middle of the room and the ornaments would be moved about. All these odd events carried on for the full eight years we lived in the house. It got so bad that I refused to go into the cellar and paid my brother to scrub the cellar steps for me. My husband always made sure that there was enough coal upstairs for me each day before he went to work.

Although we had a very busy social life neither of us was a heavy drinker. In all the eight years in "our dream home" my mother-in-law babysat for us on only one occasion. My mother babysat for us most weeks but never said anything until we moved out, when she admitted she had heard marching and crying noises. She didn't like to say anything because she felt that she had pushed us into buying the house originally. We had never told her about the peculiar goings-on we had experienced although she was aware of the wall phenomenon.

I never liked to take a bath when I was alone in the property, so arranged for someone always to be around whenever I bathed. Eventually my husband realised the weird happenings in our home were getting me down and so when we heard through the grapevine that the Corporation was planning to widen Wakefield Road my husband asked if they wanted to buy our strange but beautiful house. Someone came to see the property and immediately agreed to buy it – we settled on a price and moved out to live on the other side of Bradford.

After a short time the Corporation put tenants into the property, they couldn't believe how lucky they were to rent such a beautiful house, but less than three months later they suddenly moved out. A second lot of tenants did not stay long either. I have no idea what happened to them but I do know that finally the house was razed to the ground. It was never used for road widening but I understand that Morrison's supermarket now stands on the site.'

West Riddlesden Hall

West Riddlesden Hall, Leach Way, Keighley is believed to have been built by the Montalt or Maude family in the early part of the 15th century. On 22 September 1576, whilst visiting his daughter Isobel at her home in Baildon, Thomas Maude of West Riddlesden Hall died. His extensive lands and properties were divided between his children. Properties at West Riddlesden, Morton and Morton Banks were held of John Paslaw of Wiswall (the ill-fated abbot of Whalley who was hanged). Eventually the estate passed to Anne (née Maude), wife of John Leach of Moorhouse, West Morton in 1658. It was her son Thomas Leach who built the present West Riddlesden Hall. In his residency the Elizabethan manor underwent major structural repairs and a further wing was added. Set high in a roof of the Great Hall, Leach's initials and the date 1687 are carved by his own hand.

'Bingley Chapel'

In 1662 Oliver Heywood, a Nonconformist preacher of Coley near Halifax, took refuge at West Riddlesden Hall to escape death at the hands of his persecutors. He had been excommunicated for refusing to conform to the new prayer book foisted onto the clergy. Heywood baptised Thomas Leach's son David at West Riddlesden Hall in 1678. Finding a platform for the expression of his opinions, he continued to patronise the hall regularly. An entry in his diary for 23 March 1680 records that he 'presented the spell-bound assembly with a sermon based on Job 14,13 and afterwards stayed the night'. Leeds Sessions allowed West Riddlesden Hall to be registered for religious purposes in 1689. This was the first year of the Bill of Rights and Toleration Act passed by Parliament. The hall became known as Bingley Chapel and both townspeople and villagers travelled regularly to its doors to take part in Sabbath day devotions. By 1695 the 'Bingley Chapel' congregation had abandoned the hall after finding suitable premises elsewhere in Bingley.

The Maude Legend

One of the Maude heirs had seven sons and one daughter. The girl danced at each of her brother's weddings and in each case the bridegroom was struck down with some form of pestilence and died without an heir. Having outlived them all, she is supposed to have married into the Leach family of Bingley some time in the 17th century. She died aged about fifty years. The Leach family continued to reside at West Riddlesden until 1854. New streets there have adopted the Leach connection.

Brontë Connection

Sarah Sidgwick was the sister of Fred Greenwood of Ryshworth Hall, Crossflats. It was their father, John Greenwood of Knowle (now a funeral parlour), Keighley, who purchased West Riddlesden Hall in 1809. Whilst carrying out some alterations he used a staircase window in which to display his own coat-of-arms. Mr John Benson Sidgwick of Stonegappe, Lothersdale near Skipton took up residence at the hall as tenant around 1856. His working life had been spent as a cotton manufacturer. He died in May 1872. His widow Sarah Sidgwick lived on at the hall until her death on the 27 December 1887. Whilst living at Stonegappe Mrs Sidgwick employed Miss Charlotte Brontë as governess to her children in May 1839. But Miss Brontë was very unhappy in the Sidgwick's home. She used some of her experiences with the family as background for her novels. Mrs Sidgwick's great nephew, Arthur C. Benson, saw his great-aunt in a different light. He describes a visit to the hall as a small child in 1874 and gives a glowing account of Sarah Sidgwick. He writes, 'Just before I went to Eton, my father, then Chancellor of Lincoln, took Martin, my elder brother, and myself to visit our relations in the North. We went first to West Riddlesden Hall, near Keighley, where my great-aunt, Mrs John Sidgwick, then lived. It was an old manor house, with quiet, spacious gardens, bordered by a canal, with the moors behind. I remembered the stained glass, with the arms of Montaltes, in the great staircase window, and a long low room with an alcove formed by a little projection over the porch where we slept; my uncle John Benson Sidgwick, had been dead some time, and my only knowledge of him was derived from a photograph, which represented him sitting at ease on an arm-chair, with a black velvet skull cap on his head, and his patriarchal snowy beard grow-ing over his chest. My great-aunt Sarah, a Greenwood of Swarcliffe, was a little woman with a sweet face, who received us with gentle cordiality, and won our hearts at once; I remember her telling us that she used to call my father "the little Bishop" when he was a boy. My cousin, Charles Sidgwick, was master of the house, and there was also there "Tiffy" Drury, his sister, with her children; we fished for crawfish in the canal, and paid a visit to Old Riddlesden, a stately old house, now a farm, with large monastic barns.'

Ghost of Soldier

Just after the Second World War, two young Keighley boys were playing in a field ad-jacent to West Riddlesden Hall. In the distance they heard the roar of a motorbike en-gine approaching. As the vehicle came into view the boys saw a solider dressed in full German uniform seated on the bike. He circled the field a few times before disappear-ing into thin air.

Family Disappears

Until the day he died Bawdenin Silsden claimed to be the true owner of Beggars Val-ley (Stonegappe). The Bawden family had owned the property since 1591. Stonegappe, a desolate and solitary place in the winter, had once sheltered Bawdenin's Uncle and Aunt Bawden and their young son. One night, while the can-dles still burned, the whole family mysteriously vanished. Despite extensive enquires no trace was ever found of them. It was a popular belief that they had been kidnapped and murdered. Bawdenin's father claimed to be the natural heir and immediately moved his family into Stonegappe. A short time after the Bawdens' disappearance strangers arrived at the house claiming the property and lands as their own. On pro-duction of a will the Silsdens were ousted. Each time the estate was offered for sale the Silsdens attempted to claim the property; each time they failed. A land deed of 1775-6 records W. Bawden as resident at Stonegappe when he was awarded 16 acres from High Stile as far as Stonegappe Gate.

Stonegappe Sold

The Sidgwick family owned Stonegappe from 1796 until they removed to West Riddlesden Hall, Keighley in 1847. They sold Stonegappe (Charlotte Brontë's Gates-head Manor) to a Mr Black from Bradford. Black's sister-in-law married Frederick Delius, who composed a number of famous musical scores here.

Murders!

Local legend tells of a young maidservant murdered at Stonegappe. Her killer hid the body at the bottom of a well. Close by the old house another maid died at the hands of her lover. Her last words to him were, 'The ferns will tell of thy deed.'

Ancient Marley

Within the tiny hamlet of Marley lies Marley Hall. The name came from Peter de

Marthley, a lord of the manor of Morton in 1316. It is sited about a mile from the town of Bingley on the south side, overlooking the River Aire. The Druids' Altar casts a dark presence over the rear of the hall. An almost perfect round (burial?) mound known locally as Primrose Hill stands to the left of Marley and Hollins Wood or Blue Bell Wood to the rear. An ancient British trackway once ran northwards through Middle Hollins to Marley until an alternative highway was cut. Not far away at Castlefields was a river crossing called The Bridge of the Earth. The alchemist Lord Clifford Henry 10th passed this way from Skipton Castle to London by way of nearby Bell Bank Wood in May 1526. Amazingly, the passing centuries have done nothing to change the tiny hamlet. William Martheley of Marley was a juror at the Court of the Knights held in Bingley in 1415 and a will dated 19 June 1537 mentions a George Paslaw of Marley. In the 16th century the Maude and Currer families owned Marley Hall. John Maude died within its walls in 1564. Four years afterwards the property passed to Hugh Currer of Kildwick. Amongst the Ferrand manuscripts is an indenture dated 1571 granted by Francis Paslaw to Arthur Currer, yeoman of Marley, allowing leave to gather timber to build one house.

Saviles and Paslaws

'What became of this Manor till its acquisition by Sir John Savile later on, has up to this time been an inscrutable mystery...'

An indenture was made in 1512 between Alexander Paslaw and Sir Thomas Pek, parson of Thornhill, that Paslaw should pay rent to Master Henry Savile for land at Riddlesden and Morton Banks. Seven years afterwards another indenture was made between Master Henry Savile of Thornhill and Walter Paslaw of Riddlesden. This granted Paslaw further leave to lease part of the Manor of Riddlesden. Sir Richard Tempest (Knyght) and John Lacy of Crumwelbothome validated this document. The Saviles, I believe, hailed from the Halifax branch of the family who were acquainted with John Dee the famous astrologer from 1583. A note amongst zodiacal symbols in Dee's diary on 14 June 1596 confirms this, 'Mr Harry Savile, the antiquary, cam to me June 15, I wrote by Mr Harry Savile of the bouk (Bank, Beacon Hill) dwelling at Hallyfax, to Christopher Saxon ad Dunningley.' St Andrew's parish registers record a Miss Savile of Marley marrying a Mr Dean at Keighley in 1606.

Rebuilt in Stone

In 1627 John Savile, Lord of the Manor at Morton, rebuilt Marley Hall in stone. It had five gables until it underwent drastic alterations at the turn of the 19th century. Savile decorated two of the hall's mullion windows with his coat-of-arms depicting three owls upon a bend. It is to be hoped that the noble family was not superstitious for lore says the owl is an unlucky bird – an omen of impending doom. Shakespeare penned the line, 'The owl shriek'd at thy birth, an evil sign!' Above the front entrance Savile's coat-of-arms and his initials are set in stone. An old chronicle records a strange story of a visit to Marley Hall by a convict, Walter Calverley. John Savile received Calverley as an overnight guest en route from York to Wakefield prison. Calverley was supposed to have committed suicide in a bedchamber to avoid the grim hospitality of Wakefield jail. This story sounds suspiciously like the true story of Sir Walter Calverley who murdered his own children at his ancestral home Calverley Hall on the outskirts of Bradford in 1604-5. I do not think he was taken to Marley Hall, nor did he die here for he was pressed to death in the yard of York Castle.

Swift Justice

Savile gained a reputation as a genial host who entertained his guests in a lavish manner. Labouring under the misapprehension that Savile was a magistrate, a delegation of Bingley villagers arrived at his door one evening and interrupted a grand party. Unable to shake the villagers from their conviction he was forced to abandon his entertainment to judge a murderer apprehended in Bingley that day. Savile, in his haste to return to the festivities, tried and convicted the hapless prisoner within the hour. The victim was immediately taken out and hanged on Bingley Gallows. The mob's grisly entertainment secured the knight's speedy return home. John Savile himself was fined on a number of occasions for failing to mark his boundaries with the sign of the double cross, which identified him as a Knight of the Cross.

Marley's Secrets

The Barker family lived at Marley Hall between the First and Second World Wars. One of the bedchambers is supposed to have been slept in by Oliver Cromwell. The Barkers referred to this room next to the kitchen as 'Oliver's room'. In the 1930s Mr and Mrs Barker granted J.J. Brigg permission to excavate the cellar in search of a legendary tunnel. The secret tunnel was supposed to link Marley with East Riddlesden Hall. Walter Paslaw (related to Whalley's Abbot Palsaw) was said to have built a passage to escape religious persecution during the Pilgrimage of Grace. A small opening partly hidden by an hexagonal stone on the cellar floor was believed to be the entrance to the underground tunnel. It was said to lead into a vault somewhere in the churchyard on the opposite side of the River Aire. Brigg's workmen removed a stone dairy table from the centre of the cellar and set to work. Having dug down a foot or two they were disappointed: their labours revealed nothing but clay. Abandoning his explorations, Brigg left still convinced there was some truth to the old legend. In a letter to the *Keighley News* in 1951 Godfrey Chadwick reported finding a passageway beneath the hall's cellar. Mr Chadwick thought this hidden escape route was possibly used for espionage purposes by Royalist sympathisers. Interestingly, a carved Jacobean oak settle built into a wall which backed on to a front passageway allowed those who stood upon it to reach a hidden recess above the main door of the room. This may have been used as a priest hole to hide a visiting Catholic priest for spies were everywhere in the days when the old religion was outlawed.

Dancing Ghosts

Through the passing centuries three female ghosts linking arms have been reported to fade away into the cellar floor. Some believe them to be the ghosts of John Savile's frivolous daughters.

Henry Litton dressed as a fool, playing the part of a jester.

The Savile Jester

Sil (or Sim) o' Marley, the Saviles' jester, was sent out from the hall on an errand to deliver pies to ploughmen working in the fields. On his way there Silly Sil convinced himself he heard the bells of Bingley Church ring out, 'e-a-t t-h-e p-i-e-s, S-i-l; e-a-t t-h-e p-i-e-s, S-i-l.' To which he thought, 'Yes, and I will; yes I will.' By the time the jester reached the hungry ploughmen there were only a few crumbs left!

Fall from Grace

Preacher Oliver Heywood chronicled each bit of juicy tittle-tattle that chanced his way. His fire and brimstone sermons gained him entry into many of the large houses in the West Riding, including Marley Hall. He was privy to secrets, which he eagerly committed to his diary. An entry dated 13 August 1672 discloses, 'I being in Bingley parish at severall times they were discoursing of the decay there is of persons of quality. Mr Fairbank the minister there said to me there is a rot among the gentry, and I can say since I knew that place there is a decay of these houses and family's: Mr Savile of Marley...Mr Bins of Rushworth...Some are in debt, some imprisoned, some rooted out, title name, some dead, posterity beggars, oh what unthriftines, wickedness, sloth, and gods curse for the same; this is a good lesson, Jno, 3, 33, Zech 5, 4.'

Last Savile

Heywood condemned Robert Savile as a 'wastrel'. Savile, a weak, dissipated character, mortgaged his inheritance to indulge in a life of debauchery. In 1666 he sold his equity in Marley Hall and its lands to that prince of landocrats and misers, Samuel Sunderland of Hill-End Farm, Harden. Heywood describes Savile as living a, 'sharking wandering life, dying as he lived in an Ale House at Elland on 8th January 1669. He had gone to the "Nutter oth Coat" whereupon he sate downe in a chaire, dyed immediately of impostume as is thought.'

Curiosities

Samuel Sunderland rented Marley Hall to Joshua Walker. After Sunderland's death the property fell to Robert Parker of Brownsholme. He married a Miss Rooks of Esholt. Walker was promptly evicted and the couple took up residence at Marley Hall. Parker housed many archaeological and antiquarian curiosities here including 'coynes and medalls, and other curyosities and rarities of ye like kind'. Amongst the 'curyosities and rarities of ye like kind' was a pedigree of King James from Adam. Robert Parker contributed towards the cost of building materials for Keighley Boys' Grammar School. On the 19 January 1714 after a dispute over the proposed length of the foundations, Parker withdrew his patronage. He and his family left Marley, re-moving to Carlton near Skipton, 'Where his collection appears to have been the centre of much attraction as it certainly deserved to be, if its lingering stories of its contents are at all credible.' Parker died in 1718 and left his store of curiosities to Mr Brearcliffe of Halifax and to, 'Thomas Parker, son of Edward Parker, Esq., of Brownsholme Hall, my nephew, all my books, mathematical instruments, my collection of ancient coynes and medalls, and other curyosties and rarities of ye like kind.' Members of the Parker family resided at Marley Hall until it was sold off in 1842 to Mrs Sarah Ferrand.

Brownsholme Parkers

A relative of Robert Parker of the same name lived at Extwistle Hall in the Burnley area in 1718. He was returning home late one evening after attending a secret rendez-vous when he was forced to hide in the shadow of a forest tree when he saw an unex-pected light shining brightly in the darkness of the night. Moments later a silent procession of goblins carrying a coffin passed him. Parker peered at the inscription on the lid and was horrified to see his own name written on it in bold letters. Soon after the doomed man was caught in a rainstorm. He rushed home, took off his soaking wet coat and held it up close to a roaring log fire. Suddenly a loud blast ripped through the room. It transpired that Parker had forgotten to take out of his pocket a quantity of gun-powder and shot. Dying from his injuries, he fulfilled the goblin's prophecy. Edward Parker, another relative, lived at Huntsroyd and was kidnapped by Roundheads and hidden at Thornton near Bradford until his family stumped up £13 for his release. His father was taken to Bradford prison. A ransom of £200 was paid and he was instantly set free.

Brownsholme Skull

A member of the Parker family hailed as a martyr was beheaded for his part in the Pil-grimage of Grace. His severed head was carried back to the ancestral home and hidden away. Edward, one of the Parker boys, was on holiday from Harrow. He removed the head and buried it in the garden as a prank. He was soon to regret his actions for the hall began to fall in on itself. The timbers mouldered, the roof fell in and the walls buckled, causing the worried occupants to move out. Edward Parker eventually admitted what he had done. The skull was hastily returned to its rightful place in the Tudor Hall court cupboard. Edward's father called in workmen to reinstate the four-hundred-year-old property to its former glory.

Doomed Marley Manor, Bingley

Marley Manor

'Oh! Old Marley, Old Marley your doom is complete.'

Marley Manor, thought to be one of Yorkshire's oldest buildings, 'stood in a hamlet, which is no more than a handful of old buildings on the west-side of the railway between Keighley and Bingley.' The rambling old manor stood close to a narrow, winding stream separating Marley Manor from Marley Hall. Inside the old manor an impressive three-tiered fireplace held a chimney nook large enough to roast an ox, conceal a 'massing priest' or hold the last supper since it could seat thirteen people around its ingle. Those of us who are more superstitious would not dream of sitting in any company numbering thirteen souls, for the first person to rise to take his or her leave will die within the following twelve months as Matthew Arnold found to his cost. The Wooley family in their day loved and cherished the rambling, antiquated house. Tenants for almost two decades, they did their best to restore the old place with what little cash they could spare. Some time after Mr Wooley's death it was noted that a cottage adjoining the manor 'must have been in ruins twenty years ago...possessed no drainage, there was no water laid on, no plaster on the walls, and it was very damp'. After the Wooley family departed Marley Manor stood uninhabited as it had fallen into terrible disrepair. In 1937 a proposal to save the manor and connecting cottage was brought to the attention of the owners, Keighley Council. Councillor Mr E. Merrill thought the property not worth saving. County Alderman J.J. Brigg argued against this but it was recommended that the manor and cottage be left to fall into ruin.

Sometime during the 1940s two schoolboys walking from Keighley to Bingley stopped off at the old manor. Exploring the ruins they climbed down into one of the cellars to escape the heat of the day. However, they did not stay in the cellar long as a chill air wrapped around them. The children suddenly felt frightened to death and ran away as fast as their legs would carry them. When the demolition team arrived to dismantle the old manor they found ancient, carved oak chests and heavy furniture sheltering beneath its stout rafters. The fine antique panelling and oaken doors were ripped out and oaken floors removed. A workman was offered the wood for £15 – an offer he refused. Outside a stone trough measuring 30cms square was built into the rear wall. During the dark days of the Black Plague coins were transferred through its water. This process was believed to be superior to the common method of sterilising coins in vinegar. The water was relied upon to stave off the effects of the plague.

Farnley Hall

This Leeds property has a wonderful Elizabethan timber frame. At the front of the historic building was the inscription, 'Builded in the year of our Lord, 1586, and in the reign of the Queen 28, by Sir Thomas Danby, knight.' Farnley, the seat of the Harrington family for six centuries, was demolished in 1756 and the materials sold. A new mansion sprang up in its place. Five years later a small chapel of ease replaced the antiquated chapel standing in the grounds. Thomas Whitaker a respected antiquarian commented, 'It is owing unquestionably, to the aristocratical genius of the place, where every rood of land when leased was sure of a tenant, little less of four hundred acres of native wood, is described as Silva Pascua, should have been permitted to remain to the present day.' Unfortunately progress caught up with Farnley Hall's surrounding woodland and it was destroyed in the middle of the 1800s.

Haworth Old Hall

Villagers in older times described Haworth's Old Hall in hushed whispers as, 't'owd haunted hall'. The property, it is supposed, was the seat of the Emmott family who came originally from Laneshawbridge. It was erected at the bottom end of Haworth using stout timbers in about 1641. The family owned the hall for 284 years before they sold it to Haworth Co-op Society during the 1920s. It has been claimed that the hall had been used as a courthouse sometime during its chequered history.

Old Squire's Ghost

An old Haworthite once heard in the dark hours, 'the well-known voice of the old northern squire, in the lawn, close by the haunted hall... she has heard, not only the voice but the step, of the old squire pacing along the old oak gallery of the now deserted hall!' Revd James Whalley said it lay empty in 1869.

Religious Connections?

Monks of Kirkstall (Christall) Abbey once owned many properties around Keighley and were thought to have resided in Haworth before taking up residence at the abbey. An ancient Norman church and graveyard were rumoured to have been built on the Old Hall site. According to local lore a monk was walled up in the front elevation on the left of the entrance, opposite the main bar. Sadly, there appears to be no evidence to support such a tale.

Burning of Haworth

The Knight Sir Richard Tancred of Whixley rode by Church Gate without incident at the burning of Haworth village. Tancred is recorded as ordering the destruction of Haworth and Heptonstall. A feared adversary in battle, he was knighted on 21 May 1642 at York. He died in 1668, aged 60.

Ghosts Galore

One day in spring 1995, manageress Barbara Brooke was checking her rotas as usual when she fancied she saw the figure of a monk floating past her surrounded by a bluish haze. A little while later she saw an identical apparition disappear through the kitchen wall. Mrs Brooke found her office in an upstairs room to have a heavy atmosphere. Gerald Dodd, a local psychic, called at the hall in the hope of communicating with the restless spirit. After visiting Mrs Brooke's office he told reporter Alistair Shand, 'While upstairs I was drawn to a room. I went in and could feel choking. It was as if I was being suffocated.' A man claiming to be a ghost hunter reported to the owner of the hall that he had seen a young girl dressed in an old-fashioned yellow dress standing on the stairs.

Secret Tunnels

A secret tunnel is supposed to link the hall's cellar to that of the Black Bull at the top of Main Street. There is also rumoured to be a further tunnel that runs from deep within its cellars, under fields ending at the bottom of Bridgehouse Lane and coming out close to the beck. Two more underground passages appear in older tales. These tunnels were supposedly trodden by a procession of monks holding aloft lighted rushes as they muttered low chants en route to Haworth Parish Church. Entry to these two tunnels was thought by a previous owner to lie hidden within a huge, arched fireplace situated in the main dining room.

Tudor Fireplaces

During excavations two old stone fireplaces dating back to the Tudor period were uncovered – one was once used as an oven The main dining room was believed to have been the site of the old hall kitchen. An ancient stone floor lies hidden under the present floor. In the last century Halliwell Sutcliffe, a colourful local writer, described the hall as holding secrets within and without its walls buried by generations past. Sutcliffe visited the building in the 1870s when it was divided into two cottages.

A smooth-faced stone dating somewhere between 1730 and 1830 was taken from an old stone fireplace in 1969. It bears a strange inscription, 'Go> Mary and Pifs'. This relic hangs on a stairway wall and is on view to the curious or visitors ascending the stairs.

Old Manor House, Haworth

The Manor House was built about 1700. A reckless Lord of the Manor resided within its walls. The old story runs that the lord met with his friend and neighbour to imbibe ale at the friend's expense. Late into the night, having exhausted a barrel, he was encouraged by his sly companion to sign a deed of gift in order to confer his land with manorial rights to his host. The following morning the lord realised what he had done and begged his neighbour to tear up the deed. His entreaties fell on deaf ears and he was ousted. Today hotel guests make use of part of the original building but it is now almost lost in a larger extension.

Oakworth Hall

Historian Frank Rhodes thought the original hall to have been erected by the Copley family. The Lord of Oakworth Manor at the time the hall may have been built was Alvery Copley. The Manor of Oakworth at this time was thought to lie between Sykes Lane on one side and the Manor of Scholes, near Pickles Hill, on the other. Copley sold the Manor of Scholes to thirty freeholders in 1618. By 1844 the Ferrands had successfully claimed shooting rights there. A stone tablet which is situated at the back of the building by the main road shows a man on horseback together with three small animals. The animals are thought to be the goats of the Copley arms. A lintel above an entrance door bears the markings of a cup and ring stone thought to be over 2000 years old! A date of 1702 is carved into a lintel on the Providence Lane side. Those standing in the doorway here in times past would have observed the busy comings and goings of a little cobbler's shop next door to William Clough's storerooms. Both the Court Rolls of Haworth and Heaton's Worsted Industries say that William Clough occupied the hall in 1708. His initials 'WC' appear above the old shop. In later years James Haggas and a son of Mr Wheathead's used the property as a woolsorters' storeroom, importing the wool from Lincolnshire.

Changes Afoot

In 1883 the hall, four cottages, some farm buildings and land were sold by John Sugden of Dockroyd (related to Sir Isaac Holden's wife Sarah) 'by the direction of Elizabeth Blamires, and Martha Craven, of Oakworth'. Richard Longden Hattersley and Edwin G. Hattersley purchased the estate for £3510. In 1913 the Speight brothers bought Oakworth Hall. They sold it to the Yorkshire Penny Bank in 1936. Douglas Berry, a bank worker, bought the property from the bank when it closed in the early 1950s. Renovations revealed a fine, arched stone fireplace, which measured more than 3 metres across in the dining room near the old salt cellar. The kitchen oven is reputed to be the oldest in Yorkshire. Walls and oak beams were found to be 60cms thick and all the doors and windows fashioned from good solid oak. A boulder 60cms in width was taken out from a wall on the first floor where a doorway was being made. A stone quern bearing the date 1674 was found in the garden in 1955.

The Sugdens and the Cravens

'Quakers William Dewberry and Thomas Stubbs came from Ive Delves in

Warley to Stanbury to Christopher Smith's then to Oakworth Hall where old
Abraham Moore received them and the message.'

In the early part of the 19th century, Mr Sugden of Oakworth Hall hired a Quaker Craven living at Goodley to carry out building work at Lane Ends Mill. When the job was almost completed Sugden refused to pay Mr Craven. The master mason returned to Goodley and told his wife the news. His wife said, 'Thou must go on wi' the work and I'll see Sugden.' On going to Oakworth Hall she found Sugden enjoying his home comforts. She told him, 'Thou hast ruined my husband and thou hast ruined my children and me but I'll tell thee what it is, thou wilt have to come to our house and ask for some milk and bread.' From that day on every task that Sugden turned his hand to went badly for him. Almost penniless he pondered on the Quakeress's words. Hoping to break the curse he knocked at the Cravens' cottage door. The mistress, knowing her prophecy had been fulfilled, bid him, 'Come in, I know what thou art coming for. I'll give thee it without asking, and thou shalt have it new baked and milk warmed.' After promising to right the wrong he had done to Craven, Sugden's fortunes were restored to him.

Lanehead Cake

'Cream ½lb butter, 1lb lard and 2lb sugar; dissolve 3 teaspoons of carbonate of soda into enough buttermilk and leave to stand. Add 3lb flour, ½ teaspoon of grated nutmeg, two teaspoons of cinnamon, 3lb dates and 4oz candied peel to the creamed butter and sugar then slowly beat in milk make into a soft dough. Bake in medium oven.' This old Yorkshire Quaker recipe will keep fresh for months if stored in an airtight tin.

A Nail in Time

After moving into Oakworth Hall the Kent family felt very much at home in its friendly, warm atmosphere. One night a violent thunderstorm awoke Mr Kent. Unable to sleep he went to his bedroom window. For reasons he could not explain he felt compelled to check the upstairs rooms. There he found water pouring in from the roof. Coming down to breakfast the following morning he was surprised to find a rusty nail placed carefully on the side of his plate.

Oakworth Ghosts

Three converted cottages at Oakworth Hall are said to have shared the same mischievous ghost. At certain times items belonging to one household were substituted for those of another. A visitor to Oakworth Hall in 1983, Mr Ron Danvers told the *Keighley News* he saw what he thought was 'a strange greyish apparition'. He watched a bent figure in the shape of a man shuffle across the room before it disappeared.

Sir Isaac Holden

Born of mining stock at Hurlett on 7 May 1807, Isaac Holden was destined to become a Liberal Member of Parliament for the Keighley Division in 1885. Sir Isaac was a man blessed with both an enquiring mind and quirky nature.

Lucifer Matches

During the year of 1825 John Walker, a poor native of Stockton-on-Tees, was busy experimenting with a lighting mixture. He managed to produce the first striking match but neglected to patent his discovery. This was unfortunate for him as Samuel Jones stole Walker's invention and patented it for himself in 1828, calling it the Lucifer match. Isaac Holden had by 'the result of a happy thought' produced the first modern friction match in October 1829. This spelled the end to Walker's inferior invention. Holden generously gave John Walker the patent. Isaac gave a full account of his chemical experiments relating to his match invention to a Select Committee on Patents in the House of Commons.

Prophetic Dream

Whilst working in France in 1849, Holden began to search for a site from which to operate a worsted mill. In a dream, he journeyed alone to a village named St Denis. As he drew near the town he beheld many narrow, winding streets and almost at once became aware of another footfall echoing his own. Emerging out of the darkness a figure hurried toward him. Beckoning Holden to follow him, the silent stranger led him to a doorway of a mill whereupon he took from his pocket a candle, tinderbox and large iron key. The light from the candle reflected against the lock as the heavy oak door

Sir Isaac Holden, robed in a magician's gown *(The Yorkshireman)*

slowly creaked open. As soon as he awoke the next morning Isaac Holden knew his search for the site from which to build his new worsted empire had ended. Thinking of nothing else but his nocturnal vision he travelled to St Denis that very day. Reaching the town as darkness was beginning to fall he met with the custodian of an empty mill and, just as his dream prophesied, viewed his prospective purchase by candlelight. It was from this mill and two later acquisitions at Croix and Rheims that Holden was to build his fortune.

Oakworth Sugdens

After marrying his second wife – mill girl Sarah Sugden of Dockroyd – Holden moved into her home at Oakworth. 'It was a house with a short central passage or hall, parlour and dining-room, three bedrooms above and a return wing behind.' Holden had obtained the building and land from his brothers-in-law: a York Wesleyan Minister Peter Sugden and Robert Newsholme Sugden of Dockroyd, Oakworth on 30 December 1872. The old Sugden family home was destroyed to make way for the wonderful mansion that was to be Oakworth House.

Oakworth House

'The erection and laying out of Oakworth House, winter gardens and conservatories were commenced about 1864, and occupied over ten years...the original estimate of five thousand pounds ran up to eighty thousand pounds.' The former roadway being close to the house had to be diverted. Sir Isaac applied to the Quarter Sessions and received permission to make up a new road much further away from his new mansion, which he preferred to call Liberty Hall.

He was forced to purchase two cottages which stood in the way of his plans at a premium price. The magnificent winter gardens viewed from the 21-bedroomed mansion delighted, amongst others, high profile men such as the Duke of Devonshire, Lord Rosebery, John Bright and Andrew Carnegie. The latter honoured Keighley when he chose the town to build the first ever public library in the land. An article in the *Keighley News* praised Holden, 'With characteristic generosity Sir Isaac for many years has thrown open to visitors the winter garden and grounds around his home. The poorest were welcome, and on Saturdays and fine afternoons the stream of workpeople, men, women, and children, from the surrounding districts could be seen enjoying the beautiful surroundings so freely placed at their disposal. The boon thus conferred upon the poor was not a small one. The winter garden – a pleasure ground of half an acre in extent – was situated at the back of the house and covered with glass. In the centre rose a large dome of stained glass, and panels of richly coloured glass, ornamental ironwork, artistic gilding, and mosaic floors, executed by Italian craftsmen, gave the structure lightness and richness. A large part of the site was excavated out of the solid rock, and at the far end of the garden the natural face of the rock was converted by the skill of French workman into a scene of rugged beauty. To supply the garden with flowers in bloom and cultivate grapes, bananas, peaches, &c., there were forty glass houses, covering an area of three acres, and employing a band of some twenty gardeners. Beyond the grounds immediately surrounding the house large tracts of moorland were reclaimed and planted, forming a park of great beauty.' Guests enjoyed the benefits of a unique system whereby 'carefully-studied contrivances, a constant and equal breathing in and out of the rooms was secured, so that the atmosphere in every part of the house was entirely changed in periods varying from half an hour to three-quarters of an hour.' The first telephone communication system in Keighley was installed at Oakworth House.

'Grand Old Man of Oakworth'

In May 1897 Keighley Corporation picked out Holden (an advanced Radical) from three other worthies on which to confer the prestigious title of Freedom of the Borough. His long-time friend Joseph Constantine of Hermit Hole, Keighley, once a child labourer in a mill on the banks of the River Worth, described Holden as being, 'one of the best specimens of an Englishman and a devoted dietist.' Holden said of himself, 'I never stop indoors for the weather, either for snow, hail or rain: and it does not matter whether it is hot or cold, I never shorten my walks.' Almost until the day of his death on 13 August 1897 Holden could be found tramping over the heather-decked moors so beloved of the Brontës. As his funeral cortège passed through the streets of Bradford on its way to Undercliffe Cemetery, the Town Hall bells tolled a melancholy death knell. On his tombstone are the words, 'Extant Recte Factis Praemis,' meaning, 'Rewards exist for right actions.'

An oil portrait of Holden by Mr James Charles and paid for by public subscription in 1891, 'pictured him seated at the side of his desk in his library at Oakworth House, and on the desk was shewn an open volume and some chemical apparatus. The artist has caught one of those happy expressions often seen to beam on Mr Holden's countenance.'

House Abandoned

Holden's daughter, Mrs Alfred Illingworth of Daisy Hill, Bradford, inherited the mansion. During her ownership the once thriving centre for innovation, sponsorship and patronage stood neglected and forsaken. The mansion's fine interior, which had inspired both the illustrious and the working class, was stripped bare. Amongst the many treasures, including Sèvres ware and fine Japanese metalwork, Lady Holden's well-polished clogs were removed from the commissioned chiffonier on which they had rested. Here they had reminded Lady Holden of the time when she was plain Miss Sarah Sugden – a humble factory lass. Mr Frank Illingworth eventually sold the £80,000 mansion and grounds to Oakworth Council in 1907 for the sum of 8d (3p) per square yard.

Oakworth Blaze

The demolition of Oakworth House then began. During the early hours of Sunday, 7 February 1909 flames all but consumed the fabric of Holden's home. It appears that the demolition team, using a room near the library as a joiner's shop, piled the fire high with rubbish the previous evening. This set a beam of wood smouldering. Keighley Fire Brigade refused to answer a distress call to save the already blighted mansion as Oakworth Council did not subscribe to their service. The fire reduced Holden's vision of the future to nothing but blackened stone. This last vestige of the jewel in the worsted empire crown was swept away some four years later by, 'the hands of destroyers more conscientious still, by whom its stones are being gradually scattered, to be put to other uses.' An extract from the *Keighley News* 1909 optimistically records, 'And thus, though the Hall itself is falling, there is every prospect that from its ashes there may rise a charming village that will be a delight to the eye and a boon to the district.' The location is now a pleasant park and sports area.

Mysterious Symbol

At the rear of the property is a series of curious, winding, man-made concrete caverns. There is even a wishing chair. Etched deep into the ground is a six-pointed intertwined pentagram with six circles contained within each outer point. Within the centre, a grid marks out sixteen spaces. Could this strange symbol be the 'carved stone representing a constellation of the stars' that the late D.M. of Baildon included in his unfinished manuscript within a chapter he entitled *The Altar of Hell?*

Eldwick Hall

This Bingley hall, once home to a jester, bears a date of 1696. In 1755 Ben Harboyne, a wealthy Lisbon banker, watched helplessly as his whole family were 'swallowed up' in an earthquake. The shock 'turned his mind' and so he was escorted back to Bingley from Lisbon and kept chained up like a dog by the keeper of Eldwick Hall until the day he died. An unnamed man was supposed to have been killed by the hand of his own brother at the hall. The story came out after Joe Raistrick found a number of human remains beneath the barn floor in 1770. Raistrick's own son William lost his life when returning home from his devotions at Bingley Church one Sunday. Without a single thought for his own safety he jumped into the mill-dam at Eldwick and saved a girl from drowning. Unfortunately, William did not survive the incident.

Joseph Hartley, the son of William of Helwick Hall (Eldwick), was lost in a snowstorm on 16 November 1791 when coming from Halifax market. He was buried at Bingley, leaving a widow and a young son named John. Hartley Hartley, a descendant, had as his motto 'Heartily, Heartily, as to the Lord'. A famous sharpshooter lived at the hall in 1830.

Uncra Roman Fort

Long before the River Aire changed its course in about AD78, a Roman fort is believed to have existed between East Riddlesden and Marley Hall, near Keighley. The road to the fort is thought to have stretched along Hog Holes Lane, Long Lee, cutting along Parkwood Top before its decent to Uncra and Marley. Here it passed over the ford at the River Aire to climb the steep slopes of Morton Banks and beyond. The farmstead of Uncra was supposed to have been erected over the fort's foundations. From the August pages of the *Keighley News* 1883 a clue to the site of Uncra Farmstead may be gleaned. Mr F. Morgan, a tenant of Uncra Farm, reported smoke rising from a haystack, the property of Mr Wallbank of High Shann Farm. The haystack was in a field by the River Aire, close to his farmstead and bordered by Keighley Corporation tip and the local gasworks.

Marley or Uncra Bridge

A severe drought in the 1850s at Uncra near Marley revealed an ancient oak and sycamore bridge, 120cms wide and 18 metres across. It rested 'upon strong uprights fixed into three blocks of masonry with large-headed nails and wood pegs'. During the 1920s antiquarians digging at the site recovered a large block of stone with a hole in the centre. Masonry dispersed on the water's edge was thought to be 'the central pier, the river having changed its course since the bridge was erected'. Horsfall Turner in his *History of Ancient Bingley* said of Marloe/Marley Bridge, 'I have no memorandum to show this Bridge was destroyed.' The *Sessions Rolls* of 1650 to 1700 reveal that, 'the ford through the water where carts and carriages with wyne and oil and iron pass from the city of York to the Market Town of Keighley is worn with pitts so as to be very dangerous to passengers.' In January 1687 the wooden bridge was restored at a cost of £230. In 1929 Mr C. Bailey of East Riddlesden Hall granted permission to dig part of the Aire and its banks in this location during a drought. A number of faced stones were found in the mud, about 60cms higher than the course of the river running between Marley and Riddlesden Hall. This was close by the present course of the river near How Beck. Excavation on the North bank uncovered the sycamore central trestle sighted by antiquarians way back in the 1850s. The trestle was removed from the site and presented to Keighley Museum by its finders. It was transferred to Cliffe Castle but has since disappeared, perhaps disintegrating after being dredged from the riverbed. With only obscure references to the existence of the ancient cart ways and bridge to Uncra, had it not been for two very dry spells all may have lain hidden forever from sight.

Vanished Without Trace

The dreaded Ninth Roman Legion, a body of 5000 men, was stationed somewhere near Uncra in AD117 according to two local amateur archaeologists in the 1980s. They said they believed the whole legion to have been massacred within a two-mile radius of Crossflatts. Two coffers, one containing gold and the other bronze coins, are supposed to have been hurriedly secreted near the banks of the River Aire by Roman paymasters. *The Yorkshire Archaeological Society* is sceptical about this theory although the archaeologists have found, with the aid of a metal detector, several fragments of metal which had once been part of a spear, a metal skirt tailpiece and a medallion. They were dug from ground close to Druids' Altar, a plateau high above Uncra and Marley.

Roman Eagle

In the summer of 1917, a Mr Bennet discovered a small bronze eagle in almost perfect condition in a newly ploughed field to the north of Parkwood Top Farm, Keighley. The area is identified on the 1919 OS map as enclosure 528. This spot is only a mile or so distant from where the old Roman road from Manchester to Ilkley once ran. Bennet handed the Bronze figure over to Keighley Museum. Expert Alex Curle from the Museum of Antiquities had no doubt as to its Roman authenticity. He thought it might have been a finial for a staff. Again at Parkwood, a hoard of Roman coins was found by a man named Robert Lister in Edwardian times.

Ancient Family

The first Keighley name to be chronicled in an early charter was that of Ralph Kighley. 'The antient family of the Kighleys hence had their name, one of which called Henry de Kigheley in a *Close Roll* dated 21 Edward 1 1293 shows Henry as having quittance of the common summons of the eyre in Yorkshire...'

This same Henry procured from Edward I the privilege of holding a market each Saturday and a fair in the Keighley Manor on 27 October. The Lords of the Manor of Keighley after 1316 are listed as Richard Kighley (Ketley), Richard Utley, John Vaux and John Twaites. The will of Thomas Kighlay, the Rector of Kingston in Somerset, dated 13 November 1395-6 leaves property ' to Robert, dwelling at Kighlay Hall.'

Kighlay Weds a Cavendish

Henry Kighlay of Inskip, whose will is dated about 1 April 1568, had two daughters outlive him. One married Thomas Worlsey Esq., the other daughter, Ann, married William Cavendish, Baron of Hardwick. Ann Kighlay owned the moiety of the Manor of Keighley and six dovecotes but there was no mention of a property in her father's will. An old account says, '...the Keighleys of Yorkshire, an ancient and chivalrous family, long since extinct in the male line, but whose co-heirs (interred under a splen-

Utley House, Keighley – was this the site of Keighley Hall?

The old mansion house, High Street, Keighley – another contender for the lost Keighley ancestral home.

did monument at Hant Hucknall, near Hardwick in Derbyshire) transferred the manor of Keighley, together with the estate, at the close of the 16th century, to the family of Cavendish...'

The exact site of the Keighley Manor House is not known but there are several contenders for the title.

Manor Farm

Norman de Kyghley is recorded through the centuries as having lived at Utley. An extract from the *History of Worcester and Yorkshire* describes a substantial property being built over the original site of the manor (although I think this is unlikely). This building is known as Manor Farm, High Utley. A lintel bears the legend EAS. WB 1677.

Great Large Buildings

In June 1667, after a pilgrimage to the tomb of Gilbertus de Kyghley, an anonymous seeker, 'inquired for the manor house at Keighley, belonging to this family, and was shown a poor cottage (at Utley) where a simple schoolmaster lived, where they informed me stood formerly the Hall, and greate large buildings, but now converted into meadows and orchards and gardens.'

Utley House

The late local historian Clifford Whone of Thwaites Brow wrote a letter on the subject of Utley House to the *Keighley News* in October 1953. 'Many Keighley ratepayers beside myself must have been grieved to learn that Utley House is now on the market. Perhaps they also wonder, as I do, if it is with a good conscience that our Town Council has offered for sale a historic house bequeathed to them for preservation. The late John Clapham, by whose will the town received this legacy, belonged to one of our oldest families whose story abounds in interest...in 1703 Isaac Clapham and his wife, Mary, built Utley House and its architecture is truly representative of its times. There is reason to believe that it stands on the site of the ancient manor house occupied by "Nicholaus de Kyghelay' whose name heads the Keighley Poll Tax List of 1379." The

Idle Hall was thought by two eminent local historians to have stood on the site of the White Bear Inn at Idle.

18th-century Utley House stands on Birchwood Road. The house was constructed of stone, having four-foot thick walls, mullion windows and an impressive arched kitchen fireplace. In 1945 the council considered opening it as a museum to show off a collection of antique furniture and antiquarian books stored within. However an offer to purchase the building for £650 was viewed as a more attractive option and the bequest of John Clapham to the town fell into private ownership as easily as the few hundred pounds fell into the town council's coffers.' Utley House is a Grade 11 listed building.

Keighley High Street
Keighley Manor House is supposed to have stood in Rectory Row, High Street. Mr John Smith notified the council of his intention to convert a mansion house into five shops and submitted a building plan to the town council (no. 1087) dated Tuesday 18 September 1877.

Killington Castle
A Victorian book *Keighley Past and Present* records another possible contender for Keighley's ancestral seat as being somewhere between Parkwood and Park Lane, close to fields bearing the names 'The Parks' and 'Broad Parks'. A hand-written note attached to the *Harleian manuscripts* describe the site thus, 'In a commanding position, on the edge of a plateau, at the top of Parkwood, stands a quaint old cottage, formerly thatched, which has been occupied by the same family for more than a century.

The present occupant states that his grandfather told him it had always been known as "Killington Castle", (could he have meant Kiglington?) a name that is surely significant.' Indications of a much larger and grander building were in evidence about the cottage such as several thick foundation walls and the like. The field walls were unusual in that the stone was of large blocks faced on one side. The Keighley family had once owned the land.

Idle Hall in Idle Hands

'Let no man go to Idle expecting that the rustics will wait upon him cap in hand.' The Catholic Plumptons owned the manor of Idle and Roecliffe after the Norman Conquest. In 1310 they gave many acres of Idle land to the Esholt nunnery. Nigel de Plumpton was buried at Esholt in accordance with his wishes. A hundred years later Sir Robert Plumpton – a foreman to the king – wed the Archbishop of York's sister. Their son was beheaded in 1405 for joining a secret society against King Henry IV. Sir Ingham Clifford married into the Roecliffe side of the Plumpton family. Dying childless, the lands at Roecliffe then fell into the hands of Lord George Clifford of Skipton Castle. Lands surveyed at this time (1583-4) informed Clifford, 'the Manor House, then called Idle Hall, was greatly decayed.' Yet 'in convenient repaire for the use of those tenants (widow Isabel Dawson and Ralph Radford) who dwell therein...being at the north-east corner of the town, near unto a well (Town or Low Well)... it had a pretty lodge wherein the keeper dwelt when deer were kept there.' Widow Dawson died at the hall in September 1602. The old hall, which also housed Idle Court in the 1600s, is supposed to have stood about half way up High Street Place. Most of the manor was destroyed but part of the structure was eventually transformed into the Manor House Inn. A terrified villager reported seeing the ghost dog Guytrash at a well here. Both Horsfall Turner and William Cudworth said the hall might have been situated on the site of the White Bear Inn (named after an Elizabethan man-of-war built in 1564) at the top of High Street, opposite the New Inn.

Sometime in 1800 William Story found a quantity of Roman coins and human bones in stone coffins when a plough first turned the ground near the summit of Idle Hill. Beacons were lit here in times of war and it was thought to have been a Roman campsite.

Legend of Frizinghall

Frizinghall, one of the oldest suburbs of Bradford, took its name from Raoul de Frizing, a companion in times of war to William the Conqueror. His loyalty was rewarded when he received from William a grant of land. Raoul built himself a mansion and named it Frizing Hall. Around the 13th century a descendant of his, Sir Robert de Frizing, an adventurer, rode out one warm summer's day. Passing the door of a lonely cottage some five miles distant from his ancestral home he chanced upon an old man and his teenage daughter. Sir Robert thought the maiden the most beautiful thing he had ever seen and immediately ordered two of his men to carry her off to his mansion.

That night her captor visited his pretty prisoner and she pleaded with him to let her go. Sir Robert endeavoured to bribe her with offers of wealth and position but still she refused him. At length she told him that if he kept her against her will she would kill herself and come back to haunt him from the grave. The Baron laughed, telling her they would speak again the following day.

The girl plunged the blade of a knife deep into her heart during the night. The next day her bloody, lifeless form was found and Sir Robert informed of the girl's suicide. Just as he was looking sadly at the dead girl her father arrived. Seeing the corpse of his beautiful child he turned to Sir Robert and screamed, 'Cursed be thou and thine house! Within twelve months of this day shalt thou be laid a corpse, the last of thy name; thy house shall fall away and crumble into dust, until not one single stone remains to show the place where it now stands!' With these words the old man fell dead at the horrified Baron's feet. Father and daughter were together carried to one grave.

Sir Robert began to meditate upon the old man's dying words. Try as he might he was unable to forget the curse. Faithful servants guarded their master from harm day and night. He became a recluse and refused to venture outside his own front door. Weeks turned into months until only one day was left before the anniversary of the dreaded curse. Sir Robert decided that he was at last safe so went out into the sunshine. He lay down in a meadow and slept the sleep of the dead in the heat of the morning sunshine. When he awoke he complained of a sore ear, which got worse as the day wore on. Before the close of night the pain became so unbearable that the Baron in his agony threw himself from a high balcony and died of his injuries. It later transpired that as he slept in the meadow an insect had crawled into his ear and eaten its way to his brain. The mansion was afterwards abandoned, left to rot and decay. In time the site became lost forever, thus fulfilling the old man's curse.

Leeds, 1800

Mayhall said the 'groves, green lanes, and fields (of Leeds) have been replaced by warehouses, mills factories, foundries, railway stations, houses, &c.' It has already been seen that Leeds, as mentioned in the Domesday Book, was restricted to Briggate, Kirkgate, and Swinegate. 'The mud and wattled houses, roofed with thatch, which formed the early dwellings of the inhabitants, gave place to timber houses, one of which, Rockley Hall in Lowerhead-row, the residence of an opulent family, was in existence down to the beginning of the present century. It was built entirely of timber, and was of a very antique form, consisting of a centre and two wings, with a pointed doorway at the lower end of the central part. Instead of deals, or boards, the floors were oak planks, of so considerable a thickness, that joists were subsequently made of them. These timber houses were succeeded by another class of houses built of a perishable argillaceous kind of stone found in the neighbourhood. Then followed brick houses, the first built in Leeds, (1628) being known as the Red Hall, in Upperhead-row. Larger and more elegant edifices have replaced most of the old buildings in the town. In Briggate, and other parts of the town, a few old houses may yet be seen; but they are scarcely noticed except by the curious.' Moot Hall, a very ancient Leeds public building erected in 1615, was pulled down in 1825 to make way for new buildings. Near Gott's factory was a place named Monk Pits. The location of the factory in 1800 was named Bene Ing, meaning a field of prayers.

Howley Wolves

Old stories tell of a high-born lady resting near a well that served to quench the thirst of Howley Hall residents when she was set upon by fierce wolves and devoured. After this unfortunate lady's terrible end the well was re-named St Anne's Well in her memory. During this century the ghost of a woman (perhaps Lady Anne?) was been seen wandering the ruins of ancient Howley Hall (blown up in 1730) dressed in a dark dress. A red veil hid her face and shoulders.

Swift Nick

In the reign of Charles II, the notorious highwayman Nick Nevison (alias John Brace/y) murdered landlord Fletcher in a field near Howley Hall. A small stone was erected inscribed, 'Here Nevison killed Fletcher, 1684.' The stone was removed to the grounds of the hall for safe-keeping. Nevison died on the gallows at Micklegate Bar, York , 4 May 1685.

Bibliography

Andrews, William, *Old-time Punishments*, 1891.

Baildon, W., Paley, *Baidons of Baildon Vol.2.*, 1926.

Bannister, Frank, *The Annals of Tawden*, 1922.

Benson, Arthur C., *Account of Sidgwick family*.

Bentley, *Description of the Halifax Gibbet*.

Bogg, Edmund, *The Old Kingdom of Elmet*. 1902.

Bottomley, Gordon, *The Mickle Drede and other Verses*, 1896.

Brigg J.J., *The Brigg Collection*.

Brontë, Branwell, *Caroline, Percy*, 1837.

Brontë, Charlotte, *Shirley*, 1849, *James Taylor correspondence*, 1851.

Brontë, Emily, *Redbreast in the Morning*, Feb.1837.

Burnley, James, *Yorkshire Stories Re-told, Bradford Scrapbook*, 1875-6.

Byles, William, *Post Office Directory, Bradford Plan*, 1887-8

Carr, James Revd, *Annals and Stories of Colne and neighbourhood*, 1876.

Collyer, Revd Robert, *Old Job Senior*...

Constantine, Joseph, *Fifty Years of the Water Cure, Second Ed.* 1893.

Cooper, Asley Sir, *Diary of*, 1828.

Crabtree, Revd Henry, *Melinus Rusticus Almanack*, 1685.

Craven, Joseph, *A Brontë Moorland Village and its People*, 1907.

Chrysostom, St, *'We attend them with lamps...'* AD400.

Cryer, Silas, *The Life of Job Senior*, 1865.

Cudworth, William, *Round About Bradford*, 1876.

Dawson, W.H., *Loose Leaves of Craven History*, 1891. *Loose Leaves in Craven*, 1906.

Denton, J, *Prepare to meet thy God*, 1809.

Dixon, J.H., *Craven Minstrel's Legend of Peter King*, 1881.

Doyle, Conan, Sir Arthur, *History of Spiritualism*.

Eccles, Joseph, *Full Moon*.

Elmsley, Doris, *Bolling Hall Lodge*, 1997.

Fawcett, Stephen, *Bradford Legends*, 1872, *and A collection of poems*, 1868.

Fieldhouse, Harry, *Old Bradford Illustrated*, 1889.

Foster, J., *'Tis well to walk...'* 1881.

Gay, Pastorals III, *'I'll speed me to the pond...'*

Gatty, Mrs Alfred, *The Book of Sun-dials*, 1900.

Gent, Thomas, *The Ancient and Modern History of the loyal town of Ripon*, 1733.

Gaskell, Elizabeth, Cleghorn, *The Life of Charlotte Brontë*, 1860.

Gillingham, James, *Errors of Spiritualism*, 1922.

Gott, Benjamin, *Suicide note,* 1833.

Grundy, F.H., *Pictures of the Past,* 1879.

Harrison, Thomas, *Life and Vagaries of Jack Lobb.*

Heaton, William, *Lost Child on the Moorlands,* 1862.

Heap, Moses, *Diary of,* 1824-1913.

Henrietta, *Letter to Keighley News,* 1868.

Heywood, Oliver, *Journals of,* 1672 – 1680.

Hodgson, H.R., *The Society of Friends in Bradford,* 1926.

Hone, William, *Hones Table Book,* 1828.

Hoylus End *Bill o 'th. (William Wright) Th ' History o ' Haworth Railway... Oppnin' Serrimony.* 1902.

Illingworth, Jonas, 1877. *Full Account of old Mark's remains, The Denholme Ten, The Late Mark Illingworth,*

James, John, *History and Topography of Bradford,* 1841.

Jollie, Mr, *The Surey Demoniak,* 1697.

Jones's, *Mercantile Directory,* 1863.

Keighley, William, *Keighley Past and Present,* 1858.

Keighley, *Year Book,* 1894, 1903.

Laycock, Ben, *Life and Sufferings, Persecution and Punishments,* 1856.

Leach, James (alias Pie), *Diary of,* 1850.

Leeds Pottery, *Motto,* 1780.

Leyland, Francis A., *The Brontë Family,* 1886.

Lofthouse, Mrs, *Public Hangings,* 1864.

Lund David, *Will of,* 1903.

Magee, Revd J.A.C., *'... keep away from the séance-room...'*

Mayhall's, *Annals Vol. I,.* 1860. *Vol II,.* 1866.

Mechanics' Institute, *Records, BK2 2/5/F3,* 1820-1926

Midgley, Samuel, *Halifax and its Gibbet Law,* 1708.

Molles, *Living Library,* 1612.

Quarles, *Death has no advantage...*

R.W.K., *Bolton Abbey,* 1862.

Scaife, Joseph, *Stray thoughts by a spiritialist,* c1853.

Scott, E.K., *Fox hunting in Bingley.*

Scruton, William, *Pen and Pictures,* 1891.

Schiller, Frederick, *Verses on Illingworth tombstone.*

Slater, Frank, *The Spectre Hoseman,* 1918.

Speight, Harry (alias Jonnie Grey), *Airedale,* 1891.

Smith, John, *Life of Jack Lobb.*

Smith, John, *Mansion House plan no. 1087A, 1109A,* 1877.

Smith, Samuel, *God is love,* c1776.

Sutcliffe, Halliwell, *By Moor and Fell,* 1899.

Taylor, The Water Poet, *Halifax poem.*

Taylor, Zachary, *Letter.*

Thompson, Tommy, *The saying of the Skipton Nominy.*

Turner, Horsfall, J., *Annals of Wakefield Prison,* 1904.

Vaughan, Father B., *'Camouflage it as you will...'*

Wakefield, *Chronicles of,* 1869.

Watson, John Revd., *History and antiquities of the parish of Halifax,* 1775.

Watters, Mary, Keighley Library, *BK1 3/2/1658 Reel 200,* 1701.

Wesley, John, *Journal of,* 1761.

Whalley, Revd James, *The Wild Moor,* 1869.

Whittaker, Thomas Dunham, *The History and antiquities of the Deanery of Craven,* 1812.

Wood, Thomas, *Diary of,* 1822-1880.

Wrone, Clifford, *Keighley History,* 1953.

Young, Edward, *'Life's little stage...'.*

Government Departments
Birkenhead, Liverpool and Keighley and Birkenhead Register offices; West Yorkshire Archive Service; Wakefield, Bradford District Archives; Home Office Record Management Services; Public Record office (PRO), Kew; Borough of Keighley; *Special Keighley Constable Accounts,* 1815-1817.

Historical Archives and Libraries
The British Library, London; Keighley, Bradford, Hull, Colne, Thornton, Skipton, Leeds, Liverpool, Hoylake, Birkenhead and Rugby Libraries; Cheshire Record office; The Gold Coast and Albert Genealogical Society Inc, Australia; National Archives and Records, Washington D.C.; Chief Registry Office, Hamburg, Germany; and the Metropolitan Police Service, London..

Museums
The Craven Museum, Skipton; Cliffe Castle Museum, Keighley; Bolling Hall Museum, Bradford.

Newspapers and Periodicals
The Keighley News, Keighley Herald, Telegraph & Argus, Yorkshire Post, The Evening Post, Chronicle Newspapers, Bradford Observer, Yorkshire Observer, Leeds Intelligencer, Leeds Mercury, Yorkshire Spiritual Telegraph, Keighley Visitor, The Times, Craven Herald, Pioneer, Preston Chronicle, Bradford and Halifax, Wakefield and Keighley Reporter, Bradford Review, Yorkshire Notes and Queries, Vol. 1-4, The Yorkshire County Magazine, 1891 and the Halifax Guardian. The Yorkshireman.

Religious Matter
Bramley Overseer Accounts; Haworth Church Registers; The Society of Friends, Bradford; St James Parish Church, Thornton; Old Bell Chapel (original St. James), Bradford Parish Church; St Mary's Todmorden; St Mary's, Charlton, nr Skipton; Kildwick Church; Skipton Parish Church; Heptonstall Church; Leeds parish church; Holy Trinity, Leeds; Wesleyan Infant Day Book, Keighley; Spiritual Temple, Heber Street, Keighley; Jubilee Souvenir, assorted penny pamphlets and The Liverpool Catholic Almanac 1899; Silsden Archdeacon Court 1752 and St. Bartholomew's Church, Colne; Burial Register of Baptisms and Burials 1774-1789 as transcribed by Gladys Whittaker and W.M. Spencer 1969; Biblical Texts, Deut. 13.12. Hebrew IV, I Leviticus 19, 31. Malachi 3 v 5, Relevations 4, Jno., 3,33, Zech 5, 4., Job 14, 13. Psalms 4 and 16.

Index of Place Names

TOWNS & VILLAGES OF BRITAIN: WEST YORKSHIRE

John Spencer's book is the essential guide to West Yorkshire as seen through the colourful history of its towns and villages. Although written in a lively, readable style - it's comprehensive and presented in an easy-to-use reference book format. Over 300 entries cover all the main settlements of the county, highlighting the key buildings, landscape and famous personalities of the area, together with associated folklore. Includes natural history sites and walk suggestions to open up the area both to visitors, and residents interested in their local history. *£8.95*

JOURNEY THROUGH YORKSHIRE: History, customs and beauty of Yorkshire

"Kenneth Fields writes entertainingly and informatively, lacing personal experiences with constant reminders of Yorkshire's unique qualities and features - a book to relish, a tempting travelogue through a richly endowed county." THE KESWICK REMINDER *£7.95*

BEST TEA SHOP WALKS IN WEST YORKSHIRE

Tea shop walkers June and Norman Buckley present the perfect companion for lazy days in West Yorkshire: pleasant strolls with afternoon tea in typical Yorkshire surroundings. *£6.95*

TEA SHOP WALKS IN THE YORKSHIRE DALES

Enjoy a stroll in the Yorkshire Dales rounded off with afternoon tea in a specially selected teashop. "a tantalising mixture of walks and eating places... a delightful concoction of exercise and culinary indulgence"
£6.95

YORKSHIRE DALES WALKS WITH CHILDREN

Packed with interest and information for youngsters, this is the first book of walks in the Yorkshire Dales specifically aimed at parents and children. On these 21 circular routes - all less than 5 miles long- you'll find that children actually want to join you!
£6.95

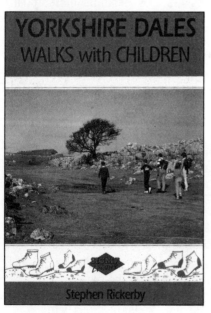

Our catalogue includes a wide range of "Tea Shop Walks" and "Walks for Children" in many locations the length and breadth of Britain. Ask for your copy today!

All of our books are available through your local bookseller. In case of difficulty, or for a free catalogue, please contact:
SIGMA LEISURE,
1 SOUTH OAK LANE,
WILMSLOW,
CHESHIRE SK9 6AR.
Phone: 01625-531035;
Fax: 01625-536800.
E-mail: sigma.press@zetnet.co.uk .
Web site: http//www.sigmapress.co.uk

VISA and MASTERCARD welcome.